Lotus Notes®/ Domino™ 5 System Administration

Tony Aveyard
Karen Fishwick
Jay Forlini
Karl Wabst

New Riders

201 West 103rd Street, Indianapolis, Indiana 46290

CLP FAST TRACK: LOTUS NOTES/DOMINO 5 SYSTEM ADMINISTRATION

International Standard Book Number: 0-7357-0878-9

Library of Congress Catalog Card Number: 99-066594

Printed in the United States of America

First Printing: June, 2000

04   03   02   01   00   7   6   5   4   3   2   1

Interpretation of the printing code: The rightmost dou-
ble-digit number is the year of the book's printing; the
rightmost single-digit number is the number of the
book's printing. For example, the printing code 00-1
shows that the first printing of the book occurred in
2000.

TRADEMARKS

WARNING AND DISCLAIMER

Publisher
David Dwyer

Executive Editor
Al Valvano

Acquisitions Editor
Nancy Maragioglio

Managing Editor
Sarah Kearns

Development Editors
Ami Frank Sullivan
Chris Zahn

Project Editor
Lori Lyons

Copy Editor
Daryl Kessler

Technical Reviewer
Mitchell Cunningham

Indexer
Joy Dean Lee

Proofreader
Marcia Deboy

Compositor
Gina Rexrode

Contents at a Glance

TABLE OF CONTENTS

Section 2: Implementing a Domino R5 Infrastructure: Exam 521

ABOUT THE AUTHORS

Tony Aveyard lives in Cincinnati, Ohio, with his wife Kathi, daughter Marie, and son Garet. The other two family members are a dog, Tango, and Randi, an attack cat. He has been actively involved in the IT industry for twenty years and has been a Domino Administrator for the past five years. In real life he works for Entex in Mason, Ohio, as a Senior Intranet/Internet System Engineer, but his secret ambition in life is to be a full-time fiction writer. FPS computer games are a serious passion, and he thinks that Raven Software is the greatest computer game development company in the world.

Karen Fishwick is currently employed at Farlink Communications Ltd., a small consulting and services organization based in Ottawa, Canada. As a Principal CLP and CLI, Karen has been providing training and consulting services in the Notes/Domino arena for over five years. She has been involved in various administration and development initiatives for many Ottawa-based clients and has trained hundreds of students all across Canada. When she's not working, Karen enjoys spending time with her husband and her twin babies.

Jay Forlini started working with computers at IBM while finishing his business degree at Kennesaw State University in Georgia. He has been involved with Lotus Notes in some fashion for more than seven years. He began as a Level 1 instructor in 1993 and he often assisted with administration and development projects when he was not in the classroom. He has been certified as an administrator for versions R3, R4, and R5. He is also the lead author for *Lotus Notes and Domino 4.5 Professional Reference*, New Riders. For the past two years, he has been working with Equifax, Inc. as Director of Systems and Development.

Karl Wabst is an independent consultant specializing in network computing. He has, over the last 11 years, worked with Notes & Domino, Windows NT, AIX, OS/2, and Novell as a network architect, administrator, and applications developer. During that time, Karl has participated in large-scale commercial projects with IBM, Lotus Consulting, Bell Labs, and AT&T. Karl has also worked on the architecture and administration of several large corporate Notes/Domino projects, including Hyundai Motor Corp. in South Korea, Wesley Jessen in the U.K., and SmithKline Beecham in PA.

After several years working on Wall Street in corporate finance, it became apparent that there was a great need for fast, accurate information flow between companies. As a result, Karl became involved with network computing as a NetWare & Notes administrator. Seeing the need for people with both technical and business acumen, Karl founded Eagle Mountain Computing, Inc. in 1997. Since then, he spends most of his time searching the Internet for new opportunities and turning those into real-life adventures.

This is Karl's third professional writing endeavor. He contributed to New Riders' recent *Domino System Administration* as well Que's *Special Edition Using Lotus Notes 4*. He currently resides in Fort Worth, TX. Karl can be reached at `karl.wabst@att.net`.

ABOUT THE TECHNICAL REVIEWER

Mitchell Cunningham has been working with Lotus Notes and Domino for a little over four years. As a full-time Certified Lotus Instructor with PBSC Computer Training Centres in the Greater Toronto Area, Mitch has had the good fortune and privilege of training thousands of Lotus Notes and Domino administrators and developers. When he is not in the classroom teaching others about the coolest application on the planet, Mitch loves to spend time with his darling bride and two young daughters.

DEDICATION

From Tony Aveyard: My contributions to this book are dedicated to my lovely wife Kathi and my two wonderful kids, Marie and Garet. Thanks for all your patience while my life-long dream came true before your eyes. I would also like to thank my friend Marcus Mullins, who has helped me keep the dream alive, and God for giving me the strength to make it a reality.

From Karen Fishwick: I wish to dedicate this book to my husband, Warren, who has always supported me 100%.

ACKNOWLEDGMENTS

From Tony Aveyard: I would like to thank my development editors, Ami Sullivan and Chris Zahn of New Riders, for their patience and help during the writing of this book. I would also like to especially honor my acquisitions editor, Nancy Maragioglio. Nancy, you have made my first experience in technical writing a true pleasure, and all of your care and support have been greatly appreciated.

From Karen Fishwick: I wish to thank Nancy Maragioglio, whose enthusiasm and professionalism always makes every project very enjoyable.

From Karl Wabst: I'd like to thank all of those people I have had the fortune to work with over the years, each in their own way pushing and enabling me to become better in my chosen profession. Special thanks to Paul Greenberg, whose friendship and encouragement made my writings possible. Also, thanks to Jean Hess whose presence, patience, and support have helped to keep life interesting.

TELL US WHAT YOU THINK!

As the reader of this book, *you* are our most important critic and commentator. We value your opinion and want to know what we're doing right, what we could do better, what areas you'd like to see us publish in, and any other words of wisdom you're willing to pass our way.

As the Executive Editor for the Certification team at New Riders Publishing, I welcome your comments. You can fax, email, or write me directly to let me know what you did or didn't like about this book—as well as what we can do to make our books stronger.

Please note that I cannot help you with technical problems related to the topic of this book, and that due to the high volume of mail I receive, I might not be able to reply to every message.

When you write, please be sure to include this book's title, author, and ISBN number (found on the back cover of the book above the bar code), as well as your name and phone or fax number. I will carefully review your comments and share them with the author and editors who worked on the book.

Fax: 317-581-4663

Email: nrfeedback@newriders.com

Mail: Al Valvano
Certification
New Riders
201 West 103rd Street
Indianapolis, IN 46290 USA

Introduction

The CLP Fast Track series is written as a study aid for people preparing for the Certified Lotus Professional exams. The series is intended to help reinforce and clarify information with which the student is already familiar. This series is not intended to be a single source for student preparation, but rather a review of information and set of practice tests to help increase the likelihood of success when taking the actual exam.

WHO SHOULD READ THIS BOOK

The *CLP Fast Track: Lotus Notes/Domino 5 System Administration* book in the *CLP Fast Track* series is specifically intended to help students prepare for Lotus' System Administration track, comprised of Exam #520: Maintaining Domino R5 Servers and Users, Exam #521: Implementing a Domino R5 Infrastructure, and Exam #522: Deploying Domino R5 Applications. Successful completion of Exam #520: Maintaining Domino R5 Servers and Users qualifies the candidate as a Certified Lotus Specialist. Successful completion of all three exams earns the candidate the Certified Lotus Professional designation.

HOW THIS BOOK HELPS YOU

This book is designed to help you make the most of your study time by presenting concise summaries of information that you need to understand to succeed on the exam.

HOW TO USE THIS BOOK

When you feel like you're pretty prepared for the exam(s), use this book as a test of your knowledge. After you have taken the practice tests and feel confident about the material on which you were tested, you are ready to schedule your exam. Use this book for a final quick review just before taking the test to make sure that all the important concepts are set in your mind.

WHAT THE EXAMS COVER

EXAM #520: MAINTAINING DOMINO R5 SERVERS AND USERS

Competencies:

Monitor, Maintain and Troubleshoot:

- Domino Applications
- Domino Directories, Users, Groups
- Domino Messaging and Replication
- Domino Servers
- Domino Systems

EXAM #521: IMPLEMENTING A DOMINO R5 INFRASTRUCTURE

Competencies:

- Creating/Registering Systems Resources
- Installing
- Setting Up Infrastructure, Servers, Workstations
- Setting Up/Configuring Database Resources
- Setting Up/Configuring Distribution and Monitoring
- Setting Up/Configuring Domino Infrastructure Security

EXAM #522: DEPLOYING DOMINO R5 APPLICATIONS

Competencies:

- Database Architecture
- Domino Infrastructure

HARDWARE AND SOFTWARE RECOMMENDED FOR PREPARATION

As a self-paced study guide, much of this book expects you to use Domino 5. The computer configurations for the System Administration track coverage in this book are described as follows:

A PC with an Intel 80486 or Pentium Processor

An operating system capable of running your version of Domino R5

16MB RAM, 24MB or greater recommended

150MB minimum server hard disk space, 300MB or greater recommended

VGA (or Super VGA) video adapter

VGA (or Super VGA) monitor

Mouse or equivalent pointing device

Two-speed (or faster) CD-ROM drive

Network Interface Card (NIC) (if networked, though not necessary)

I

WHAT'S IMPORTANT TO KNOW ABOUT THE EXAMS

The exams required for certification as a Certified Lotus Specialist (CLP) Domino R5 System Administrator are 520, 521, and 522.

Part I of this book is designed to help you make the most of your study time by presenting concise summaries of information that you need to understand to succeed on the exams.

Part I is divided into three sections, with each section covering a specific exam. Each chapter within the sections then covers a specific exam objective area as outlined by Lotus.

**Section 1: Maintaining Domino R5 Servers and
         Users: Exam 520   7**

**Section 2: Implementing a Domino R5 Infrastructure:
         Exam 521   197**

Section 3: Deploying Domino R5 Applications: Exam 522   329

SECTION 1: MAINTAINING DOMINO R5 SERVERS AND USERS: EXAM 520

ABOUT THE EXAM

Exam Number	**520**
Minutes Allowed	**60**
Single-Answer Questions	**No**
Multiple Answer with Correct Number Given	**Yes**
Multiple Answer without Correct Number Given	**No**
Choices of A–D	**Yes**
Choices of A–E	**No**
Scenario-Based Questions	**Yes**
Objective Categories	**Yes**

CHAPTER 1

Monitoring, Maintaining, and Troubleshooting Domino Applications

The coverage of the objectives for this chapter is organized under four broader topic areas. Those topics include the following:

- Working with Domino Databases
- Working with Domino Agents
- Monitoring and Troubleshooting Calendaring and Scheduling
- Working with Domino Log Files

WORKING WITH DOMINO DATABASES

This section will cover the various aspects of database management. As an administer, you will be required to perform periodic tasks that involve issues such as databases that need to be upgraded or moved to different locations. Instances may also occur where databases are corrupt and require an administer to repair the damage. This section will address these issues, as well as others.

Upgrading Databases

After upgrading a server to Domino R5, you can upgrade the databases on that server to R5 database format (On-Disk Structure, or ODS) and design (template). These two steps—upgrading database format and upgrading database design—are independent of each other. Because the ODS does not replicate, you can leave the design of a database based on an R4 template and upgrade the database format on that server to R5 ODS. Upgrading the database design means that you have decided to use design features that can be accessed and used only by R5 clients. Pre-R5 clients cannot use the new R5 design features.

Upgrading a database to the R5 ODS allows you to take advantage of all of the benefits that R5 offers associated with improved database performance. For more information on how to improve database performance in R5, see the later section "Optimizing and Troubleshooting Application Performance Problems."

Performing the Database Upgrade

After you install Domino R5 on a server, you can upgrade the format of databases on that server. Compacting a database using a Domino R5 server upgrades the database format or ODS to Release 5. The Database Properties box under R5 lists the current ODS version.

Compacting a database to Release 5 format can be done in one of two ways:

- Issuing the compact command at the server console

- Using the Notes client to compact the database using Database Properties

Upgrading to R5 ODS Using the Server Console

Perform the following steps from the Domino server:

1. Upgrade the application server to Domino Release 5.

2. Launch the upgraded server.

3. At the server console, type `load compact databaseName.nsf`, where *databaseName*.nsf is the file name of the database you want to compact to R5 format.

Compacting a Database Using the Notes Client

Perform the following steps from the Notes client:

1. Open the database, or select the database from the workspace.

2. Open the Database Properties dialog box by selecting Database, Properties from the File menu.

3. Click on the Info tab.

4. Click the Compact button.

If a user compacts a database on the server using a Notes client, the server compacts the database for the client. Thus, a Release 5 Domino server compacts the database using R5 compaction and an R4 Domino server compacts the database using R4 compaction. If the user compacts a local database, then the compaction is performed locally by the client software.

Keeping a Database in Release 4 Format

Any Notes client can access a database hosted on a Domino server, regardless of the release the client or server is running or the release format the database uses. However, Notes clients cannot access or use database features from later releases; for example, a Release 4 Notes client can access a Release 5 database on a Domino server, but it cannot access or use R5 features in that database.

If a database is stored on the local drive of a client, only clients of the same release and later can access it. For example, a database in Release 4 format can be accessed locally by a Release 4 or Release 5 Notes client, but not by a Release 3 client.

Domino servers can host only those applications in their release format and earlier formats. For example, an R4 server can host an R4 or R3 database, but not an R5 database.

To create a Release 5 application that can be accessed locally by R4 clients and stored on R4 servers, give it the extension .NS4 in the File Name field when creating the database. To keep a database in Release 4 format so it can be accessed locally by R4 clients or stored on an R4 server, change the database's extension to .NS4 via the operating system before compacting to R5 ODS or make a new replica of the database using the extension .NS4. Note that this strategy will work only for server-based databases; if the database is stored locally and is compacted by an R5 client, then the resulting R5 ODS cannot be read by an R4 client.

Other Issues Affecting the Database Upgrade Process

There are a number of things you can do to make the upgrade process for databases run more smoothly. First, you should run Fixup on your R4 databases prior to upgrading them. Running the Fixup task on the server prevents most errors that interfere with compaction to the new database format.

In R5, users may experience an initial delay when accessing upgraded databases for the first time. This occurs because all database views rebuild on initial access due to the updated View version in this release. To prevent this, run Updall -R on the database to rebuild the views.

Last, if you have already upgraded an application or database to R5 format (ODS), you can roll back to an earlier ODS version by using Compact -R or by creating a new replica or copy of the database in R4 format, using the .NS4 extension. Notes clients from Release 4 can access Release 5 databases on Release 5 servers, but you cannot use a Release 5 database on a Domino server running an earlier version of the software.

The Release 5 database format does not replicate, and Release 4 servers ignore unsupported Release 5 features, so you can safely replicate a database replica that has been upgraded to Release 5 database format with a replica that has not.

Adding and Moving Databases

In the R5 Domino Administrator, Lotus has provided a consolidated, intuitive interface to use when managing Domino databases. This new client has allowed Lotus to remove unnecessary end-user client constructs while focusing on providing only the tools needed by an administrator in the field. Managing databases has never been easier than with the R5 Domino Administrator.

The Files tab of the Domino administrator provides many of the tools described in this chapter. To access the Files tab, perform the following steps:

1. Launch the Domino Administrator client.

2. Choose a server from the list of servers to administer.

3. Select the Files tab. A list of available databases should appear on the left in the Files pane. Select one or more databases in the Files pane.

4. Choose the appropriate tool from the list of tools on the right.

Moving Databases

It may be necessary for an administrator to move a database from one server to another—for example, to distribute databases evenly among servers. There are two ways to accomplish this task:

- Use the Domino Administrator to move the database(s)

- Move the database(s) manually

It is important to note that neither of these processes should be used to move mail databases.

Using the Domino Administrator to Move Databases

To use the Files tab of the Domino Administrator to move databases, you must first set up and configure the Administration Process.

Assuming that the Administration Process is running on both the source and destination servers, perform the following steps to move a database:

1. Make sure that you have Create Database access in the Server document of the destination server and at least Manager with Delete Documents access in the access control list (ACL) of the databases on the source server.

2. Ensure that the source server (or another server that replicates with the source server and has a replica of the database) has Create Replica access in the ACL of the destination server.

3. Make sure that the destination server has at least Reader access in the ACL of the replica on the source server.

4. From the Domino Administrator, in the Server pane on the left, select the server that stores the databases you want to move. To expand the pane, click the server's icon.

5. Select the Files tab.

6. Select one or more databases to move in the Files pane.

7. In the Tools pane on the right, select Database, Move. Or drag the selected database(s) to the Move tool.

8. Select one or more destination servers. To select a server that does not appear in the list, click Other, specify the hierarchical server name, then click OK.

9. Click OK again. A dialog box shows the number of databases processed and indicates whether any errors occurred. See the status bar for more information.

10. If the source server is not a cluster server, you must approve the deletion of each original source database after the Administration

Process completes the "Non Cluster Move Replica" request, which creates a replica at the new location. To do this, follow these steps:

- Make sure that you have Editor access to the Administration Requests database (ADMIN4.NSF).

- Open the Administration Requests database.

- Select the Pending Administrator Approval view.

- Open the "Approve Deletion of Moved Replica" request for each source database that you moved, click Edit Document, Approve File Deletion, Yes, Save and Close.

11. Notify users that you've moved the database.

Moving Databases Manually

This procedure should be used to move a database to a server in another Notes domain, to move a database when you don't have access to the Domino Administrator, or when the Administration process is not configured for the source and destination servers. Prior to R5, this was the only way to move a database. Perform the following steps:

1. Make sure that you have Create Replica access in the Server document of the destination server.

2. Make sure you have Manager with Delete Documents access in the ACL of the original database.

3. Choose File, Replication, New Replica to create a replica of the database on the destination server.

4. Make note of the file name and path of the original database. You'll include this information when you notify users of the move.

5. Choose File, Database, Delete to delete the original database.

6. If the database receives mail, change the Mail-In Database document in the Domino Directory to reflect the new location.

7. In the ACLs of any replicas of the database, remove the name of the server that you moved the database from and add the name of the destination server.

8. Notify users that you have moved the database.

Notifying Users of a Moved Database

After you move a database, create a new database with the same file name and path as the database before you moved it. In the new database, create a form and document that provides the following information:

- Title of the original database
- File name and path of the original database
- Date of the move
- Reason for the move
- Server currently storing the database
- New file name and path of the database
- A database link to point the users to the moved database automatically

When users open this database, they'll see information about the move.

Deleting Databases

To keep a server performing efficiently and to free disk space it is sometimes necessary to delete databases that are no longer active. To delete databases from a cluster server, use the Domino Administrator. To delete databases on non-cluster servers, select the databases and delete them manually.

Deleting a Replica in a Cluster

Perform the following steps to delete a replica database in a cluster of servers:

1. Make sure you have Manager access in the database ACL.
2. From the Domino Administrator, in the Server pane on the left, select the server that stores the replicas you want to delete. To expand the pane, click the server's icon.
3. Click the Files tab.
4. Select the folder containing the replicas you want to delete.

5. In the Files window, select the replicas you want to delete.

6. In the Tools pane on the right, select Database, Cluster. Or, drag the selected replicas to the Cluster tool.

7. Select Pending Delete.

8. Click OK to mark the database for deletion.

Deleting a Database That Is Not in a Cluster

Perform the following steps when you want to delete databases that aren't in a cluster. Databases can be deleted by anyone who has manager access in the database ACL, regardless of whether or not they are an administrator of the server that stores the database.

1. Make sure that you have Manager access in the database ACL.

2. Notify users of the impending deletion and the reason for it.

3. If there are no replicas of the database, make an archive copy of it.

4. Record the file name and path of the original database. This allows you to replace the deleted database with a new database that notifies users that the original database has been deleted.

5. Select the database icon.

6. Select File, Database, Delete, and then click Yes to confirm the deletion.

7. Delete any Mail-In Database documents associated with the deleted database.

8. Remove references to the database in database libraries and portfolios.

9. Notify users that you have deleted the database.

It should be understood that notifying users of a deleted database follows the same steps as notifying users of a moved database. See the previous topic in this chapter for full instructions.

Monitoring and Repairing Databases

There are many tasks that can be performed by an administrator to keep a database in good working order. The server performs some of these tasks automatically, whereas others need to be configured by or manually managed by the administrator. Many of these tasks need to be executed on a daily basis; others can be safely performed on an occasional basis.

The following sections provide descriptions of the maintenance tasks, along with recommendations of how often a task should be executed.

Monitor Replication if a Database Replicates

Replication should be monitored on a daily basis, and can be done in any number of different ways. First, the administrator should monitor the replication history of a database. By choosing File, Replication, History, the administrator can obtain a list of each successful replication session for a database, which is useful for determining at a glance if a replication is occurring. Also, the administrator should look at the Replication Events view of the log file (LOG.NSF), which shows details about replication events between servers. Finally, the administrator can set up a replication monitor for a specific database, which notifies you when replication of a database hasn't occurred within a specified time period. For more information on monitoring database replication, see Chapter 3, "Monitoring, Maintaining, and Troubleshooting Domino Messaging and Replication."

Check for and Consolidate Replication or Save Conflicts

This check should be performed on a daily basis for large, active databases and on a weekly basis for other databases. Resolving replication and save conflicts is a manual process and can usually be avoided by carefully controlling application and document access. To consolidate a conflict, merge information into one document and remove the other document. Conflicts are easiest to consolidate soon after they occur, while the conflict document is still closely synchronized with the information in the main document. It's important to consolidate replication or save conflicts quickly, so users can access the correct information.

When resolving a conflict, every attempt should be made to consolidate changes into the main document, rather than in the conflict document(s); this method avoids a scenario in which the conflict document becomes orphaned and ensures that the main document is the one to be replicated to other replica copies of the database.

Monitor Database Activity

Monitoring of database activity should be done regularly, usually on a weekly basis. Database usage statistics are generated by the statlog task on the server, and are logged to the Database - Usage and Database - Sizes views of the LOG.NSF and also to the Info tab of the Database Properties box. If database activity is high and users report performance problems, do any of the following:

- Set database properties that improve performance. This topic is discussed in detail in the later section "Optimizing and Troubleshooting Application Performance Problems"

- Create a replica of the database on another server or, if possible, one within a server cluster.

- Move the database to a more powerful server.

- Move the database to disk that is less heavily used, or if it's a large database, to its own disk.

Monitor Database Size

The following methods can all be used to monitor database size and used space in a database:

- Using the Domino Administrator Files tab

- Using the log file (LOG.NSF)

- Using the Database Properties box

In addition to these methods, you can use the Statistics Collector task to generate File Statistics reports that report database size and statistics on space used for databases. For more information about the Statistics Collector task, see Domino 5 Administration Help.

Using the Domino Administrator Files Tab

1. In the Server pane of the Domino Administrator, select the server that stores the files you want to monitor. To expand the Server pane, click the server's icon.

2. Click the Files tab.

3. Display the files you want to monitor.

4. The files window displays this information relating to file size:

   • **Size.** The current size of the file in bytes.

   • **Max Size.** The maximum database size limit in gigabytes, which was set when the database was created. Applies only to Release 4 format databases.

   • **Quota.** An optional database size limit set by the administrator. Quotas and warnings are set using the Files tab of the Domino Administrator. Choose the databases in the Files list for which you want to set quotas and/or warnings. From the Databases tool, choose Quotas, and complete the necessary information in the Set Quotas dialog box. When a database has reached its quota, the user receives a warning dialog box and no further data can be saved to the database file.

   • **Warning.** An optional size threshold set by the administrator that triggers a warning message in the log file (LOG.NSF) when a database is approaching a size quota.

Note that the display of column information in the Files tab is controlled by the administrator by choosing File, Preferences, Administration Preferences, Files. The administrator can then add, remove, or reorder any file information.

Using the Log File (LOG.NSF)

1. From the Domino Administrator, on the Server pane on the left, select the server that stores the files to monitor. To expand the pane, select the Servers icon.

2. Click the Server, Analysis tab.

3. Expand Notes Log, Database, Sizes. This view sorts databases by size, from largest to smallest, and calculates the total size of all databases on the server, in kilobytes.

4. Open a document for a specific database to see the size of the database as well as the size of each view in the database. A view that has a size of 0KB is inactive and you should consider deleting it.

5. If size quotas are set for databases, select Notes Log, Miscellaneous Events and open recent documents to search for the messages `Warning, database has exceeded its size warning threshold` and `Cannot allocate database object` — `database would exceed its disk quota`. The first message indicates that a database is approaching its size quota, and the second that the database has exceeded it. In either case, take steps to reduce the size of the database.

Using the Database Properties Box

If you're not a system administrator or you don't have access to the Domino Administrator client software, perform the following steps from the Notes client:

1. Open the database and choose File, Database, Properties.

2. Click the Info tab to see the size of the database.

3. Click % Used to display the percent of database space in use.

Run the Updall Task on the Server

Running the Updall task updates all views and full-text indexes in the database, allowing users to access and search for data more quickly. By default, the Updall task runs on the server daily at 2 a.m., as specified in the NOTES.INI file. The administrator can force the Updall task to run at any time, which may cause delays for users as server activity increases. See the Domino 5 Administration Help database for more information on how Updall runs and for a list of available switches.

Run the Designer Task on the Server

To use a consistent design for multiple databases, database designers can associate databases or elements within databases with a master template. Designers can manually synchronize databases with a master template, but more often they rely on the Designer task to do this. When a master template design changes, the Designer task updates all databases that inherit their designs from the master template. Designer runs daily by default at 1 a.m. The Updall task then updates the view indexes of data-bases changed by Designer. The administrator at the server console can invoke the Designer task manually by typing `load designer`, or on the Status tab of the Domino Administrator using the Task, Start tool.

For a server's Designer task to update databases, you must create a replica of the master template on each server that stores databases that inherit from the master template.

You can't run the Designer task against a specific database or folder. It runs only against all databases on a server.

Run the Compact Task

When documents and attachments are deleted from a database, Domino tries to reuse the unused space rather than immediately reducing the file size. Sometimes Domino won't be able to reuse the space or, due to fragmentation, can't reuse the space effectively, until you compact the database. Note that Release 5 is much better at reusing space in Release 5 format databases, so compacting is needed less often than in past releases.

There are three styles of compacting used in Release 5:

- In-place compacting with space recovery
- In-place compacting with space recovery and reduction in file size
- Copy-style compacting

It is recommended that you compact Release 5 format databases weekly or monthly using the -B option to recover disk space. If you use a Release 5-certified backup utility, remember to run it after compacting is complete. Although converting Release 4 format databases to Release 5 is recommended, if you retain some Release 4 format databases, generally you should compact them weekly using the -R option; since users can't edit documents during this process, run Compact during off-hours. The first two methods of compacting do not prevent users from reading and editing information during the compact process.

Monitor the Database Cache

To minimize delays that occur when users, servers, or API programs open and close databases on a server, each server maintains a database cache. When a database closes and there are no users or processes using the database, Domino puts the database in the cache so it can close it quickly. The database remains in the cache until it's opened again or for about 15 to 20 minutes, whichever comes first. Databases in the cache can be opened quickly.

By default, the number of databases that the cache can store simultaneously is the greater of these values:

- The value of the NSF_Buffer_Pool_Size setting in the NOTES.INI file, divided by 300KB

- 25

To change this limit, add the NSF_DbCache_Maxentries setting to the NOTES.INI file or increase physical memory. Increasing the database cache size improves system performance but requires additional memory. The minimum number of databases allowed in the cache at one time is 25; the maximum is 10,000.

Repairing Corrupted or Damaged Databases

If you encounter database corruption in a database, you can use any of the methods in the following list to try to fix the problem. Because corruption is much less of an issue for logged, Release 5 databases, these methods are primarily used for solving corruption problems in Release 4 databases and in unlogged Release 5 databases.

- Run Fixup to fix corrupted views and documents.

- Run Updall to fix corrupted views and full-text indexes; if a corrupted view is the problem, try Updall before trying Fixup.

- Run Compact to fix corruption problems that Fixup doesn't correct; if the database is a Release 5 database, use the -C option.

- Press Shift+F9 to rebuild one view; press Ctrl+Shift+F9 to rebuild all views in a database.

- Create a replica of the database.

Using the Fixup Task

When you restart a server, the server quickly searches for any Release 4 format databases and any unlogged Release 5 databases that were modified but improperly closed because of a server failure, power failure, hardware failure, and so on. A few minutes after server startup is complete, the Fixup task then runs on these databases to attempt to fix any inconsistencies that resulted from partially written operations caused by a failure. When users attempt to access one of these databases and Fixup hasn't yet run on the database, the users see the message This database cannot be opened because a consistency check of it is in progress. A similar Fixup process occurs when you restart a Notes client.

Multiple Fixup tasks run simultaneously at server startup to reduce the time required to fix databases. The number of Fixup tasks that Domino runs by default at startup is equal to two times the number of processors available on the server. Although this default behavior should be adequate in most circumstances, you can edit the NOTES.INI file to include the Fixup_Tasks setting. The actual number of tasks run is the smaller of the configured number of tasks that can run and the number of databases that require fixing. For example, if you set Fixup_Tasks to 4 but only one database requires fixing, then only one Fixup task runs.

Keep in mind that after you convert Release 4 databases to Release 5 and set up transaction logging, Fixup is not needed or used to bring databases back to a consistent state. Transaction Logging is discussed in detail in the next section, "Backing Up and Restoring Databases."

The following list outlines the different methods available to run Fixup. Each of these methods enables you to customize how Fixup runs:

- Use the Fixup tool in the Files tab of the Domino Administrator to run Fixup on multiple databases.

- Use the Task, Start tool in the Domino Administrator.

- Use a console command and type Load Fixup, along with any relevant parameters and switches.

- Use a Program document to schedule the Fixup task on the server.

Backing Up and Restoring Databases

There are several methods that can be used to back up and restore or recover databases. Some of these methods are more reliable or efficient than others. The following paragraphs describe the different methods and their respective advantages and disadvantages.

Creating a Backup by Using the Database – Copy Method

One of the most rudimentary ways to back up a database is to make a copy of the database in another location, preferably on another server or drive. To restore the database, you would simply recopy it back to the desired location. This method is easy to use but is not practical for large numbers of databases. End-users or designers could use this method to keep their own local backups of specific databases. It is important to note that the new copy can never be synchronized with the old copy, as the two are not replicas.

To make a copy of a database, perform the following steps:

1. Make sure that you have the Create New Databases privilege in the Server Access section of the Server Document in the Domino Directory.

2. Choose File, Database, New Copy.

3. Next to Server, click the arrow to display a list of servers. Then select the server on which you want to place the copy, or choose Local to make a copy on the local disk.

4. Next to Title, enter a title for the database.

5. Next to File Name, enter the path and file name of the database. Limit the file name to eight characters plus the NSF extension.

6. Choose Database Design and Documents to copy the database design and all documents.

7. At this point, you may perform any of the following optional steps:

   - Choose Access Control List to copy the ACL.

   - Select Create Full Text Index to create a full-text index on the new copy.

- Create a full-text index now or at a later date.

- Choose Encryption to encrypt the new copy of the database.

- To allow a database to grow beyond the default 1GB limit, click Size Limit, select a size option, and click OK. This option applies only to Release 4 format databases.

Creating a Backup with the New Replica Method

Creating a replica of a database is similar to creating a copy, with the exception that replicas can replicate to synchronize documents, whereas copies can't. The pros and cons of creating a replica as a backup are similar to creating copies—this process can be fairly tedious and isn't recommended for large numbers of databases.

You can use either of these methods to create replicas:

- Use the Administration Process to create replicas of multiple databases on multiple destination servers.

- Manually create one replica of a database if you don't have access to the Domino Administrator or if you want to adjust replication and other settings as you create the replica.

For more information about the steps involved in creating replicas, consult Chapter 3, or refer to the Domino 5 Administration Help database.

Using Transaction Logging with a Third-Party Backup Utility to Back Up and Restore Databases

Domino supports transaction logging and recovery. With this feature enabled, the system captures database changes and writes them to the transaction log. Then if a system or media failure occurs, you can use the transaction log and a third-party backup utility to recover your databases.

A single transaction is a series of changes made to a database on a server—for example, a transaction might include opening a new document, adding text, and saving the document.

In most situations, you no longer need to run the Fixup task to recover databases following a system failure. Excluding Fixup results in quicker server restarts, because Fixup must check every document in each database while transaction log recovery applies or undoes only those transactions not written to disk at the time of the system failure.

Transaction logging provides three main benefits:

- ◆ Transaction logging saves processing time because it allows Domino to defer database updates to disk during periods of high server activity. Transactions are recorded sequentially in the log files, which is much quicker than database updates to random, non-sequential parts of a disk. Because the transactions are already recorded, Domino can safely defer database updates until a period of low server activity.

- ◆ Using transaction logging simplifies your daily backup procedure. You can use a third-party backup utility to perform daily incremental backups of the transaction logs, rather than perform full database backups.

- ◆ Transaction logging works with databases in Domino Release 5 format but not with databases that use formats from earlier releases. After you enable transaction logging, all databases in Release 5 format are automatically logged. To check database formats, use the Files tab in Domino Administrator.

To use all of the features of transaction logging and recovery, you need a third-party backup utility that supports Domino Release 5 and transaction logging. It should also be noted that for reasons of fault tolerance, the log path specified for transaction logging should be pointing to a dedicated device that is mirrored with a dedicated controller. The transaction log should never be written to the same device that stores the Domino server executable or data files.

Setting Up Transaction Logging

Perform the following steps to set up transaction logging for a particular server:

1. Ensure that all databases to be logged reside in the Domino data directory, either at the root or in subdirectories.

2. From the Domino Administrator, click the Configuration tab.

3. In the Use Directory On field, choose the server's name.

4. In the left pane, expand the Server category, and then click Current Server Document.

5. Click the Transactional Logging tab.

6. In the Transaction Logging field, choose Enabled. Accept the default choices in the other fields, or make changes to configure the way you want the logging to work, and then save the document.

Disabling of Transaction Logging

After you set up transaction logging, all databases that are in Domino Release 5 format are logged. Although it is not recommended, you can disable transaction logging of specific databases. For example, you might disable logging of a database that stores only attached files, because changes to those files are not recorded as transactions.

Disabling logging is not recommended because you need to run the Fixup task in order to recover databases following a system failure.

To disable transaction logging for a specific database, follow these steps:

1. Perform any of the following options:

   ◆ When creating a new database, choose Disable Transaction Logging in the Advanced Databases Options dialog box.

   ◆ For an existing database, choose Disable Transaction Logging in the Database Properties box.

   ◆ In Domino Administrator, select a database on the Files tab, choose Tools, Database, Advanced Properties, and then choose Disable Transaction Logging.

   ◆ Use the Compact task with the -t parameter.

2. Ensure that all users have closed the database.

3. Use the dbcache command with the flush parameter to close the database in the database cache.

4. Open the database.

Scheduling Backups of Transaction Logs and Logged Databases

Backups are essential for recovering from a media failure. If you have a third-party backup utility, you should schedule the following:

- Daily incremental backups of the transaction log.

- Archiving of transaction log files. If you use the archive logging style, use a third-party backup utility to schedule archiving of log files.

- Weekly full database backups. Each week, it is recommended to run the Compact task with the option to reduce file size. Because this compaction style changes each database's DBIID, you should schedule compaction with a full database backup.

Monitoring, Modifying, and Troubleshooting Database Access Control

Every database has an access control list (ACL) that specifies the level of access users and servers have to a database. Although the names of access levels are the same for users and servers, those assigned to users determine the tasks that users can perform in a database, whereas those assigned to servers determine what information within the database the servers can replicate. Only someone with Manager access can create or modify the ACL.

To control the access rights of Notes users, select the access level, user type, and access level privileges for each user in a database. You can set default entries in the ACL when you create the database. You may also assign roles if the database designer determines this level of access refinement is needed by the application. Work with the designer and user representatives of the application to plan the correct access level before you put a database into production.

For each user name, server name, or group name in an ACL, you can specify the following:

- An access level
- Access level privileges or refinements to the access level

- A user type
- Roles

The following sections identify common database access problems along with a variety of possible solutions.

Users Cannot Access the Database

Users may not be able to access databases for the following reasons:

- **The server storing the database is temporarily down.** Check with the Domino administrator and tell users when the database is expected to be available again.

- **Users don't have the appropriate access.** Check the database access control list (ACL) to make sure users have the necessary access to the database. Check with the Domino administrator to ensure that users have access to the Domino server that stores the database.

- **Server backup is occurring during work hours.** Users may be unable to access a server that is being backed up during work hours because a full backup may require significant disk I/O capacity. Ask the Domino administrator to schedule backups to occur overnight, if possible.

- **The server is continuously updating a full-text index.** If a database is large and active, database performance can be slow if the server updates a full-text index too frequently. Change the full-text index update frequency if necessary.

Users Experience a Delay when Accessing the Database

Users may experience a delay when accessing databases for the following reasons:

- **The database is heavily used.** View the user activity to determine whether the database is heavily used. This option is on the Information tab of the Database Properties dialog box. Check the server to see if its hardware and memory are powerful enough to support the user activity for the database. If the server is not powerful enough, you may need to upgrade hardware or memory on the server. You can also create an additional replica of the database so all users are not always using the same one. If disk contention is a problem, move the database to a less heavily used disk.

- **There are too many views.** If the database contains many views, consider consolidating some of them. For example, you can consolidate views by creating alternative collations in the same view, rather than using separate views. Database performance can suffer when a database contains many views.

- **View indexes are being refreshed too frequently.** If the database is heavily used or contains many documents, refresh view indexes less frequently, if possible.

- **The database design is complex.** A complex database design can cause performance problems. Work with the designer to redesign or minimize performance problems.

- **The database cache needs adjustment.** If you are a system administrator, monitor the database cache on the server that stores the database to see if it's working effectively. If necessary, increase the number of the databases the cache can hold. The NSF buffer pool size may also need to be increased.

Resolving Conflicts when Names Are Assigned to More than One Access Level

It's possible to assign users or servers more than one level of access to a database. Table 1.1 describes access level conflicts and how Notes resolves the conflicts.

TABLE 1.1

CONFLICT LEVELS AND NOTES RESOLUTIONS

Access Level Conflict	Resolution
A name is listed in an ACL individually and as a member of a group	The access level assigned to the individual name takes precedence over the access level for the group, even if the individual access level is lower than the group level.
A name is included in two or more groups	The name receives the access of the group with the highest access.

continues

TABLE 1.1   continued

Access Level Conflict	Resolution
A name appears in an ACL and in access lists associated with forms, views, or sections	The ACL controls database access; design element access lists refine this access to a lower level. For example, if a user has Author access to a database but is not listed in the access list for a form in the database, the user cannot use the form to create a document.

Understanding and Troubleshooting Database Access from a Web Client

The Domino server uses a different process to authenticate users using Web clients than it does to authenticate Notes clients. Users using the Notes client software are authenticated by the server using their Notes ID file. A user who accesses a Domino server using a Web browser doesn't have an ID file; instead, he is "approved" by the server in one of four ways:

- As an anonymous user
- With name-and-password authentication
- With session-based name-and-password authentication
- With SSL authentication

Anonymous Access

To set up Internet/intranet clients for anonymous access, you set up the server for anonymous access in the server document and then set up database ACLs to include the entry "Anonymous." If you do not allow anonymous access and clients try to access the server anonymously, the clients receive an Authorization failure message.

Name-and-Password Authentication

Setting up name-and-password access involves creating Person documents in the Domino Directory for Internet/intranet users. Domino authenticates Web users in the following cases:

- When they attempt to do something for which access is restricted
- When session-based authentication is enabled
- If anonymous access is not allowed on the server

For example, when a user tries to open a database that has an ACL with No Access as the Default, Domino challenges the user for a valid user name and password. Authentication succeeds only if the user provides a name and password that matches the name and password stored in the user's Person document and if the database ACL gives access to that user. Anonymous users are not authenticated.

Session-Based Name and Password Authentication

A *session* is the time during which a Web client is actively logged on to a server. Session-based name-and-password security includes additional functionality that is not available with basic name-and-password authentication. You use the Server document in the Domino Directory to specify settings that enable and control session authentication. Session-based authentication makes use of cookies to track user information and allows for customized login forms, http user login information, and forced expiration of idle users' credentials. Refer to the Domino 5 Administration Help database for more information about how to set up this type of authentication.

Optimizing and Troubleshooting Application Performance Problems

Even with careful server maintenance, you may occasionally encounter unexpected system problems. You can reduce database performance problems by using the following:

- Release 5 databases, which are faster than Release 4 databases

- Transaction-based logging and recovery

- Disk-tuning procedures, such as disk defragmentation and disk-space reallocation

Some of the recommended solutions involve changing the database design. You should always test design changes on a template or a copy of the database before applying them to the production copy.

Properly setting the following database properties can improve the performance of an active database. Setting these properties on many databases or on one, large, active database can also improve server performance.

In addition, some of these property settings also help reduce the size of databases. Although in many cases large databases perform significantly better in this release of Domino, reducing database size can still improve performance as well as save disk space.

Display Images after Documents

To quickly display documents that contain images, select the Basics database property "Display images after loading." Then Notes users can read the text while the images load. If you don't load images after text, Notes loads images in the order in which they appear in a document; if an image appears first, Notes loads it before displaying text. With large images or slow connections, loading images in order may slow the display of the document.

This setting applies only when using Notes to view databases; Web browser settings control the display of images to Web browser users.

Prevent the Use of Stored Forms

To ensure that a document always displays correctly, you can store the form with the document. However, storing a form with every document uses system memory and may require as much as 20 times more disk space than not doing so. To save memory and disk space, you may want to prevent the use of stored forms, especially if users experience performance problems when trying to read the documents. To prevent the use of stored forms, deselect the Basics database property "Allow use of stored forms in this database." Before preventing the use of stored forms, make sure you understand how this design feature works and how the database uses it.

Don't Maintain Unread Marks

Maintaining unread marks in a database requires system resources and can significantly slow database performance. For some databases, unread marks aren't useful—for example, reference databases such as the help databases provided with Domino, administration databases such as the Domino Directory, or databases such as the log file (LOG.NSF) that are continually updated. In these types of databases, consider disabling unread marks. To disable unread marks, select the Advanced database property "Don't maintain unread marks."

Associate Document Tables with Forms for View Updates

When updating a view, Domino refers to tables of document information. These tables are stored internally in the database. By default, during view updates and rebuilds, Domino searches each table for documents that appear in the view being updated. To update views more efficiently, select the Advanced database property "Document table bitmap optimization." This property associates tables with the forms used by the documents the tables contain. Then during a view update, Domino searches only the tables associated with the forms used by documents in the view being updated. This significantly improves the performance of view updates, especially updates of small views within large databases—for example, the Connections view in the Domino Directory.

This property works only for views that use Form= as part of the selection criteria. There's a slight performance cost to maintaining the table/form association; however, when updating small views in large databases, the benefits offset the cost.

Prevent Overwriting of Deleted Data

When data is deleted from databases, Domino, by default, overwrites the deleted data on disk with a pattern. This pattern prevents an unauthorized user from using a utility to access the data. This overwriting causes disk I/O and can affect database performance.

Preventing the overwriting of deleted data is appropriate in these circumstances:

- The data is already secure—for example, the database is on a server in a locked room.

- Deleted space in the database is constantly reallocated—for example, in a system database such as MAIL.BOX.

- Data security isn't an issue—for example, in an informal discussion database.

To prevent the overwriting of deleted data, select the Advanced database property "Don't overwrite free space."

Don't Maintain "Accessed (In This File)" Document Property

The Document Properties box displays the property "Accessed (In this file)" which can show the date a document was last modified or read. The Advanced database property "Maintain LastAccessed property" controls whether the "Accessed (In this file)" property is updated if the last document access was a read. Maintaining the "Accessed (In this file)" property for reads causes disk I/O that wouldn't otherwise occur.

By default, the database property "Maintain LastAccessed property" is not selected, meaning the "Accessed (In this file)" property isn't updated when the last document access was a read, but only when the last access was a document modification. Change the default behavior by selecting "Maintain LastAccessed property."

You should select "Maintain LastAccessed property" if you use the document archiving tool, available in the Database Properties box, to delete documents based on days of inactivity.

Disable Specialized Response Hierarchy Information

By default every document stores information that associates it with a parent document or a response document. Only the @functions @AllChildren and @AllDescendants, which are often used in view selection and replication formulas, use this stored information. Maintaining this information has a significant, negative effect on database performance.

To improve database performance, disable the response hierarchy information in databases that don't use these @functions by selecting the Advanced database property "Don't support specialized response hierarchy."

Disabling the response hierarchy information has no effect on views and replication formulas that display information hierarchically without using @AllChildren and @AllDescendants.

Prevent Headline Monitoring

Users can set up headline monitoring to automatically monitor databases for information that interests them. Monitoring a database this way affects performance, especially if many users do this. To prevent users from monitoring a database, select the Advanced database property "Don't allow headline monitoring."

Administrators can also use the Security section of a Server document in the Domino Directory to control headline monitoring at the server level.

Limit the Size of $UpdatedBy Fields

Every document includes an $UpdatedBy field that stores, by default, the name of the user or server associated with each document-editing session. Storing a complete edit history consumes disk space and slows view updates and replication. To conserve disk space and improve database performance, use the Advanced database property "Limit entries in $UpdatedBy fields" to specify the number of entries that the $UpdatedBy field can contain. When the $UpdatedBy field reaches this limit, the oldest entry is removed to make room for the newest entry.

Limit the Size of $Revisions Fields

Every document includes a $Revisions field that stores, by default, the date and time of each document-editing session. Domino uses this field to resolve replication or save conflicts that occur when two users simultaneously edit the same document on one replica or edit the same document on different replicas between replications.

By default, the $Revisions field stores a history of up to 500 edit sessions, each of which requires 8 bytes of disk space. Over time, $Revisions fields can grow large, taking up disk space and slowing view updates and replication. To conserve disk space and improve database performance, use the Advanced database property "Limit entries in $Revisions fields" to specify the number of entries that the $Revisions field can contain. When the $Revisions field reaches this limit, the oldest entry is removed to make room for the newest entry.

Consider limiting the entries in $Revisions fields on a database with all of the following characteristics:

- ◆ The database contains many documents
- ◆ The database replicates often or has no replicas
- ◆ The database contains documents that are not often edited

A suggested limit is 10 entries. If you set the limit lower than 10, you run the risk of increased replication or save conflicts.

WORKING WITH DOMINO AGENTS

Domino contains a powerful agent technology that gives you the ability to create automated tasks that range from simple to complex. To help you control the power of these agents, Domino enables you to specify restrictions that affect how the agent runs.

Controlling Agent Execution

The key thing to remember is that an agent can run only if the user has the appropriate rights—rights in the database ACL where the agent will run, rights to run a particular type of agent, and rights to do what the agent is written to do.

The difficulty lies in trying to figure out which user's rights are checked when the agent is run. An agent user may simply initiate the execution of the agent, or be the *invoker*. The user may also be the one who created or modified the agent, or the *creator*. The creator is sometimes referred to as the *signer* of the agent. The signer is the person who last saved the agent. The key is that the invoker and the creator may or may not be the same user. Depending on the type of agent and where the agent is run, sometimes the rights of the invoker are checked, and sometimes the creator's rights are checked.

Checking Database ACL Rights

Users with at least Reader access to a database can run agents, but the agents they run or create can update only those documents to which they have at least Editor access. After it is determined that the invoker of the agent has the rights to run the agent, the rights of the creator of the agent are used to determine what the agent can do.

Agent Restrictions

After the user's rights in the database ACL have been checked, the next step is to verify that the user can run a particular type of agent. Different types of security controls exist for different types of agents, which depend on what type of code the agents runs, whether it's personal or shared, and whether it's an embedded agent.

Agent Types

Agents can run four different types of code: simple actions, formulas, LotusScript, or Java. Each type of code is associated with different security mechanisms.

Simple agents and formula agents have no restrictions on who can run them. The ACL rights of the database where the agent was created dictate the documents the agent can access.

LotusScript and Java agents have two modes of operation: restricted and unrestricted. Restricted access is the more common access and allows a user to run agents with some features disabled (for example, file I/O). Unrestricted access allows all features of LotusScript or Java to be used, which means that Notes security can be circumvented. Therefore, unrestricted access should be given to only trusted individuals, usually to senior developers.

Specify restrictions for LotusScript and Java agents in the Security section of the server document, using the fields Run Restricted LotusScript/Java Agents and Run Unrestricted LotusScript/Java Agents. If either field is blank, then *no* users may run these agents with restricted/unrestricted access on this system. If either of the fields is filled in, then the user must be in the field to have restricted/unrestricted access.

Personal Versus Shared Agents

Any of the four types of agents can be personal or shared. A shared agent can be seen and run by anyone who has access to the database that contains the agents, including the agent creator. Personal or private agents can be seen and run only by the agent creator. If users have Designer access or higher to a database, they can create shared agents; otherwise, they can create only personal agents.

The Run Personal Agents field in the Security section of the server document determines whether a user can run a personal agent. If the field is blank, then all users may run personal agents. If the field is filled in, the user must be explicitly listed in the field to be able to run personal agents. Personal agents cannot be accessed through the Web client.

Embedded Agents

Agents can invoke other agents, and it is possible for the creators of these agents to be different. With embedded agents, the restrictions that apply to the top-level agent propagate to the embedded agents.

Server Access

An additional consideration is whether the user has the rights to do what the agent is written to do. For example, if the agent is written to update documents on another server, the user must have access to that server. For all agents, Notes uses the fields Access Server and Not Access Server in the Security section of the Server document to verify that users have the proper access rights to the server.

Situations That Affect How Agents Run

Agent restrictions may change according to where you're running the agent: on the desktop or server, in the foreground or background, or on the Notes client or Web client.

Desktop or Server

An agent is running on a server if it is part of an agent on a server-based database and the agent has one of the following triggers:

- Before new mail arrives

- After new mail arrives

- When documents have been created or modified

- On schedule hourly, daily, weekly, or monthly

When an agent runs on a server, all restriction and ACL checks are operational, except when the server is "Local." All other agents (invoked via the following menu options: the "Actions menu," the "Agents list," or "When documents have been pasted.") run on the workstation, regardless of whether the database itself is on a workstation or a server. When the agent is run locally on the workstation, the restriction checks are bypassed. When an agent runs on the Web, Notes performs all the restriction and ACL checks, because Web agents always run on the server.

Foreground or Background

If the agent is triggered through the Notes user interface (manually through the Actions menu or from the Agent list), Notes is running the agent in the *foreground*. If the agent is invoked through a schedule or by an event (such as a document update or the arrival of new mail), Notes is running the agent in the *background*. The foreground/background concept does not apply to the agents invoked through the Web where agents always run on the Web server, which is a combination of the foreground/background environment.

On the Notes Client

When the server background agent is triggered from the Notes client (via a schedule or event), the agent always runs with the rights of the agent creator. To see who the agent creator is, look at the Agent Properties infobox on either the Info tab or in the contents of the $UpdatedBy field on the Fields tab. To change the agent creator, you need to edit and save the agent while logged in as a person who will appear as the agent creator.

On the Web Client

On the Web client, as with the Notes client, the agent restrictions are determined by the agent creator. However, Notes uses either the database rights of the agent invoker or the agent creator to verify database access. By default, a Web user runs agents with the rights of the agent creator. However, you can specify that a Web user run an agent as himself/herself by selecting the Run Agent as Web User option in the agent's properties Infobox on the Design tab. When Run Agent as Web User is selected, the Web user is prompted to log in with a name and password. Then, the user name is used to check for rights in the database ACL.

You can create agents only through a Notes client, not a Web client. Only shared agents can run on the Web client. The Web does not have a scheduling mechanism, so agents that run on the Web cannot be run at a predefined time. The When Should this Agent Run option available during agent creation applies only to agents run from the Notes client. The option Which Documents Should it Act On determines which documents the agent will operate on. It applies to both agents invoked from the Notes client as well as on the Web client. The following four options are not supported on the Web:

- All Unread Documents in View
- All Documents in View
- Selected Documents
- Pasted Documents

Understanding the Agent Manager

After you have the appropriate rights, you're all set if your agent is run manually (for example, from the Actions menu or from a button on a form). However, there are more factors to consider if you've designed an event-triggered or scheduled agent because now it's up to the Agent Manager to run your agent.

The Agent Manager is the background server program that manages and runs agents on a server. It determines who can run the agents, where they should run, and when they should run. It sets up the context for the agents to run in, checks security, and handles loading, invocation, caching, error reporting, and logging. Depending on the type of agent, the Agent Manager may perform database operations for simple actions, evaluate formulas, or call back-end classes. For event-triggered agents, the Agent Manager monitors events and then determines when the agents should be invoked. It also watches the clock and invokes scheduled agents when the right time comes.

Improving Agent Manager Performance

Every time an agent runs, it uses server resources. To control when scheduled and event-triggered agents run, you specify settings in the

Server document and in the NOTES.INI file. Customizing when agents run may conserve server resources, but it may also delay when agents run.

Controlling How Often Agent Manager Runs Agents

The following NOTES.INI settings affect how often the Agent Manager executes agents. In general, the more frequently agents run, the sooner they perform their tasks. Running agents more frequently, however, may increase demand on server resources and adversely affect overall system performance.

+ **AMgr_DocUpdateAgentMinInterval.** Specifies the minimum elapsed time, in minutes, between the executions of the same document update-triggered agent. This lets you control the time interval between executions of a given agent. The default is 30 minutes. A longer interval can result in the agent running less often, reducing server demand. If document update events are infrequent, you can reduce the delay.

+ **AMgr_DocUpdateEventDelay.** Specifies the time, in minutes, that the Agent Manager delays before scheduling a document update-triggered agent after a document update event. The default is 5 minutes. The delay time ensures that the agent runs no more often than the specified interval, regardless of how frequently document update events occur. When the agent executes, it will also process all additional events (if any) that occurred during the interval. A longer interval results in the agent running less often, thus reducing demand for server time. If document update events are infrequent, however, you can reduce the delay to ensure that the agent runs soon after the event occurs.

+ **AMgr_NewMailAgentMinInterval.** Specifies the minimum elapsed time, in minutes, between executions of the same new mail-triggered agent. The default is 0 (no interval between executions). Entering an interval can result in the agent running less frequently.

+ **AMgr_NewMailEventDelay.** Specifies the time (in minutes) that the Agent Manager delays before scheduling a new mail-triggered agent after new mail is delivered. The default is 1 minute. Similar to AMgr_DocUpdateEventDelay, the delay time ensures that the agent runs no more often than the specified interval.

- **DominoAsynchronizeAgents.** Specifies whether Web agents triggered by browser clients can run at the same time (asynchronously). The default is zero (only one agent can run at a time). Set this to 1 to allow multiple agents to run simultaneously, which can result in faster execution of agents; however, a high number of agents executing at the same time can slow overall system performance.

Controlling How Quickly the Agent Manager Queues Agents

The Agent Manager periodically checks to see whether it has any new agents that it needs to schedule. These NOTES.INI settings control how quickly an agent gets into the schedule queue.

1. **AMgr_SchedulingInterval.** Specifies a delay (in minutes) between runnings of the Agent Manager's scheduler. Valid values are 1 minute to 60 minutes. The default value is 1 minute.

2. **AMgr_UntriggeredMailInterval.** Specifies a delay (in minutes) between runnings of the Agent Manager's check for untriggered mail. Valid values are 1 minute to 1,440 minutes (the number of minutes in a day). The default value is 60 minutes.

Controlling When the Agent Manager Runs Agents

When you create or modify an event-triggered agent, the Agent Manager schedules it to run immediately. This ensures that the agent can quickly process new documents. These NOTES.INI settings let you specify a time interval between subsequent executions of the agent. This can prevent repeated executions of the agent—for example, because of a rapid series of triggering events:

1. **AMgr_DocUpdateEventDelay.** Specifies a delay of execution (in minutes) that the Agent Manager includes in the schedule for a document update-triggered agent after a document update event. The default is 5 minutes.

2. **AMgr_NewMailEventDelay.** Specifies a delay of execution (in minutes) that the Agent Manager includes in the schedule for a new mail-triggered agent after a new mail message is delivered. The default is 1 minute.

3. **AMgr_DocUpdateAgentMinInterval.** Specifies the minimum elapsed time (in minutes) between executions of the same document update-triggered agent. The default is 30 minutes.

4. **AMgr_NewMailAgentMinInterval.** Specifies the minimum elapsed time (in minutes) between executions of the same new mail-triggered agent. The default is 0.

Monitoring the Load on the Agent Manager

Domino Release 4.6 and earlier releases include the field "Max % busy before delay" in the Server document. This field limits the percentage of time the Agent Manager can use to run agents. When this limit is exceeded, the Agent Manager delays agent execution. To improve Agent Manager performance, Domino Release 5 does not include this limitation. You can, however, still use this field for Domino Release 4.6 and earlier releases.

If your server attempts to schedule agents at a rate faster than the Agent Manager can run them, the message AMgr: Agent scheduling is paused appears on the console. The Agent Manager will not schedule any new agents until the server processes some agents that are already scheduled. Therefore, the running of new agents may be slightly delayed.

Controlling How Many Concurrent Agents Are Running

You can relieve a heavily loaded Agent Manager by allowing agents to run concurrently. To do this, modify the Max Concurrent Agents fields in the Server Tasks/Agent Manager section of the Server document. Values greater than 1 allow more than one agent to run at the same time. Valid values are 1 through 10. Default values are 1 for daytime and 2 for nighttime.

An Agent Executive runs each concurrent agent. To see a snapshot of the Agent Manager status, including the number of Agent Executives currently running, enter the command `tell amgr status` at the server console.

Tools for Troubleshooting the Agent Manager and Agents

Whenever an agent won't run, check the Agent Log to see when the agent last ran and whether it completed. For additional information, check the server console or the Miscellaneous events in the log file (LOG.NSF) for messages from the Agent Manager.

Log File

To enable agent logging in the log file (LOG.NSF), edit the NOTES.INI file to include the Log_AgentManager setting, which specifies whether or not the start of agent execution is recorded in the log file and displayed on the server console. It's important to monitor the server console or log for information from the Agent Manager because error and warning messages generated by the Agent Manager on behalf of the agent, as well as output—for example, print statements—generated by a background agent, appear on the console and in the Miscellaneous events view of the log (LOG.NSF).

The Agent Log

The Agent Log is a view in a database that shows the last time an agent ran and describes if the agent completed or not.

In order to view the Agent Log, execute the following steps:

1. In the database, choose View, Agents.

2. In the Design view that lists all the agents, choose the agent.

3. Choose Agent, Log.

Using Console Commands to Debug Agents

The following is a list of Tell commands that can be used to monitor agent activity on the server:

- **Tell Amgr Pause.** Pauses scheduling of agents.

- **Tell Amgr Resume.** Resumes scheduling of agents.

- **Tell Amgr Schedule.** Shows the schedule for all agents scheduled to run for the current day. In addition, the command shows the agent trigger type, the time the agent is scheduled to run, the name of the agent, and the name of the database on which the database runs. Checking the Agent Manager schedule lets you determine whether an agent is waiting in one of the Agent Manager queues.

  Agent Manager queues:

  E - Agents eligible to run

  S - Agents scheduled to run

  V - Event-triggered agents waiting for their events to occur

  Trigger types:

  S - Agent is scheduled to run

  M - Agent is a new mail-triggered agent

  U - Agent is a new/updated document-triggered agent

- **Tell Amgr Status.** Shows a snapshot of the Agent Manager queues and displays the Agent Manager settings in the Server document.

- **Tell Amgr Quit.** Stops the Agent Manager on a server.

MONITORING, MAINTAINING, AND TROUBLESHOOTING CALENDARING AND SCHEDULING

Domino's calendar and scheduling features enable users to check the free time of other users, schedule meetings with them, and reserve resources such as conference rooms and equipment. You can also define information on holidays particular to your organization or country. Users import this information directly into their personal calendars.

The Domino Server Tasks that Make Calendaring and Scheduling Run

The calendar and scheduling features use the Schedule Manager (Sched task), the Calendar Connector (Calconn task), and the Free Time system (a combination of Sched, Calconn, and nnotes tasks) to operate. When you install Domino on a server (any server except a Directory server), the Sched and Calconn tasks are automatically added to the server's NOTES.INI file. When you start the server for the first time, the Schedule Manager creates a Free Time database (BUSYTIME.NSF for non-clustered mail servers and CLUBUSY.NSF for clustered mail servers) and creates an entry in the database for each user who has filled out a Calendar profile and whose mail file is on that server or on one of the clustered servers.

Each user can keep a personal calendar and create a Calendar Profile that identifies who may access the user's free time information and specifies when the user is available for meetings. When users invite other users to meetings, the Free Time system performs the free time lookups. The Free Time system also searches for and returns information on the availability of resources. If the lookup involves searching in Free Time systems on different servers or scheduling applications, the Calendar Connector sends out the queries. When users schedule appointments in their calendars and book resources, the Schedule Manager task collects and updates that information in the Free Time database.

Troubleshooting Calendaring and Scheduling Problems

The following topics describe problems and errors that occur with scheduling meetings or resources.

Free Time Information Is Not Available

If, while scheduling a meeting, a user can't look up free time for a particular invitee because the invitee's schedule is grayed out in the Free Time dialog box or if no users' free time information can be accessed and the message No scheduling information for the requested users could be found at this time appears, use these tips to troubleshoot the problem.

- Check that the invitee's name is spelled correctly on the meeting invitation. If the invitee belongs to a different domain, be sure to specify the invitee's full hierarchical name, including the domain name.

- Check that Domino Release 4.5 or higher is installed on the invitee's mail server.

- Make sure that the mail server is running. Free time lookups fail if Domino cannot access the free time database on the invitee's mail server because the server is down. If the server isn't running, the user can still complete invitation processing, including sending and receiving meeting-related messages with the invitee. Also, lookups for other invitees with free time databases on other servers still work.

- Check that the Schedule Manager task is running on the mail server.

- Check that the invitee saved his or her Calendar Profile after upgrading the design to the Domino Release 4.5 or higher mail template.

- Check that the user is included in the list of users who can read the invitee's Free time Schedule in the Calendar Profile.

- Check that the free time lookup finds schedule information for users whose mail servers are in a foreign or adjacent domain. If it fails to do so, make sure a valid Domain document exists. In addition, check the Calendar Server field in the Domain document to make sure a valid calendar server has been defined for the domain.

- Check that the mail servers are running the same protocol. The mail servers must run the same protocol so that the servers can connect to each other to perform a free-time lookup.

No Resource/Room Found for Time and/or Capacity Requirements

The message No resource/room found for time and/or capacity requirements may appear when a user creates a reservation in the Resource Reservation database. This message indicates that the Site Profile name for that particular resource includes a comma—for example, Acme, East. Re-create the Site Profile name without the comma—for example, Acme East.

Can't Find User in Name and Address Book

If this message appears, the entry used in the $BusyName field in a calendar entry for the Note ID reported in the log doesn't exist in the Domino Directory. This situation typically arises when a user leaves the company and no longer exists in the Domino Directory. To resolve this error, find the document associated with the NoteID and delete the document.

Cannot Perform this Action Locally

This message appears when you try to create a Site Profile in the Resource Reservation database locally on the server. To avoid this message, when you open the Resource Reservation database, specify the actual server instead of "Local."

WORKING WITH DOMINO LOG FILES

Every Domino server has a log file (LOG.NSF) that reports all server activity and provides detailed information about databases and users on the server. The log file is created automatically when you start a server for the first time; in fact, you cannot start a server without it. Administrators can perform the following tasks associated with the Log:

- ◆ View the log file
- ◆ Search the log file
- ◆ Record additional information in the log file
- ◆ Control the size of the log file

Viewing the Log File

Perform the following steps to view information in the log file:

1. From the Domino Administrator, click the Server, Analysis tab.

2. Select the server that stores the log file you want to view.

3. Click Notes Log.

4. Click the desired view.

5. Open the desired document.

Searching the Log File

You can search the log file (LOG.NSF) for documents containing specific words using the database analysis tool. You can specify a search string of any length containing any type of character. The search is not case sensitive—that is, aa is the same as AA. For example, you can search for all documents containing: "9:00:00," "Starting," and "Ending." Domino places any document containing one of these words in a Results database whose name and location you choose. The template for the Results database is LOGA4.NTF.

The Results database contains one view, Log Events, categorized by server. It shows the dates and times of events, their sources (events or console messages), and the text of messages. The view doesn't display times for server console messages. Create the Results database on your local workstation so that it won't conflict with searches conducted by other administrators. To search the logs on multiple servers, perform separate searches. For each search, choose "Append to this database" to collect all of the results in a single database.

Steps to Follow to Search the Log File

1. From the Domino Administrator, click the Server, Analysis tab.

2. Click Analyze, and then click Log.

3. Click Results Database, select the server to store the database, and specify a title and file name for the database.

4. If a Results database already exists, choose one of these, and then click OK:

   ♦ Overwrite this database to remove any previous entries.

   ♦ Append to this database to add the new entries to the existing ones.

5. Enter the number of days' worth of activity to search.

6. Type individual words for which you want to search, separating each with a comma. You can enter only individual words, not phrases.

7. Do one of the following:

   ◆ Click Start to search the log file but keep the Results database closed.

   ◆ Click Start and Open to search the log file, and then immediately open the Results database to view the results.

Recording Additional Information in the Log File

By default, the log file records information about the Domino system. However, you can record additional information in the log file—for example, when you are troubleshooting a specific system problem.

When you record additional information in the log file, you choose a logging level that specifies the amount of detail that is recorded in the log file. If you set a high logging level, the log file may become quite large. Therefore, after you troubleshoot the problem, remember to reset the logging level.

The following is a list of specific tasks and the settings used to generate additional logging for those tasks:

   ◆ **Agent manager.** Add "Log_AgentManager" in NOTES.INI.

   ◆ **Indexer activity.** Add "Log_Update" in NOTES.INI.

   ◆ **Mail routing.** Add "Mail_Log_To_MiscEvents" in NOTES.INI.

   ◆ **Messages generated when views are rebuilt.** Add "Log_View_Events" in NOTES.INI.

   ◆ **Modem and Script I/O.** Choose File, Preferences, User Preferences, Ports, COMx Options.

   ◆ **NNTP server.** Choose one of the three logging options listed in the "NNTP log level" field on the Internet Protocols, NNTP tab of the Server document.

   ◆ **Replication.** Add "Log_Replication" in NOTES.INI.

- **Server tasks.** Add "Log_Tasks" in NOTES.INI.

- **Traced network connections.** Choose File, Preferences, Notes Preferences, Ports, Trace.

- **User sessions.** Add "Log_Sessions" in NOTES.INI.

- **Web Navigator.** Choose one of the three logging options in the "Retriever log level" field on the Server Tasks, Web Retriever tab of the Server document.

Controlling the Size of the Log File

Because the log file (LOG.NSF) can become quite large, it's important to manage its size. For example, if you are troubleshooting a problem and set the logging level to Verbose, the log file will contain a large amount of information for that activity. If you set a high logging level during troubleshooting, reset the logging level after you solve the problem.

To control the size of the log file automatically, use these settings:

- The Log setting in the NOTES.INI file controls when documents are automatically deleted from the log file. By default, documents are deleted after seven days.

- Edit the Database Properties of the log file to include the setting "Archive all documents not modified or updated after *x* days." This option is found in the Archive Settings button on the Basics tab.

Working with the Domino Web Server Log (DOMLOG.NSF)

The Domino Web server log (DOMLOG.NSF) logs all Domino Web server activity and tracks this information about each HTTP request:

- Date and time the request was made

- User's IP address (or the DNS address if DNS lookup is enabled in the Server document)

- User's name (if the user supplied a name and password to access the server)

- Status code the server returns to the browser to indicate its success or failure in generating the request

- Length of the information, in bytes, sent from the server to the browser

- Type of data accessed by the user—for example, text/html or image/gif

- HTTP request sent to the server from the browser

- Type of browser used to access the server

- Internal and Common Gateway Interface (CGI) program errors

- URL the user visited to gain access to a page on this site

- Server's IP address or DNS name

- Amount of time, in milliseconds, to process the request

You can log Domino Web server information in the Domino Web server log (DOMLOG.NSF), in text files, or in both the Domino Web server log and text files. Logging to text files is useful when the site is large and busy or when the site uses a third-party HTTP server-reporting and management tool. In addition, you can set up workflow events—for example, set up an event that sends mail when a page is accessed more than a specific number of times—to help manage the information in the database. Logging to a database is somewhat slower than logging to text files, especially at very busy sites. If you use the Web server log, you can use Notes features to analyze the results.

Setting up the Domino Web Server Log

Domino creates the Web server log database when the HTTP task starts after you enable logging. You can customize the design of the Domino Web server log to analyze log file results. Perform the following steps to enable logging to this Notes database:

1. From the Domino Administrator, click the Configuration tab.

2. Open the Server document for the Web server.

3. Click the Internet Protocols, HTTP tab.

4. Select Enabled in the Domlog.nsf field.

5. Complete the optional fields.

6. Save the document and then restart the HTTP task so that the changes take effect.

Viewing the Domino Web Server Log

Perform the following steps to view the Web server log, after enabling logging:

1. From the Domino Administrator, click the Files tab.

2. Open the Domino Web server database (DOMLOG.NSF).

3. Click Requests to display request documents, and then click a request document to display its content.

Using Text Files for Domino Web Server Logging

In addition to, or instead of, logging Domino Web server information to the Domino Web server log (DOMLOG.NSF), you can record logging information in text files that Domino stores, by default, in the data directory. If you enable text-file logging, Domino, by default, creates a new log file each day using the date for the file name.

The following is a list of the text files generated by the logging process along with a description of what each file records:

◆ **ACCESS.** Date and time of the request; user's IP address (or the DNS address if DNS lookup is enabled in the Server document); user's name (if the user supplied a name and password to access the server); HTTP request sent to the server from the browser; status code the server returns to the browser to indicate its success or failure in generating the request

◆ **AGENT.** Date and time of the request; type of browser used to access the server; status code the server returns to the browser to indicate its success or failure in generating the request

◆ **ERROR.** Internal server errors

◆ **CGI-ERROR.** Standard errors (stderr) from CGI programs

◆ **REFERER.** Date and time of the request; URL the user visited to gain access to a page on this site; status code the server returns to the browser to indicate its success or failure in generating the request

Setting Up Text Files for Domino Web Server Logging

To save disk space, periodically check the size of log files and delete the log files you no longer need. If the server is not running when Domino needs to create the new log file, Domino creates the log file the next time the server starts. Perform the following steps to enable text file logging:

1. From the Domino Administrator, click the Configuration tab.

2. Open the Server document for the Web server.

3. Click the Internet Protocols, HTTP tab.

4. In the Log Files field, choose Enabled.

5. Complete all fields appropriately.

   Refer to the Domino R5 Administration Help database for more information on each specific field.

WHAT IS IMPORTANT TO KNOW

- Understand the different ways to upgrade databases to the R5 ODS, as well as the different scenarios for hosting different versions of databases on various client and server versions.

- Know the different ways to move and delete databases.

- Understand and know all the ways to repair and monitor databases, especially with regard to server tasks such as Updall, Compact, Designer, Fixup, and so on.

- Know how to use the Domino Administrator client to monitor databases with the Files tab.

- Understand how to back up and restore databases, especially with regard to transaction logging.

- Be aware of the different scenarios that could occur with regard to troubleshooting database access. Familiarize yourself with all the sections of the ACL. Know the difference between Notes- and Web-based authentication.

- Recognize the different kinds of performance problems that can occur with applications. Familiarize yourself with all of the options on the Advanced tab of the Database Properties box.

- Know the difference between the types of agents that can run on the server, as well as how agents run based on a variety of scenarios: desktop versus server, foreground versus background, and so on.

- Understand all the intricacies of how the Agent Manager runs on the server and the different settings that control its execution.

- Be aware of the different tools available for troubleshooting the Agent Manager and agents.

- Understand the server tasks that make Calendaring and Scheduling work, as well as the different problems that can occur and how to troubleshoot them.

- Know the differences between the Log file (LOG.NSF) and the Domino Web Server Log (DOMLOG.NSF).

- Know how to view, search, and interpret information logged to all log files.

OBJECTIVES

▶ Localize Address Books in Multi-Cultural Settings

▶ Maintain Directory Configuration

▶ Maintain Groups

▶ Maintain Notes User IDs (Re-Certify, Move, Rename, Recover)

▶ Monitor/Maintain Users (Add, Remove, Upgrade)

▶ Troubleshoot Directory Problems

▶ Troubleshoot User Problems

CHAPTER *2*

Monitoring, Maintaining, and Troubleshooting Domino Directories, Users, and Groups

This chapter will explain the various tools provided for monitoring and maintaining the server. Domino release version 5 has been redesigned, and the name and address book have been replaced by a new database called the Domino Directory. The default name for the Domino Directory remains NAMES.NSF.

LOCALIZING ADDRESS BOOKS IN MULTI-CULTURAL SETTINGS

Domino release 5 is designed for use in a Notes environment running various release versions. The Directory template has been designed to be compatible with previous servers running version 3 and version 4. Upgrade your first server to version 5, and then replicate the new design to your other servers to assure compatibility.

A powerful feature of Domino release version 5 is its capability to use alternate names for users in the Domino directory. A user now has the ability to have two assigned names. The first name would be the user's name that is internationally recognizable. The second name would be recognizable in the user's native language, using their native language and character set. This would be helpful in name searches in the Domino Directory.

NOTE   Lotus will periodically release maintenance updates of the Notes servers that will provide new features and address common problems. If you decide to upgrade to a new point release—for example, from 4.6.1 to 4.6.2—Domino will prompt you to replace the design of your Directory. Proceed with the installation of the software for the point release, but do not answer Yes when prompted to replace the design of the address book, or it will revert to a release 4.x version and lose the added functionality from your ODS release 5 structure.

MAINTAINING A DIRECTORY CONFIGURATION

The following sections address the issues involved in maintaining a directory configuration. Directory profiles are discussed.

Using the Domino Directory Profile

The Domino Directory Profile is created when you open your upgraded Directory file, either with a Notes client or a Web client, such as Internet Explorer. The default parameters are defined by the Directory Profile. The steps in the following section are used to define custom settings in the Profile.

Setting Up the Public Directory Profile

The Public Directory is used to define miscellaneous settings in the Domino Directory. Setting up the Public Directory is accomplished by performing the following steps:

1. From the Domino Administrator, in the Server pane on the left, select the server that stores the replica of the Domino Directory you want to modify. If you don't see the Server pane, click the Server tab.

2. Select the Files tab.

3. Select the Domino Directory and double-click to open it. This file is called NAMES.NSF by default.

4. Choose Actions—Edit Directory Profile.

5. The fields in the profile screen consist of the following six options:

    ♦ **Domain Defined by This Public Directory.** The name of the Domino Directory is defined by this field. Domino automatically fills it out at the time you set up your server.

    ♦ **Directory Catalog File Name for Domain.** This field is an optional field. Use this field to define the file name of the server directory catalog for the domain. This field should be the same for each server that has replica of the directory catalog.

    ♦ **Sort All New Groups by Default.** This field has two options: Yes and No.

    Choosing Yes will sort the members of each new group as you create them.

    Choosing No, which is the default action, will cause each group to display members in the order in which you create them. You can override this choice and sort members of a specific group at any time.

- **Use More Secure Internet Passwords.** This field has two options: Yes and No.

  Choosing Yes, which is the default action, provides increased security using encryption for the values stored in the Internet Password field found in the person documents for each user.

  Choosing No will revert to encryption available with previous versions of Domino.

- **Allow the Creation of Alternate Language Information Documents.** This field has two options: Yes and No.

  Choosing Yes, which is the default action, allows Alternate Language Information documents to be created that support LDAP clients and allows them to search for information in an alternate language.

  Choosing No will stop Alternate Language Information documents from being created

- **List of Administrators Who Are Allowed to Create Cross Domain Configuration Documents in the Administration Process Requests Database.** Use this field to define users who can create Cross Domain Configuration documents. These documents will permit the Administration Process to process requests between Notes domains.

The new Domino Directory contains new views and has been modified to remove certain views. New views in the Domino Directory include the following:

- External Domain Information

- Holiday

- Web Configurations

The People view contains one new view:

- Alternate Language Information

The Domino Directory incorporates the following hidden views:

- $LDAPCN
- $LDAPG
- $PeopleGroupsByCorpHier
- $PeopleGroupsByPhonetic
- $RegisterGroups
- $ExternalDomainNetworkAddress
- $ExternalDomainConfigurations
- $ExternalDomainServerConfigurations
- $Holidays
- $LDAPHier
- $LDAPS
- $PeopleGroupsByLang

Deleted views in the Domino Directory include views that were integrated in release 4:

- $ACLMONITOR
- $RepMonitors
- $Thresholds
- $NamesFieldLookup

The Domino Directory has incorporated new forms. These forms include the following:

- External Domain Network Information
- Configuration Settings (formerly Domain Configuration)
- Holiday

The Domino Directory also provides the new, hidden forms. These forms are available only when using developmental routines during database development:

- (AlternateLanguageInformation)
- (ExternalDomainNetworkAddress)
- (FileProtection)
- (FileProtectionDialog)
- (Mapping)
- (VirtualServer)
- ($MessageSettings)
- (InternetMail)

MAINTAINING GROUPS

Groups are used in Notes to simplify the logical ordering of users, servers, and other groups, that share similar characteristics. For example, let's assume that you have a group of people that have left the company, and for security reasons you want to make sure that none of these ex-employees has access to the Notes server. These users would be entered in the Deny Access group and their server access would be prohibited. Take a look at some of the specific tasks involved in this sort of maintenance.

Editing a Group

Editing all fields in a group document requires the user to have Editor access in the ACL of the Domino Directory. To edit just the group type, description, and member fields, however, a user requires only Author access in the ACL of the Domino Directory and *one* of the following:

- He must have the role of group modifier in the Domino Directory.

- His name must be listed (explicitly or in a group context) in either the owners or administrators field. Please note as well that to edit a group document, there is no need for a user to possess document creator rights as defined in the ACL refinement section of the ACL dialog box. The following steps walk you through the process of editing a group.

1. From the Domino Administrator, click the People & Groups tab.

2. Select a group name.

3. Click Edit Group.

4. Change the following fields:

   ◆ **Group Name.** Use this field to change the name of the field that will be displayed in the View pane in the Group view of the Directory

   ◆ **Group Type.** Select one of the following group types:

   Multipurpose. Used for groups that will perform various functions, such as mail, ACL access, and so on

   Mail Only. Used for groups that define users in specific mailing lists

   Access Control List Only. Used for groups that add only ACL's

   Deny List Only. Used to define users that are denied access to the server

   Servers Only. Used to define groups containing only servers

   ◆ **Members.** Use this field to add members to your group.

Adding members can be completed by utilizing the following steps:

1. Type the fully qualified name in the Member field.

2. Select an address book by pushing the down arrow hotspot and selecting a user from an address book and clicking on the Add button. You could also accomplish this by copying and pasting a user from the Username field of the Directory.

With group renaming, simultaneous occurrences of the new and old names are not permitted while the name change makes its way across databases in the domain. For example, if a group name changes in the Domino Directory before it has a chance to change in a database ACL, the old group name in the database ACL is invalid. (This limitation doesn't occur with user and server renaming.)

As a work-around, you can initiate the group rename action during non-peak work hours—for example, over the weekend—or you can immediately process the requests, rather than waiting for the changes to occur according to Administration Process schedules.

How to Delete a Group

To delete a group, your access in the Domino Directory must be set to Editor or Author (with the ability to delete documents and the GroupModifier role assigned).

1. From the Domino Administrator, click People & Groups.

2. Select the group to delete from the View pane.

3. Click Delete Group. You can delete the group immediately by clicking Yes, but the active processes on the server will dictate the amount of time required when the group name is removed from other objects in the Directory.

A dialog box will appear after the group has been deleted successfully.

Also, a user can delete the document if she has Author access in the ACL and her name is listed in the Administrator or Owner field. This would alleviate the need for the user to have the GroupModifier role.

Using the Manage Groups Tool to Manage Groups

The Manage Groups option on the Tools pane provides a quick-and-easy method for managing existing Domino groups. You can open any Domino Directory to which you have Administrator-defined access, and you can then add or remove people and groups from groups as necessary. You can also view details on groups.

To use the Manage Groups tool, execute the following steps:

1. From the Domino Administrator, click the People & Groups tab.

2. From the Tools pane, click Groups, Manage.

3. Make the necessary changes in the correct fields.

The options for the fields in the Manage Groups dialog box are as follows:

- **People and Groups Look In.** This field provides a list of directories available.

- **Group Hierarchies Look In.** This field displays a list of the groups you are managing.

- **Show Me.** This field provides two choices:

  All Group Hierarchies. This field displays the group hierarchies in the selected directory.

  Only Member Hierarchies. This field displays the member hierarchies in the selected directory.

- **List Alphabetically.** This field lists all people and groups in the selected directory alphabetically.

- **List by Organization.** This field lists people and groups in the selected directory.

- **Show Group Type.** This field will limit the group type to one of the following:

  Multipurpose

  Mail Only

  Access Only

  Deny Only

  Servers

  All

Adding members to a group requires you to do the following:

1. Select the group in the Group Hierarchies pane.

2. Select the user or group from the People and Groups List.

3. Click Add.

To remove a group member from a group:

1. Select the member from the Group Hierarchies pane.

2. Click Remove.

To view a group document:

1. Select the group from the Group Hierarchies pane.
2. Click Details.

MAINTAINING NOTES USER IDS

The role of an administrator includes maintenance of user certificates contained in the user ID. User IDs are set with an expiration date at the time of creation. After a Notes ID expires it must be re-certified with a new certificate before it can continue to be used.

Re-Certifying a User ID

Re-certifying a user ID requires Author access with Create Documents access and the UserModifier role or Editor access established in the Domino Directory. The certification log must also be set for Author access with your user ID having the capability to create documents. The steps for re-certifying an ID are as follows:

1. From the Domino Administrator, click People & Groups.
2. Select the user to be re-certified, and from the Tools pane, select People, then select Re-Certify from the drop-down list box.
3. Select the certifier ID originally used to certify the selected users and click Open. When prompted for a password, enter the correct password for the certifier ID to continue.
4. Domino will now present you with the option of setting the date for expiration of the ID. The default is two years, but you can change it by typing in a new date. The second field, Only Renew Certificates That Will Expire Before, is an optional field.
5. Click Certify to complete the process. A Summary dialog box will appear stating whether re-certification was successful.
6. Click OK to continue. If re-certification was not successful, examine the certification log to identify the problem, resolve the issue, and re-certify the ID again.

Note that the required access levels for re-certification that you have out-lined apply only in the case of a manual re-certification process—that is, using the Domino Administrator, Configuration, Certification, Certify option. As was the case with editing groups, there is also no need for cre-ate document rights in this process. In addition to having access to a cer-tifier ID file, an administrator would only require the following levels of access: Reader in the Domino Directory; Author with Create Document rights in the Administration Requests database; and Author with Create Document rights in the Certification Log.

Instances may occur when a mail file will need to be moved to a differ-ent server. A server may need to be reconfigured or a user may need to be moved to another server because they have moved to another depart-ment. Moving a mail file requires that the fields Mail File Name and Mail Server be changed in the location document.

1. From the Domino Administrator, click People & Groups.

2. Select the person whose mail file you are moving.

3. Click Move Mail File.

4. Click Yes at the prompt to move the mail file.

5. Enter the new mail server name and click OK.

Completing the move will require editing the user's Person document in the Domino Directory to reflect the new Server name. The required access to change a user's Person document in the Domino Directory is Editor. The steps for moving a user to a different domain are as follows:

1. Cut and paste the user's Person document from the current Domino Directory. If you move the user's mail file to a different domain, cut and paste the Person document from the Domino Directory to the new domain's Domino Directory.

2. Make the corrections in the new Domain's Directory to reflect the new domain and server names.

NOTE If shared mail is installed and you need to delete a user, unlink the mail file from all databases where it is linked.

Using the Tools Pane to Move a User's Mail File

If you need or want to move a user's mail file, you can do it using the Tools pane. Just follow these steps:

1. From the Domino Administrator, click People & Groups.

2. The Move Mail File(s) dialog box will appear. You can select a server listed, or enter a server in the dialog box.

3. Click OK.

4. Select the directory for the new mail file server and then click OK.

Using this method for moving a mail file will make changes required to the Domino Directory without any intervention required by the Administrator to the person document.

Renaming Users

Instances occur when a user's name will have to be changed, such as when they have gotten married or an error was made at the time of creating the ID. To rename a user you must have Editor access with create documents role access or UserModifier role access to the Domino Directory. In addition, you must have at least Author access with the create documents role access defined in the Certification log. The steps to rename a user are as follows:

1. From the Domino Administrator, click the People & Groups tab.

2. Select the user requiring the name change and from the Tools pane select People, Rename.

3. Select Click Change Common Name. At this point the requestor box will appear asking for a certifier ID. Select the ID that was used to create the ID. Enter the password and click OK to continue.

4. The Rename Selected User dialog box now appears. The option is presented for expiration date of the new ID. This option may be changed.

5. You can now change the Users fist name, middle initial, and last name as required. The last field, New Qualifying Org unit, is an

optional field. This field can be used to place a unique organizational unit identifier into a user's hierarchical name without having to register the user with a physical OU certifier ID file at that OU level.

6. After all the changes have been entered, click Rename and then OK.

7. A Summary dialog box will appear stating if re-certification was successful.

8. Click OK to continue. If re-certification was not successful examine the certification log to identify the problem, resolve the issue, and re-certify the ID again.

Again, in addition to having access to a certifier ID file an administrator would only require the following levels of access: Reader in the Domino Directory; Author with create document rights in the Administration Requests database; and Author with create document rights in the Certification Log.

Recovering IDs or Passwords

Previous versions of Notes would require users who had lost their ID file or had forgotten their password to have a new ID created by the administrator, or have the administrator restore the file using the Escrow agent if it was used during ID creation. With release 5, the administrator now has the option of working with the user to recover the lost ID file.

When a user needs an ID file recovered, the following steps need to be completed:

1. Send an email request to the administrator requesting the encrypted backup ID.

2. From the client, select File, Tools, Recover ID.

3. A requestor dialog box appears prompting you to select the ID to recover. Select the user ID and click Open.

4. The next dialog box prompts you for the first password supplied to unlock the ID. Contact the administrator to get the password to unlock the ID. Lotus recommends that at least three administrators be associated with securing an ID.

5. Enter the administrator's password, and then click Enter.

6. If more than one password is required to unlock the ID, repeat steps 4 and 5 until the ID is unlocked.

7. Enter a new password, and then enter the password again to confirm the change.

8. If more than one ID file exists, the user should delete the duplicate copies and use the new, recovered ID file.

Obtaining an Administration Password for ID File Recovery

To ensure established security, the following steps should be completed by administrators and should only be done at the administrator's workstation. If a user discovers the recovery password, he will have the ability to recover any password for any user ID, so it should be protected from unauthorized use.

1. If the user has access to email, have the user send you an encrypted backup of his ID file. From the user's email request, detach the encrypted backup of the ID file.

2. If the user has stated that the ID file is damaged, send the user a copy of the ID file that should be stored from the time of ID creation.

   Using the Domino Administrator client, select the Configuration tab, and then select choose Certification—Extract Recovery Password.

3. A dialog box appears and requests the password. Enter the password and select OK to continue.

4. Specify the ID file you want to recover. This is the same ID you detached in step 1.

5. Give the user the administration password that is displayed.

Monitoring/Maintaining Users

New Notes users can be created by registering them with the Administration client or by migrating them from existing mail systems.

Adding users requires the appropriate certifier ID. The certifier ID will generate a user ID and the proper certificates to allow system access.

Setting up Notes Users requires an administrator to do the following:

- Define common settings used for workspace and user registration.
- Register users.
- Make install files available to users so that they can install and set up Notes.

Defining Default Settings for Users

Before you register new Notes users, you may want to specify default settings that Notes applies to all users you register. Default settings make user registration easy and fast and ensure that user settings are consistent.

Definable settings include the following:

- **Specific mail servers for users.**
- **Workstation security.** Data can be secured by using a default workstation execution control list (ECL) to prevent unauthorized access.

After the initial settings have been defined, they can be edited by the User Setup profile, Registration preferences, or by modifying settings in the Register Person dialog box.

Registering Users

Notes provides four methods to register users:

- Basic user registration
- Advanced user registration

+ Registration using a text file

+ Migration tools (for people using an external mail system or directory) registration

Basic Registration

Basic user registration is the quickest method for creating a user. You are
required to set user-specific settings, such as user name and password,
while providing the convenience of defining specific default settings,
including:

+ Specific settings in the Registration preferences

+ Specific settings in the Register Person dialog box

Definable settings in Basic registration include the user name and password, as well as the assignment of users to specific groups.

Advanced registration is available during Basic registration by selecting
the Advanced check box in the Register Person dialog box.

Advanced Registration

Definable settings available in Basic registration are also available in
Advanced registration. In addition, the option to change default settings and set up Advanced registration offers all the settings included
in Basic registration and more. Basic registration (and thus Advanced
registration too) allows you to change default settings and define
advanced or specific settings.

Text File Registration

Text files are used for registering groups of users. Two ways to register
users from a text file are as follows:

+ Using the Register person dialog. An entry is created for each user
  in the User Registration Queue. This method allows you to change
  user settings for each user.

+ Users can be registered directly so that the entries for them never
  appear in the User Registration Queue. If users are registered
  directly, non-user–specific settings can be defined before importing
  and registering them.

Migrating Users from External Mail Systems or Directories

Users can also be migrated from external mail systems or directories into Notes. Registration is completed by using migration tools accessed through the Migrate People button in the Register Person dialog box. After migrating them, you can modify their settings. Note that the migration tools are available using only a custom install of the Administration client software.

The following list details the types of users you can migrate into Notes:

- Lotus cc:Mail
- Microsoft Exchange
- LDIF (from an LDAP directory)
- Microsoft Mail
- Windows NT
- Novell GroupWise 4.1
- Novell GroupWise 5
- Netscape Messaging Server

> **NOTE**
> If you choose to delete a user's mail file, you must have at least Editor with Delete Documents access to the Administration Requests database and Delete Documents access to the Domino Directory.

Deleting a User Name

You can delete a user name with the Administration process by initiating a Delete Person from the Domino Administrator by using the Web Administrator, or by using the Windows NT User Manager. When you delete a user, you may want to add that user to a "termination" group to prevent the user from accessing servers. When you create a termination group, assign the group a group type of "Deny Only."

If the server is running Windows NT and a user has a Windows NT account, you can delete this account, too.

Deleting a User

To delete a user, you must have the following rights:

- Author with Delete Documents access and the UserModifier role, or Editor access to the Domino Directory

- Author with Create Documents access to the Certification Log

Also, an administrator would only require Author access in the ACL of the Domino Directory and *one* of the following: his name must be listed (explicitly or in a group context) in either the owners or administrators field or he must have person modifier role.

1. Using the Administrator client, select the People & Groups tab.

> **NOTE**
>
> If you are also deleting the user's mail file, you must have the following rights defined: access equivalent to at least Author, access to create documents in the Administration Requests database, and access to delete documents access in the Domino Directory.

2. Select the user to be deleted, and from the Tools pane select People, Delete.

3. A verification dialog box will appear. Select Yes to continue.

4. A dialog box will appear prompting you to define fields related to deleting the user.

   The available fields are as follows:

   - **What Should Happen with the User's Mail File?** This option will allow you to delete the Person document but not the mail file, to delete the mail file defined in the Person document, or delete the Person document and the mail file for the user.

   - **Add to Group.** Domino provides you with the option to add the user to a group that would stop them from accessing the server. The group name should be entered here. You can type the group name in the empty field or access the group name from the Domino Directory by accessing the button at the end of the field.

- ◆ **Delete Users Windows NT Account?** Select either the Yes or No option to delete the user's NT account.

5. Click OK.

6. The Requestor box will appear. Selecting Yes will cause the Administration Process to immediately delete all references to the user in this replica of the Domino Directory. The Administration Process will also submit a "Delete in Access Control List" request.

If No is selected, the request for deleting the user will be entered into the Administration Requests database and be deleted at the time defined by the Interval setting for the Administration Process.

Upgrading a User's Mail File

The first step in upgrading a user's mail file is to upgrade the Domino server to release 5, and the Notes clients to release 5. If users are not running release 5, new design features will be unavailable. User's mail files should be done at night or over a weekend to ensure that they are not being used. Make sure that users are aware that their mail will be unavailable while the upgrade is being done. The following steps should be completed to upgrade the user's mail database:

1. Access the Domino server screen.

2. The Domino mail route needs to be shut down to ensure that mail is not being routed to users while their mail file is upgraded. To stop the router type `tell router quit`. Then press Enter.

3. The next step is to load the mail conversion utility. Type `load convert mail\user.nsf * mail50.ntf`, substituting the user's mail file name for user.nsf. Press Enter to continue.

4. After the upgrade is complete, reload the router. Type `load router` then press Enter.

TROUBLESHOOTING DIRECTORY PROBLEMS

Troubleshooting directory problems involves stopping or managing replication or save conflicts. This section begins by discussing the two types of conflicts. Then it addresses the means by which you can stop or manage conflicts. Finally, it concludes with discussion of when you might need to use the conflict document as the new master document and how to accomplish that change.

Replication Conflicts

Two or more users editing the same document, then saving changes in different replicas between scheduled replication times will cause replication conflicts to occur. Domino uses the following criteria to determine how to save the edited documents:

- The document with the greater number of saves and edits becomes the main document and other documents will be labeled as replication conflicts.

- If the save and edit count in both documents is the same, the most recently saved document becomes the main document, and remaining documents are labeled replication conflicts.

- In the instance where a document has been edited in a database, but deleted in a replica copy, the deletion will be defined as the primary action. The exception to this instance comes about when the edited document has multiple edits or is edited after being deleted.

Save Conflicts

Two or more users editing the same document at the same time on the same server will cause a save conflict to occur. In this instance, the first document saved becomes the main document. When the second user attempts to save the document, a dialog box appears warning the users that a save conflict exists and if the user continues, the document will appear as a replication or save conflict.

Stopping the Occurrence of Conflicts

There are five ways to decrease the possibility of replication and save conflicts. When a database is created a designer can create the database with three options defined:

- When designing the database, set the Form property "Merge replication conflicts" to resolve conflicts into one master document automatically. Unfortunately, this will only work on replication conflicts; save conflicts will remain unaffected.

- When designing the database, set a Form property with versioning enabled. This will allow edited documents to become the master document.

- Create LotusScript code that resolves the conflicts.

Administrators can use two methods to stop the propagation of conflicts:

- Set database users' access no higher than Author. This will stop users from editing other user's documents, provided that multiple users are not listed in any author's data type fields in the documents.

- Design the Notes network in such a way that the minimum number of replicas are used.

Conflict Management

Administrators need to examine the Domino Directory and check for conflicts. If a conflict occurs, examine both documents, make the changes to the master document that are different, and delete the conflict. The key to conflict management is resolving the issue as quickly as possible after the occurrence. If the conflict can be resolved quickly after it has been created, the resolution will be easier because the documents will be nearly identical and the conflict will be easy to detect. Although a conflict exists, users will be unable to determine which document is the master document and will not know which document to update.

Whenever possible, use the main document as the master and remove the conflict. However, there is no reason that you cannot use the conflict as the new master. To use the existing main document as the main document, copy the different information from the conflict document, and then delete the conflict document.

Using Conflict Documents

There may be an instance where it makes more sense to use the conflict as the new master document. If that is the option, the following steps should be completed to make the conflict the new master.

1. Cut and paste the needed information from the main document into the saved document. If no information is needed from the main document, open the conflict document in edit mode and make a minor change somewhere in the document.

2. The conflict document will now become the new master document due to the changes made in edit mode. Save the document and it becomes the new master document.

3. The original main document will now appear as a conflict. Delete it.

TROUBLESHOOTING USER PROBLEMS

The most obvious problems that users will experience will be related to problems with the Domino server. If the server is down, define policies that will inform users when the server will be available for use. If the server is running and users are not able to access databases, administrators can check the following items:

- **ACLs not defined correctly.**

- **Server tasks running during peak hours of use.** Make sure that backups and system tasks are set up to run during non-working hours.

- **Load balancing is not properly defined.** Proper infrastructure planning will ensure that servers are built to support the required number of users and their requirements.

- **Poor database design.**

- **Database maintenance.** Regularly compacting database as well as other options, such as turning unread marks off, will increase database access speed.

- **System parameters.** Item, such as database cache or server tasks, can be used to maintain server performance.

- **Configuration of the location document.** Make sure all location information is entered correctly.

- **Connection document configuration.** Verify that all ports and connections are set up properly.

- **Port configuration.** Proper port access must be defined for the servers to replicate and send mail properly inside of the Notes domain.

- **User preference settings.** User preferences that are not defined properly may cause intermittent errors.

WHAT IS IMPORTANT TO KNOW

- Domino is well suited for a multi-cultural environment and allows users to have two names: one international name and one in their native language.

- Check the Lotus Web site for periodic updates and apply them as needed. Keep in mind not to upgrade the address book if you are in a multiple-version environment and have already addressed the Directory to release 5.

- The Domino Directory Profile is created when you open your upgraded Directory file, either with a Notes client or a Web client, such as Internet Explorer.

- The new Domino Directory contains new views and has been modified to remove certain views. New views in the Domino Directory include the following:

  External Domain Information

  Holiday

  Web Configurations

- The Manage Groups option on the Tools pane provides a quick-and-easy method for managing existing Domino groups.

- User IDs are set with an expiration date at the time of creation. After a Notes ID expires, it must be re-certified with a new certificate before it can continue to be used.

- Notes provides four methods to register users:

  Basic user registration

  Advanced user registration

  Registration using a text file

  Migration tools (for people using an external mail system or directory) registration

- Users can also be migrated from external mail systems or directories into Notes.

- To maintain a clean working server, things to check for trouble are as follows:

  ACLs not defined correctly.

  Server tasks running during peak hours of use.

  Load balancing is not properly defined.

Poor database design.

Database maintenance.

System parameters.

Configuration of the location document.

Connection document configuration.

Port configuration.

User preference settings.

CHAPTER 3

Monitoring, Maintaining, and Troubleshooting Domino Messaging and Replication

MONITORING AND MAINTAINING REPLICATION

Database replication can be monitored and maintained using a variety of tools. Here are some of the ways that administrators can ensure that replication is happening in a timely fashion, or that it's happening at all.

Using the Notes Log

The Replication Log entries in the Replication Events view of the log file (LOG.NSF) display detailed information about the replication of specific databases. For each database that has replicated on a specified server, a Replication Log shows the access the server has to the database; the number of documents added, deleted, and modified; the size of the data exchanged; and the name of the replica that this database replicated with. The Events section of a Replication Log shows any problems that occurred when a specific database replicated. For example, the Events section shows whether replication is disabled or the database ACL is preventing replication.

Use the Domino Administrator to view a Replication Log.

1. From the Domino Administrator, in the Server pane on the left, select the server that stores the log file you want to view. To expand the pane, click the Servers icon on the left.

2. Click the Server, Analysis tab.

3. Select Notes Log, Replication Events.

4. Open a recent Replication Log.

If you don't have access to the Domino Administrator, you can open the log by choosing File, Database, Open.

Viewing the Database Replication History

A database's replication history is stored in the Basics tab of the Database Properties dialog box. The first time one server replica successfully replicates with a replica on another server, Domino creates an entry in the replication history. The entry contains the name of the other server, as well as the date and time of the replication. Separate entries are created when a replica sends information and when a replica receives it. On each subsequent replication with a specific server, Domino updates the entry in the history to reflect the most recent replication time.

Domino uses the replication history to determine in which documents to scan for changes during the next replication. For example, if a database successfully replicated with the Server1/East/Acme server 24 hours ago, Domino replicates only those documents that were added, modified, or deleted in the replica on Server1/East/Acme within the last 24 hours.

Before replication starts between two databases, Domino checks the replication history of both databases to make sure that they agree. If they don't, Domino scans each document created or modified since the data specified in the Only Replicate Incoming Documents Saved or Modified After setting on the Other panel of the Replication Settings dialog box.

If a database doesn't replicate successfully, Domino doesn't update the replication history.

If you have Manager access to a database, you can clear the database's replication history if you think the database doesn't contain all the documents it should or if the database's replication history is not synchronized with that of other replicas. Clear the replication history only as a last resort to solve replication problems. If you clear the history, during the next replication, Domino scans each document created or modified since the data specified in the Only Replicate Incoming Documents Saved or Modified After setting on the Other panel of the Replication Settings dialog box. Scanning all these documents can be time consuming, especially over dial-up connections. If you clear the Only Replicate Incoming Documents Saved or Modified After setting, Domino scans all documents in the database.

Creating Replication Monitors

A Replication Monitor document monitors replication failures and infrequent replication activity on the Domino system. Replication monitors generate events to the Server, Analysis, Statistics Reports, Events view in the Domino Administrator. Replication monitors are usually created by administrators as part of an organization's statistics and monitoring plan. For more information on how to monitor the Domino system as a whole, see the Domino 5 Administration Help database. To create a Replication Monitor document, follow these steps:

1. From the Domino Administrator, click the Configuration tab.

2. Click Statistics & Events, Monitors, Replication.

3. Click New Replication Monitor.

4. Click the Basics tab and complete the appropriate fields that pertain to the server and database(s) being monitored.

5. Click the Other tab and next to Generate a Replication Event of Severity, click the arrow, and select a severity level.

6. Click Create a New Notification Profile for This Event.

7. Keep this monitor enabled.

8. Click OK.

Using the Database Analysis Tool to Monitor Replication

You can perform a database analysis to collect information about one or more databases from a variety of sources—the replication history, the User Activity dialog box, and the log file (LOG.NSF)—and view it in a single "results" database. You can perform a database analysis only if you have access to the Domino Administrator.

Use database analysis to collect the following information about a database:

- Replication history, as recorded in the Replication History dialog box
- User reads and writes, as recorded in the User Activity dialog box
- Document creations, edits, and deletions, as recorded in a database
- Design changes, as recorded in a database
- Replication additions, updates, and deletions, as reported in the log file (LOG.NSF)
- Mail messages delivered by the mail router

You can collect this information from multiple replicas of a database. The steps involved in performing a database analysis are as follows:

1. From the Domino Administrator, in the Server pane on the left, select the server that stores the databases you want to analyze. To expand the pane, click the Servers icon.

2. Click the Files tab.

3. Select the folder containing the databases you want to analyze.

4. In the Files window, select the databases you want to analyze.

5. In the Tools pane on the right, select Database, Analyze. Or drag the selected database(s) to the Analyze tool.

6. In the Analyze Last x Days of Activity field, enter a number representing the days' worth of information to report. You can specify up to 99; the higher the number, the longer it takes to generate the results.

7. Select one or more of the remaining options from the table.

8. Click Results. Take the following steps, and click OK:

   ◆ Specify the server, title, and file name of the database where you want to store the results. It's recommended that you create the results database on a local client rather than on a server. If multiple people generate results databases on a server, they should each specify a different file name so that the results don't conflict.

   ◆ If the specified results database already exists, click Overwrite Database to write over the existing contents, or click Append to This Database to add the new results to existing ones.

9. Click OK to run the analysis.

10. To see the results, open the database and choose one of the available views.

11. Open Database Analysis Results documents in the selected view.

It should be noted that by following the preceding steps, an analysis of any database can be performed; there is, however, an easier way to perform an analysis of the log file (LOG.NSF). To do a log analysis, simply go to the Server, Analysis tab of the Administrator. Then choose Tools, Log Analysis, and follow steps 6–11 in the preceding list.

How to Force Replication

Replication between database replicas on servers typically occurs according to schedules in Connection documents. However, there are times when you want to force replication between two replicas, rather than wait for replication to occur on schedule. For example, you might force replication when you want to test replication settings or troubleshoot replication problems. The following three methods can all be used to force the replication of one database or several databases.

Using the Server Console

If you are a server administrator, you can use the Replicate, Pull, or Push server console command to force replication between servers. Optionally, you can specify a database parameter to force replication of a specific database that two servers have in common. These commands can be entered directly at the server or by using the remote console from the Domino Administrator.

- Use the Replicate command to send changes to and receive changes from a specified server.

- Use the Pull command to receive changes from a specified server.

- Use the Push command to send changes to a specified server.

For example, to send changes to the database PRODUCTS.NSF from the server Server1/East/Acme to the server Web/East/Acme, enter the following command from the console on Server1/E/East/Acme:

```
Push Web/East/Acme Products.nsf
```

Using the Replicate Command Within the Domino Administrator

Rather than using the console's command-based interface to force replication, administrators can use the Domino Administrator's graphical user interface to issue the same replication commands as outlined in the previous section. To access this interface, perform the following steps:

1. Start up the Domino Administrator and go to the Server, Status tab.

2. From the Tools list on the right, choose Server, Replicate.

3. Make the appropriate choices within the dialog box to replicate one or all databases with a selected server.

Forcing Replication from Within the Database

Replication of a single database can be forced by anybody using a Notes client and having at least Reader access to a database.

1. Open the database.

2. Choose File, Replication, Replicate.

3. Select Replicate with Options and click OK.

4. Select the server that stores the replica with which you want to replicate.

5. Select Send Documents to Server to send updates from the replica selected on your workspace to the server selected in step 4.

6. Select Receive Documents from Server to send updates from the server selected in step 4 to the replica selected on your workspace.

7. Click OK.

REPLICATING DESIGN CHANGES

There are several ways to force design changes to propagate throughout databases within an organization. It is important to know how each of these methods works as well as the pros and cons of each method.

Refreshing or Replacing a Database Design

One way of updating a database's design involves using either a Refresh Design or Replace Design command. Both of these methods affect only design elements, and do not use replication as a means of transferring the design notes between databases.

Refreshing a design updates a database whose design is linked to a template. The Design Refresh can be effected in one of two ways:

- Manually, using the File, Database, Refresh Design command
- Automatically, by allowing the Design task to run on the server, which runs by default every night at 1 a.m.

The Replace Design command makes a database identical to a template and is the only way to distribute design changes if the database doesn't inherit its changes from a template. The only way that a database design can be replaced is by issuing the File, Database, Replace Design command. You must have Designer access or higher to the database to be able to issue this command.

Using Replication to Update a Database's Design

The replication process involves the exchange of three different types of data, in this order:

- Access Control List elements
- Design elements
- Data documents

Because design changes are automatically exchanged during replication along with Access Control List changes and data documents, the administrator need only ensure that the proper access control levels apply to each database involved in the replication process. To receive design changes from a source server, the database replica on the destination server must give the source server at least Designer access, and the source server replica must give the destination server at least Reader access. For both servers to receive design changes during replication, each server must have Designer access to the database.

RESOLVING REPLICATION AND SAVE CONFLICTS

As a Domino administrator, you will have to be on top of many details, not the least of which are replication and save conflicts. The following sections will outline the basic causes and resolutions for these conflicts, as well as some preventative medicine.

How Conflicts Occur

Multiple users can simultaneously edit the same document in one copy of a database or edit the same document in different replicas between replication sessions. When these conditions occur, Domino stores the results of one editing session in a main document and stores the results of additional editing sessions as response documents. These response documents have the title Replication or Save Conflict. Domino uses the $Revisions field, which tracks the date and time of each document editing session, to determine which document becomes the main document and which documents become responses.

A replication conflict occurs when two or more users edit the same document and save the changes in different replicas between replications. These rules determine how Domino saves the edits sessions:

- ◆ The document edited and saved the most times becomes the main document; other documents become Replication or Save Conflict documents.

- ◆ If all of the documents are edited and saved the same number of times, the document saved most recently becomes the main document, and the others become Replication or Save Conflict documents.

- ◆ If a document is edited in one replica but it is deleted in another replica, the deletion takes precedence, unless the edited document is edited more than once or the editing occurs after the deletion.

Consolidating Replication or Save Conflicts

Regularly look for and consolidate Replication or Save Conflicts. To consolidate a conflict, merge information into one document and remove the other document. Conflicts are easiest to consolidate soon after they occur, since the conflict document is still closely synchronized with the information in the main document. It's important to consolidate Replication or Save Conflicts quickly, so users have access to the correct information. To locate Replication or Save Conflicts, create a view that displays only conflict documents. Then, to see a conflict document in context with its main document, select the Replication or Save Conflict document in the view that displays conflicts, hold down the Ctrl key, and switch to the view that shows the main document.

To consolidate replication or save conflicts, you can save the main document or save the Replication or Save Conflict document.

To Save the Main Document

Saving the main document is a matter of a few simple steps:

1. Copy any information you want to save from the Replication or Save Conflict document into the main document.

2. Delete the conflict document.

To Save the Replication or Save Conflict Document

1. Do one of the following:

    ◆ Copy any information you want to save from the main document into the Replication or Save Conflict document.

    ◆ If you do not need to save any information from the main document, perform a minor edit in the Replication or Save Conflict document—for example, deleting a space.

2. Save the conflict document. The conflict document becomes a main document.

3. Delete the original main document. It is essential that steps 1 and 2 be undertaken before deleting the document. After the document has been deleted from the database, it can be retrieved only from a backup.

Preventing Replication or Save Conflicts

These techniques reduce or eliminate Replication or Save Conflicts. The first three are techniques that a database designer uses. The last three are techniques that a system administrator or database manager can use.

- Select the Form property Merge Replication Conflicts to automatically merge conflicts into one document if no fields conflict. This applies only to replication conflicts and not to save conflicts.

- Specify a Form property for versioning so that edited documents automatically become new documents.

- Use LotusScript to write a custom conflict handler.

- Assign users Author access or lower in the database ACL to prevent users from editing other users' documents.

- Keep the number of replicas to a minimum.

- If the database property Limit Entries in $Revisions Fields is set to a value greater than 0, increase the limit by specifying a greater value than the existing one or specify –1 to remove the limit.

TROUBLESHOOTING REPLICATION PROBLEMS

The following topics suggest common problems associated with scheduled replications, along with their solutions.

Total Replication Failure

Sometimes replication fails to happen at all. Most often, the problem is either a communication or network failure, or a complete server failure. Other causes could include the fact that replication may have been disabled for a specific database, or that connection documents may have been changed and are no longer working. Here is a list of possible problems along with some viable solutions:

- Check to see whether you are having network problems. Test network and dial-up connections to see whether other network services are operating.

- Check to see whether or not the Notes server is running. If the server is running, check the Server, Status tab of the Domino Administrator or issue the command "show tasks" at the server console to see whether or not the Replica task is running.

- Verify that replication has not been disabled for the database(s) in question. To do this, open the database and choose File, Replication, Settings, Other section and ensure that Temporarily Disable Replication is not checked.

- Verify that any relevant connection documents are accurate. Sometimes changes can be made to connection documents that cause replication to fail, such as changing port information or server names.

A Database Replica Does Not Contain All the Documents It Should

The following sections are a list of possibilities to explore when documents don't seem to be properly replicating between databases.

Replicas Are Different Sizes

If changes made to one replica have not yet replicated, the content of replicas may be different until replication occurs.

The Source Server Has Insufficient Access

The source server access in a destination replica ACL determines what the destination replica can receive from the source server. Give the source server higher access in the destination replica ACL if necessary.

No Destination Server in an Access List

Access lists allow only a subset of people and servers in the ACL to access documents. If such access lists exist, add the destination server to them in the source server replica. If the access list uses a role to define access, add the destination server to the role on the source server replica.

An Intermediate Server Has Insufficient Access

If replication between a source and destination server occurs through an intermediate server, make sure the source and destination server replica ACLs give the intermediate server high enough access to replicate all changes.

Replication Settings Are Filtering Documents

Some replication settings act as filters that screen out documents and features. Check the replication settings by opening the database and choosing File, Replication, Settings. For example, in the Space Savers section, the setting Remove Documents Not Modified in the Last x Days would remove any documents older than a specific date. You may discover one day that many documents have disappeared from the database based on this setting if it has been selected.

The Server Is Out of Disk Space

Check to see if the database is a Release 4 format database and has exceeded the maximum database size. Ask your Domino administrator to resolve disk space problems and if necessary, consider moving a replica to another server or deleting databases on the server.

Older Documents Weren't Replicated to a New Replica

When the replica was created, the date specified for the replication setting option Only Replicate Incoming Documents Saved or Modified After is later than it should have been. This option is on the Other panel of the File, Replication, Settings dialog box in the Notes client. Create a new replica with an earlier date specified.

Database Replicas Are Different Sizes

Database replicas may be different sizes for the reasons listed in the following sections.

Replication Settings

Some replication settings cause one replica to receive only a subset of documents and features from another replica. For example, in the File, Replication, Settings, Space Savers section, the setting Replicate a Subset of Documents may have been checked off, limiting the replication of documents within a specific view or folder.

Access Control List

The ACL may be preventing a replica from receiving all documents or design elements from a source replica. Verify that the source and destination servers have sufficient access rights within the ACL.

Read ACLs or Reader Names Fields

A destination server isn't included in a Read ACL or Readers field and therefore doesn't receive all documents from a source server replica. In this scenario, the administrator should seek help from the designer of the application who was responsible for implementing read access at the document level.

View Indexes

A view is used in one replica but not in another, and the replica containing the unused view is smaller because no index is built for the unused view.

Personal Agents, Views, or Folders

These features, used on one replica but not another, can cause a size disparity between the replicas.

Deletions Are Not Replicated

Check these replication settings in File, Replication, Settings in the Notes client:

- On the Advanced panel, the Deletions option under Replicate Incoming is not selected.
- On the Send panel, the Do Not Send Deletions Made in This Replica to Other Replicas option is selected.

Unused Space

One replica has been compacted while another has not been compacted. The compacted replica may have recovered unused whitespace and is therefore smaller than the replica that has not been compacted.

Deleted Documents Reappear

When deleted documents reappear in another replica copy of a database, typically the problem is either a purge interval prevents replication of deletions or a document edit writes over a document deletion.

A Purge Interval Prevents Replication of Deletions

When a document is deleted, it leaves behind a deletion stub. When the database replicates, Notes uses the deletion stub to identify and delete the same document in the replica.

To save disk space, Notes purges deletion stubs that remain from document deletions according to the replication setting Remove Documents Not Modified in the Last x Days. If Notes purges the deletion stubs before they have a chance to replicate, deleted documents can reappear after the next replication. This option is on the Space Saver panel of the File, Replication, Settings dialog box in the Notes client. The purge interval is one third of the value of the number recorded in the Remove Documents Not Modified in the Last x Days field.

A Document Edit Writes over a Document Deletion

When the same document is modified on different servers between replication sessions, the document that was modified most frequently takes precedence, or if both documents are modified only once, the one modified most recently takes precedence.

If a document is edited multiple times on one server and deleted on another server between replication sessions, the edited document takes precedence because it underwent the greatest number of changes, even if the deletion was the most recent change.

If somebody deletes a document on one server and then someone else updates the document on another server once between replication sessions, the edit overrides the deletion because both documents were updated once and the edit occurred after the deletion.

MONITORING AND MAINTAINING MAIL ROUTING

Domino provides three tools that you can use to monitor mail. Message tracking allows you to track specific mail messages to determine if the intended recipients received them. Mail usage reports provide the information you need to resolve mail problems and improve the efficiency of your mail network. Mail probes test and gather statistics on mail routes.

Tracking Mail Messages

Both Domino administrators and end users can track mail. Administrators can track mail sent by any user, while end users can track only messages that they themselves sent.

When you configure mail tracking, you can specify which types of information that Domino records. For example, you can specify that Domino not record message tracking information for certain users, or you can choose not to record the subject line of messages sent by specific users.

Domino records all message tracking information in the Mail Tracking Store database (MTSTORE.NSF). When an administrator or user searches for a particular message, Domino searches the Mail Tracking Store database, which is created automatically when you start the Mail Tracking program on the server.

How Mail Tracking Works

The following steps describe the process of tracking a mail message:

1. Create a query to determine whether a specific message arrived at its intended destination or to determine how far it got if delivery failed.

2. Message tracking begins on the starting server. If the message is found there, the tracking automatically continues on the next server on the route.

3. Step 2 is repeated on each "next server" until the route ends. Detailed information is provided about the processing of the message on each server.

4. Select the message and then check the delivery status, which is one of these: delivered; delivery failed; in queue; transferred; transfer failed; group expanded; unknown. For a detailed explanation of each of these terms, refer to the Domino 5 Administration Help database.

Setting Up Message Tracking and Monitoring

To set up mail tracking and monitoring, you must complete these procedures:

1. Start mail tracking (the mtc task) on the server.

2. Configure the server for message tracking.

3. Set up the Reports database (REPORTS.NSF).

Starting the MTC Task

To start the MTC task, navigate to the Server, Status tab of the Domino Administrator. From the Tools list, choose Task, Start. Select Message Tracking Collector from the list of tasks and click the Start button.

Configuring the Server for Message Tracking

Perform the following steps to configure a specific server for message tracking:

1. From the Domino Administrator, click the Configuration tab.

2. Expand the Server view.

3. In the Use Directory On field, choose Current Server.

4. Perform either step 5 or step 6, depending on whether you need to create a new Configuration Settings document.

5. To create a new Configuration Settings document:

♦ Click Configurations, and then click Add Configuration.

♦ Click the Basics tab.

♦ Click Yes in the Use These Settings as the Default Settings for All Servers check box to use this Configuration Settings document to apply to all servers. Otherwise, enter the name of a specific server or group in the Group or Server Name field.

- Leave all other fields to default.

- Click Save and Close.

6. Click Configurations, and then double-click the name of the server for which you want to enable message tracking.

7. In the Configuration Settings document, click the Router/SMTP, Message Tracking tab.

8. Click Edit Server Configuration.

9. In the Message Tracking field, choose Enabled.

10. Optionally, complete the rest of the fields, or accept the default options.

Setting Up the Reports Database

The Reports database (REPORTS.NSF) must be loaded on the server to generate mail usage reports. Typically, the Reports database is created automatically when you set up the server. For security purposes, you must perform the following steps manually:

1. View the Access Control List (ACL) and verify that the administrator of the server and the server itself are present and have manager access.

2. Use the View, Agents list box and enable all scheduled agents.

3. Give the administrator unrestricted agent access on the server by adding them to the server document under Security, Agent Restrictions, Run Unrestricted LotusScript/Java Agents.

Generating Mail Usage Reports

Over time, the Mail Tracking Store database contains historical data about messaging on the server. It may be useful to generate mail usage reports from this data. For example, you can generate reports of recent messaging activity, message volume, individual usage levels, and heavily traveled message routes.

Mail usage reports provide important information that you can use to resolve problems and improve the efficiency of the mail network. In addition, this information is valuable when you plan changes or expansions to the mail network. For example, you can generate a report that shows the top 25 largest messages or the top users by the number and size of messages. With this information, you can identify users who might be misusing your mail system. Reports showing the most popular next and previous hops can help you assess compliance with corporate mail use policies.

Domino uses the data stored in the Mail Tracking Store database (MTSTORE.NSF) to create mail usage reports. As an administrator, you can generate a one-time report, or you can generate scheduled reports. By default, Domino generates scheduled reports at midnight at the interval you specify—daily, weekly, or monthly.

The Reports database (REPORTS.NSF) stores all mail usage reports. Views in the database display reports according to report type, date, and user. In addition, a view displays all scheduled reports by interval. Perform the following steps to create a mail usage report:

1. Make sure that you set up mail monitoring.

2. Open the Reports database.

3. Click Run Report.

4. Complete all necessary fields, and then click OK. For a complete listing of all fields and their descriptions, consult the Domino 5 Administration Help database.

Alternatively, reports can be generated from the Domino Administrator. Go to the Messaging, Mail tab and choose Reports, Create Report. The report is then generated as described in the preceding steps.

Creating a Mail Probe

Using a mail probe, you can test and gather statistics on mail routes. To test a mail route, ISpy sends a mail-trace message to the mail server of the individual you specify. The probe generates a statistic that indicates the amount of time, in seconds, that it took to deliver the message. If the probe fails, the statistic has the value −1. The format of a mail probe statistic is:

QOS.Mail.*RecipientName.ResponseTime*

If the Collect task is running, the Statistics database (STATREP.NSF) stores the mail probe statistics. In addition, ISpy generates events for probes that fail. You can set up an Event Notification document to notify you when an event has occured. By default, ISpy monitors the local mail server. To monitor other Domino mail servers, you must create probe documents.

1. Make sure that you started the ISpy task on the server.

2. From the Domino Administrator, click the Configuration tab.

3. Click Statistics & Events, Probes, Mail.

4. Click New Mail Probe.

5. Click the Basics tab and complete these fields:

    ◆ **Probing Servers (Source).** Enter the server you want the probe to start from or select the server from the drop-down box.

    ◆ **Target Mail Address (Destination).** Enter the mail recipient for which you want to check the mail route or use the drop-down box to select a recipient from a Domino Directory or Address Book. Do not enter more than one individual and do not enter a group name.

6. Click the Probe tab and complete these fields:

    ◆ **Send Interval.** Enter the probe interval. This is the frequency at which probes will be sent.

    ◆ **Time Out Threshold.** Enter the time out threshold. This is the period the probing server (source) will wait for a response before logging a failure.

7. Click the Other tab, complete these fields, and then click OK.

    ◆ **Event.** Select the severity of the event you want to be generated if the probe fails.

    ◆ **Create a New Notification Profile for This Event.** You can set up notification for a custom event. If you click this button, you will be guided through the process by the Event Notification Wizard.

    ◆ **Enablement.** Select the Disable the Probe field if you want to disable this probe. You can re-enable it at any time.

HOW TO FORCE MAIL ROUTING

There are two methods that can be used by administrators to force mail to route immediately. The administrator can issue the Route command at the server console, or the Domino Administrator user interface can be used.

Using the Route Command at the Server Console

The Route command sends mail to or requests mail from a server immediately. This command overrides any mail routing schedules that you create in the Connection documents in the Domino Directory. Use the Route command for servers that are configured for Pull, Pull Push, Push, or Push Wait routing in the Connection document. Use the server's full hierarchical name, if applicable. If the server name is more than one word, enclose the entire name in quotes. For example, to force mail routing from the current server to Server1/East/Acme, open the console on the current server and issue the following command:

```
Route Server1/East/Acme
```

If no mail is queued for routing, Domino ignores the Route command. To check which servers have mail queued, enter this command at the console:

```
Tell Router Show
```

Routing Mail with the Domino Administrator

You can also route mail directly from the Server, Status tab in the Domino Administrator.

1. From the Domino Administrator, click the Server, Status tab.

2. If necessary, click Tools to display the toolbar, and then click Server, Route Mail.

3. Under Route with Server, enter the name of the server you want to route mail to, or select the name of the server from the list.

4. Click Route.

TROUBLESHOOTING MAIL ROUTING PROBLEMS

When dead or pending mail indicates a problem with mail routing or when users have problems sending or receiving mail, steps can be taken to gather information, identify the problem, and then correct it.

Checking Mail Routing Topology Maps

Mail routing topology maps are useful to track mail routing problems between servers. Administrators can also use the mail routing events view in the log file, LOG.NSF, to check for mail routing problems.

1. From the Domino Administrator, click the Messaging, Mail tab.

2. Choose one of the following:

   ◆ Mail Routing Topology by Connections

   ◆ Mail Routing Topology by Named Networks

Analyzing Delivery Failure Reports

Users should always try to resend memos for which they receive Delivery Failure Reports. To help users troubleshoot delivery failure, ask them to use steps 1–3 in the following list to send you a copy of their mail database. Sending you a copy of their mail database preserves the field properties of the reports, which you analyze as a means of troubleshooting. Alternatively, users could delegate authority to the Administrator so that the Administrator could read any delivery failure reports from within the user's mail database.

1. The user creates a new mail database on the workstation. From the menu, choose File, Database, New. Be sure to use the MAIL50.NTF template.

2. The user copies any Delivery Failure Reports from the original mail file and pastes them into the new database.

3. The user attaches the new mail database to a mail message and sends it to you.

4. You open the mail database attached to the mail message and select a Delivery Failure Report.

The Delivery Failure Report identifies the reason the delivery failed and the routing path over which the message was sent. Use this information to further investigate the problem.

Tracing the Mail Delivery Route

To troubleshoot mail routing or test mail connections, you trace a mail delivery to test whether a message can be successfully delivered without actually sending a test message.

1. From the Domino Administrator, click the Messaging, Mail tab.

2. If necessary, click Tools to display the toolbar.

3. From the toolbar, click Messaging, Send Mail Trace.

4. Complete the following fields, and then click Send:

   • **To.** The mail address of a particular user.

   • **Subject.** The subject of the trace.

   • **Send Delivery Report From.** Choose either Each Router on Path to receive a delivery report from each router on the path or Last Router Only to receive a delivery report only from the last router.

The mail trace is delivered to the Administrator's mail database, with a report indicating the path traced. The Administrator then uses this information to troubleshoot where problems have occurred along the route.

Checking the Domino Directory for Errors that Affect Mail Routing

The Domino Directory is the source of many conditions that prevent mail from routing properly. Check for these conditions and correct them, if necessary.

1. Check the replication history of the Domino Directory to ensure that changes to it are replicating properly. Make sure the Domino Directory's ACL provides servers with at least Editor access. Check for messages in the Administration Requests database, and verify that the Administration Process is set up and working properly.

2. Look for and correct any of these problems with person documents:

   ◆ There's no person document for the recipient in the Domino Directory. If necessary, register the recipient to create one.

   ◆ The mail recipient's name, mail server, or mail file is incorrect or is spelled incorrectly. Correct the entries, if necessary.

   ◆ Multiple occurrences of the recipient's name, in the Domino Directory. There may be more than one person document, a user and a group of the same name, and so on. You can add a middle initial to one of the user names if two users share the same name. You can modify a group name if it's duplicate of another.

   ◆ The recipient receives mail through a gateway. Make sure the recipient's person document contains a forwarding address.

3. Check the Server documents of the sender's and recipient's mail servers. Make sure that the names of the server, domain, and Notes named network are spelled correctly.

4. Check Connection documents for mail routing. To check mail routing connections, from the Domino Administrator, click the Messaging, Mail tab. You can see mail routing topology in two ways: Mail Routing Topology by Connections and Mail Routing Topology by Named Networks. Look for servers that can't reach a server in another Domino named network or domain. Then check the Domino Directory for these problems and edit or create the documents as necessary.

5. If mail routing occurs through a non-adjacent or foreign domain, check that the Domino Directory contains a correctly set up Non-adjacent or Foreign domain document. For a non-adjacent domain, verify that a Connection document to the intermediary, or "middle," domain also exists.

Checking the Workstations of Users Involved in Sending and/or Receiving Mail

The following workstation-based conditions could affect the way mail is being routed and should be checked:

1. Check the User Preferences (File, Preferences, User Preferences). Check the settings for Mail—for example, the Mail Program field may be set to None, which disables all mail for the user. Check the settings under ports; the port(s) necessary to send mail may be disabled.

2. Check the user's Personal Address Book for a missing view. If a view is missing, replace the design of the Personal Address Book. Choose File, Database, Replace Design and specify the Personal Address Book template, PERNAMES.NTF, not the Domino Directory template, PUBNAMES.NTF. Replacing the design deletes any non-standard private views but does not affect the data.

3. Check whether the user is using the appropriate Location document. For example, a mobile user who is working in the office may be attempting to use a Location document that is for use only when the user works at home. Another possibility is that the Location document may contain incorrect information. To check the current Location document, from the workstation, choose File, Preferences, Location Preferences. Also, check that the sender's workstation is set up with the correct mail server and mail file names by looking in Location Preferences and verifying the settings in the Home/mail server and Mail file fields.

Checking the Server for Errors that Affect Mail

Check for these conditions and correct them, if necessary:

1. Verify that the sending and receiving servers have a certificate in common. From the Domino Administrator, click the People and Groups tab. From the toolbar, click Certification, ID File. Choose the appropriate server ID file and click Open. Click Certificates to

display the certificates held by the server. Repeat for the second server. Re-certify one or both server IDs, as necessary.

2. Make sure there's enough memory and disk space on the recipient's mail server. Add memory to the server, and/or increase the disk space for swapping. Add disk space to the server.

3. Check for a corrupt mail file. On rare occasions a recipient's mail file may become corrupted. Do one of these:

   ◆ Run the Fixup task. Use this task if the database is in Domino Release 5 format and if you are *not* using transaction logging, or if the database is in Domino Release 4 format.

   ◆ Run the Fixup task with the -J option. Use this task if the database is in Domino Release 5 format and you are using transaction logging. If you use a backup utility certified for Domino Release 5 and you run Fixup -J, perform a full backup of the database as soon as Fixup finishes.

4. Check for a corrupt MAIL.BOX on the server. Run the Fixup task with the parameters specified in step 3. If the corruption still persists, shut down the server and rename MAIL.BOX—for example, rename it to BADMAIL.BOX. Then restart the server to generate a new MAIL.BOX file and copy any uncorrupted documents from BADMAIL.BOX to MAIL.BOX.

5. Check for problems with modem connections.

Checking the Shared Mail Setup

Check for these conditions and correct them, if necessary:

1. Verify that shared mail is enabled. To determine if a mail file or individual mail files in a directory use shared mail, enter this command at the console:

   `Load Object Info USERMAIL.NSF`

   USERMAIL.NSF is the name of a user's mail file or the name of a directory that contains mail files.

2. Check for a corrupt shared mail file. If you suspect the shared mail file is corrupt, you can restore the file.

3. Verify that there's enough disk space available for the shared mail file. If there isn't, you can purge obsolete message from a shared mail file.

4. Make sure the user's mail file hasn't been unlinked from the shared mail file. If necessary, relink the mail file.

For more detailed instructions on how to perform the preceding steps, consult the Domino 5 Administration Help database.

MIGRATING TO DOMINO FROM OTHER MAIL SYSTEMS

The migration tools in the Domino Administrator allow you to easily migrate information from your existing messaging and directory system to Lotus Notes and Domino Release 5. With the migration tools, you can import users from a foreign directory, register them as Notes users, and then, convert mail from supported mail systems to Notes mail. The migration tools let you migrate all users from a foreign directory or select specific users to migrate.

By default, the migration tools are not installed with the Domino Administrator; you must select the Migration Tools component during installation. If you did not install either the Domino Administrator or the migration tools when you first installed the Notes client, run the installation again.

Importing Users from a Foreign Directory

A post office directory, such as a cc:Mail post office directory or a Microsoft Exchange Address Book, stores basic information about users of the system: names, mail addresses, passwords, and so forth. During migration the migration tools extract information from the foreign directory and use it in creating person documents in the Domino Directory.

The process of importing users consists of the following component tasks:

1. **Specifying the foreign directory source.** A source directory or address book contains important information about users of the old mail system. Using the Domino Administrator, you select the type of directory and then enter the information needed to connect to it and extract information from it. You can then browse the list of available users and select those to be imported to Notes.

2. **Selecting users to migrate.** After selecting a directory to import, you can select the users and groups you want to migrate. If you are migrating from multiple systems, you can select users and groups from different foreign directories during a single session. For example, from the People and Groups Migration dialog box, you can select 10 users to migrate from a cc:Mail directory, and then select additional users from a Microsoft Exchange directory. If you select the cc:Mail directory again, the 10 users are still selected.

3. **Setting migration options.** You can set options on the People and Groups Migration dialog box to specify how information in the source directory is imported into the Domino Directory and Notes mail file. The options you set apply to all users imported from the current directory source during this session. You can select a different set of options for each directory source you import from in the session. The items available in the Migration Options list depend on the foreign directory source selected. The following import options are available:

   ◆ Generate Random Passwords

   ◆ Add Full Name Provided to the Notes Person Document

   ◆ Allow Addition of Empty Groups to Notes

   ◆ Convert Mail

   ◆ Convert Mail Only

Case Study: Migrating Microsoft Exchange Users

Notes provides migration tools to facilitate the migration to Notes from many different mail systems, such as cc:Mail, Microsoft Mail, LDIF files, and so on. This section describes the migration from Microsoft Exchange to Notes. Because each migration is slightly different, consult the Domino 5 Administration Help for examples and instructions involving other mail systems.

Using the Microsoft Exchange to Notes migration tools in the Domino Administrator, you can import Microsoft Exchange users and distribution lists from a selected server and add them to the Domino directory as Notes users and groups. The migration process does the following:

- Imports users and distribution lists from the Exchange server and creates entries for them in the Domino Directory.
- Lets you create a Notes ID and mail file for imported users.
- Migrates the contents of mailboxes (PST files) that are located in a central location, such as on the Microsoft Exchange server.

The following steps must be accomplished to move users from Microsoft Exchange to Notes:

1. Preparing to migrate users from Microsoft Exchange
2. Importing users and groups from the Microsoft Exchange directory
3. Registering migrated users

Preparing to Migrate Users from Microsoft Exchange

Before migrating users from Microsoft Exchange to Notes, complete the following tasks:

- Determine the order in which you want to convert your Exchange servers to Notes. This should be your migration schedule.
- Verify that you have purchased the appropriate Notes client license for each Microsoft Exchange user you are migrating.

- On your administrative workstation, install the Notes Release 5 Domino Administrator client and the optional Exchange Administrative migration tools. You must perform a custom installation to install the migration tools component.

- Back up Domino information.

- Verify that you have access the certifier IDs and passwords for the Domino organizations and organizational units where you are registering users.

- Verify that you have Editor, Designer, or Manager access rights to the Domino Directory on the Registration Server.

- From the administrative workstation, log in to Notes with a Notes ID that has Create Database Access on the Mail server.

- On the administrative workstation, close all applications except for Notes, and close any Notes databases.

- (Optional) Create a Notes group that you can add migrated users to.

- Send any pending Microsoft Exchange messages by making sure Synchronization has been performed on each client.

- Perform an Exchange Directory Synchronization to ensure that the Exchange directory being migrated is complete.

- Make sure the workstation running the Domino Administrator has an Outlook or Exchange client installed and an Administrator mail profile that points to the Exchange server.

Importing the Microsoft Exchange Directory

The Microsoft Exchange directory contains information for the Microsoft Exchange users who will be migrated to Notes. Notes uses the information extracted from the directory to configure migrated users for registration.

Importing the Microsoft Exchange directory involves the following:

- Connecting to the Exchange server

- Importing Microsoft Exchange users into the registration queue

Connecting to the Exchange Server

To import users to migrate, you first need to locate the Exchange server where users have their mailboxes, and log into it.

1. At the administrative workstation where you installed the Domino Administrator, insert a disk containing the appropriate certifier IDs for the organizations and organizational units where you are registering users.

2. From the Domino Administrator, click the People and Groups tab.

3. From the Tools pane, click People, Register.

4. When prompted, enter the certifier ID password and click OK.

5. Remove the disk containing the certifier ID and click OK.

6. (Optional) From the Basics pane of the Register Person—New Entry dialog box, specify a registration server if necessary, by clicking Registration Server and selecting the server that registers new users. Click OK.

7. Click Migrate People.

8. From the People and Group Migration dialog box, select Microsoft Exchange Users from the Foreign directory source list.

9. From the Choose Profile dialog box, select the administrator mail profile that connects to the Exchange server and click OK. The Exchange to Notes migration tool fails to load if you do not specify an appropriate mail profile.

Importing Microsoft Exchange Users into the Registration Queue

After the Available People/Groups dialog box displays the contents of the Microsoft Exchange server directory, select the users to import and the migration options that determine the data to migrate.

1. From the People and Groups Migration dialog box, enable options by selecting items in the Migration Options box. The options you select apply to all Microsoft Exchange users imported during this session.

2. From the Available People/Groups dialog box, select users and groups to migrate and click Add.

3. Click Migrate to place the selected users in the registration queue, and click OK to close the message that indicates the status and number of users queued for registration.

4. Click Done.

The people queued for registration now appear in the Registration status box. You are now ready to register users.

Registering Users and Completing the Migration from Exchange

After you successfully import users into the registration queue, you are ready to register them and complete the migration. Depending on the options you select, the registration process does the following:

♦ Creates a Notes Person document and Notes ID for each migrated user

♦ Creates a Notes mail file

♦ Migrates messages from the Microsoft Exchange mailbox

You can specify additional Notes registration information for users, including mail server name, license type, group membership, organizational unit, and so forth.

After the registration process has started, you cannot use the workstation for any other task until the process completes. If necessary, you can stop the registration process by pressing Ctrl + Break.

Perform the following steps to complete the migration:

1. From the Basics view of the Register Person dialog box, view the registration information for each name that appears in the Registration status box to ensure that it is correct.

2. (Optional) Click the Options button, and select the registration options to apply during this session and click OK.

3. (Optional) Specify additional registration information for users as necessary. If you created a "migration" group, open the Groups pane and assign users to this group now.

4. From the Registration status box, select users to register and click Register. The Domino Administrator attempts to register the selected users in the order in which they were added to the queue, and migrates data from their mailboxes to Notes. Users whom you do not select remain in the queue for later registration. The registration process may require a considerable amount of time, depending on the number of users, and the number and size of the mailboxes being upgraded. After the registration completes, a message informs you of the registration status. Failed registrations continue to be listed in the Registration status box with a status message indicating the reason for the failure. Correct registration settings as needed and attempt to register the user again.

5. Verify that the migration was successful.

After the migration is complete, users can run an upgrade wizard to convert local mail archives and other Microsoft Exchange data that the Domino migration tool did not process.

If you retained the default setting for the migration option Convert Mail (that is, the option remains selected), when you register migrated users, the Domino Administrator automatically converts their Microsoft Exchange mail files to Notes mail files as part of the registration process. On the Mail pane of the Register Person dialog box, the option Create Mail File Now is selected. An error message is displayed if you attempt to change this option to create mail files using the background administrative process (adminp).

WHAT IS IMPORTANT TO KNOW

- Know how to use the Notes log and the database's Replication History to monitor replication.

- Remember where to go to set up a Replication Monitor document, and how the document works to monitor replication failure.

- Know what Database Analysis is, what the options are for reporting, what the results database is and how it gets created.

- Learn and practice the three different ways to force replication.

- Understand the difference between replicating design changes and propagating design changes through a Refresh/Replace Design. Remember that replication causes the exchange of three types of data: ACL changes, design elements, and data documents, in that order.

- Know the difference between a Replication Conflict and a Save Conflict.

- Be able to explain how to consolidate Replication Conflicts, as well as how to prevent them in the first place.

- Go through the different replication troubleshooting scenarios to fully grasp how to solve replication problems.

- Know how to set up Message Tracking: What databases, tasks and steps are involved? How do you track a message? Don't confuse Message *tracking* with Message *tracing*.

- Understand the concept of mail probing using the ISpy task and how it differs from mail tracking.

- Remember the two ways to force mail routing: at the console, and using the Domino Administrator.

- Learn the different troubleshooting techniques to help solve mail routing problems—know how to trace a message.

- Understand the basic concepts involved in mail migration from another mail system to Notes mail.

- ▶ Maintain Domino Server IDs (Re-Certify, Move, Rename, Recover)
- ▶ Monitor Servers (Re-certify)
- ▶ Monitor Server Resources
- ▶ Monitor Server Tasks
- ▶ Monitor/Maintain Servers
- ▶ Monitor/Maintain Web Services
- ▶ Monitor/Maintain/Modify Server Access Control
- ▶ Reconfigure/Remap Directories and Links
- ▶ Run Program Documents
- ▶ Troubleshoot Administration Process Problems
- ▶ Troubleshoot Clustering Problems
- ▶ Troubleshoot Partitioning Problems
- ▶ Troubleshoot Server Access Problems
- ▶ Troubleshoot Server Problems

CHAPTER 4

Monitoring, Maintaining, and Troubleshooting Domino Servers

MAINTAINING DOMINO SERVER IDs

Server IDs may expire, or a server may need to be moved to another domain. The following processes will define the steps required to maintain the server ID.

To re-certify a server ID, the administrator will require Author access and the ability to create documents, as well as the role of ServerModifier. Administrators with Editor access to the Domino Directory will also be able to re-certify the server ID. Additionally, Author access with the ability to create documents in the Certification Log is required. After these conditions have been met, follow these steps to re-certify the ID file:

1. Start the Administrator client and select the Configuration tab. From the Favorites icon or the Domain icon, select the server to be re-certified.

2. Select Actions, then select Re-certify Selected Servers.

3. A dialog box will be displayed, asking you to select the certifier ID. Use the original certifier and enter the password to continue.

4. The default expiration date for the server at Registration time is 100 years, minus one day, but can be changed if required. Click Certify to complete the recertification.

In addition to having access to a certifier ID file, an administrator would require, as a minimum, Author access in the ACL of the Domino Directory and *one* of the following:

The administrator's name must be listed (explicitly or in a group context) in either the owners or administrators field *or* he must have server modifier role Author with create document rights in the Administration Requests database and Author with create document rights in the Certification Log.

MONITORING SERVER RESOURCES

The Administrator client provides server resource monitoring in real-time and on-demand modes. Disk space, memory, and status of servers can be checked for availability.

Using the Administrator client, open the Files tab. Under the Tools option select the Tools tab, and select Disk Space to display the available drives and the available space on each drive. This option is also available using the Web Administrator and by selecting Analysis, then Disk Space.

You can check the available memory by using the Web Administrator and selecting Analysis, then Memory.

You also can determine database sizes by using the Administrator client's Files tab, and examining the sizes. Databases should be compacted on a regular basis to optimize access and reduce size.

Use the Statistics tab to view real-time statistics on the Domino server.

The Domino log provides the capability to monitor the following resources:

+ Database replication
+ Available disk space
+ Available memory
+ Dial-up communications
+ Mail routing
+ User access
+ NNTP (news server) usage
+ Object Store usage
+ Passthru connections

You can change the contents of the Domino log by using log analysis. Using log analysis allows an administrator to search for specified information.

MONITORING SERVER TASKS

Server tasks are Domino utilities that perform defined functions, from maintenance to scheduled upgrades. There are various methods that an administrator can use to perform these server tasks. Server tasks can be initiated at the Domino console, in the NOTES.INI file, or through the administration client. The administration client is a key tool for running these tasks. Table 4.1 lists the utilities and descriptions of their functions.

TABLE 4.1

SERVER AND DOMINO UTILITY FUNCTIONS

Utility	Description
AdminP	Administration Process, used to automate admin tasks
Amgr	Agent Manager, processes agents on selected databases
Billing	Collects required information for billing
Calconn	Loads Calendar utility
Cataloger	Performs updates to the database catalog
Chronos	Initiates scheduled full-text indexes
Cladmin	Cluster administration process maintains cluster operations
Clbdir	Cluster Database Directory Manager, provides cluster database directory updates and updates specified databases with predetermined attributes for the cluster
Clrelp	Cluster Replicator, initiates database replication in the defined cluster
Collect	Used to collect server statistics for specified servers
Compact	Used to remove whitespace in database and optimize disk space
Designer	Modifies databases based on template upgrades
DIIOP	Permits Domino and Web browsers to access the Object Request Broker server program
Dircat	Maintains Directory catalogs
Event	Audits server events
Fixup	Repairs corrupted databases
HTTP	Allows server to provide Web-enabled databases
IMAP	Provides mail delivery services for IMAP clients
Indexer	Indexer utility, modifies databases to reflect changes in views or changes in full-text indexes
Ispy	Initiated by loading RunJava Ispy at the Server Console, generates a mail probe to provide statistics on mail routes
LDAP	Allows LDAP directory services to be enabled for LDAP clients
MTC	Message Tracking Collector, reads the files and generates summaries regarding mail traffic as the router generates log files
NNTP	Provides Domino-based news services for NNTP clients
Object	Used to provide maintenance on shared mail databases
POP3	Provides POP3 compatibility
Replica	Provides Database Replication between servers
Report	Reporter, generates server statistics
Router	Mail Delivery task

Utility	Description
Sched	Manages meeting details
Stats	Displays server statistics
Web	Utility provided for Domino server to generate Notes documents from Web pages

MONITORING/MAINTAINING SERVERS

The Domino Administrator client is a versatile tool for monitoring Domino servers. Using the Monitoring and Status tabs, an administrator can gauge the health of a server at a glance.

The Monitoring Tab

Figure 4.1 shows the Monitoring tab.

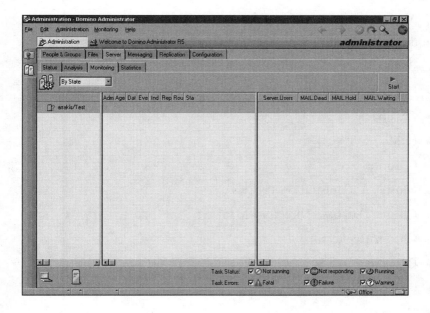

FIGURE 4.1
The Monitoring tab.

The following tasks are the default tasks:

- Admin Process
- Agent Manager
- Database Server
- Event
- Indexer
- Replicator
- Router
- Stats
- Server Users
- Mail.Dead
- Mail.Hold
- Mail.Waiting

In addition to the default tasks, the following tasks can also be added:

- Billing
- Calendar Connector
- Cataloger
- cc:Mail MTA
- Chronos
- Cluster Administration Process
- Cluster Database Directory Manager
- Cluster Replicator
- Collector
- Compactor
- Converter
- Decs Server
- Designer
- DIIOP Server

- Directory Cataloger
- Domain Indexer
- Event Monitor
- Fixup
- HTTP Web Server
- IMAP Mail Server
- Internet Cluster Manager (ICM)
- ISpy
- LDAP Server
- Maps Extractor
- Message Tracking Collector (MTC)
- NNTP News Server
- Object Store Manager
- SMTP/MIME MTA (R4 only)
- Statistics (Mail-In Stats)
- Statistics log
- Update (Database Indexer)
- Update all (Database Indexer)
- Web Retriever
- X.400 MTA
- X.400 MTA: Binary log Decoder
- X.400 MTA: MADMAN subagent

These tasks are installed based on the type of server license that was selected when the server was built.

The Monitoring tab is flexible in that various states of tasks are selectable for viewing. Different views are available for this tab. You can view by timeline or by state. Moving the mouse over certain values will cause descriptive text to appear that defines a column when it is not fully expanded. Clicking your right mouse button while selecting the columns will generate a menu that allows you to start, stop, or remove a task. The default state for each task is on. Removing the checkmark from the box next to any of the following tasks disables that task:

- Not Running
- Fatal
- Not Responding
- Failure
- Running
- Warning

The Status Tab

Figure 4.2 shows the Status tab.

The top pane displays tasks running on the server. The bottom pane displays users attached to the server, the databases they have open, and how long they have been idle, displayed in minutes.

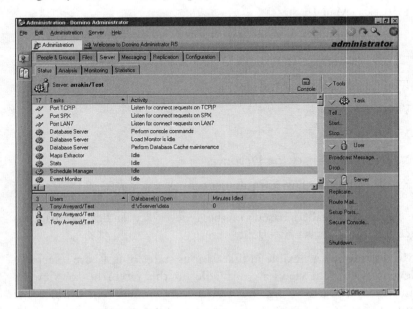

FIGURE 4.2
The Status tab.

Selecting the Tools menu on the left side of the Status screen will display options to assist in maintaining the server. These options are discussed in the next three sections.

Task

Select a task in the Tasks pane, then select Start to enable the task and Stop to disable the task. Certain tasks have variables that can be defined within the Tasks pane. Select the task and then select Tell from the Tools menu to display the definable options for the tasks.

User

The User tools allow you to drop a user from the server, or broadcast a message to a user. Select the user from the Users pane, then select either Drop User or Broadcast Message to perform these tasks.

Server

The Server tools provide quick management options for addressing server performance and configuration. The tools available under the Server tab are as follows:

- **Replicate.** Use this option to replicate all or specific databases between servers.

- **Route Mail.** This tool provides immediate mail routing between servers.

- **Setup Ports.** Communication ports can be changed or added using this tool.

- **Secure Console.** Use this tool to define the console password used to secure the server from unauthorized use.

- **Stop Port.** Select a port in the Task pane and select Stop Port to disable the port.

- **Shutdown.** This tool will shut down the Domino server.

The Status page also provides administrators access to the remote console on a server by clicking the Console button. After the remote console has been selected, selecting the Live button will provide live access to the remote server. Clicking the Tasks button will return you to the Status page.

MONITORING/MAINTAINING WEB SERVICES

New to Domino Release 5 is the capability to run HTTP services using Microsoft IIS server. Domino performs this function using a procedure call Domino Services for IIS. After the IIS server is installed correctly, if starting the Domino Server process causes the IIS server to stop responding, restart the IIS server to correct the error. Keep in mind, the Domino server ID file cannot be password protected in order for it to function as a Domino for IIS server.

While gathering requirements for Web services, you may discover that users will require the ability to display files on the Web server. If users are receiving the error Database Browsing Not Allowed, check the server document and verify that the field Allow HTTP Clients to Browse Databases is enabled. This will correct the error and permit access to the files.

Notes databases require users to have proper ACL access defined before they are permitted access. This condition remains true for Web users as well. Users who are receiving the error message Unauthorized Exception while attempting to access a database using a Web client most likely do not have properly defined ACLs to the database.

Hardware installed to ensure security to the network, such as Firewalls, can prevent users from accessing the server. The first step in troubleshooting the problem is to ping the server to ensure that the communications path is open for access. If the ping is successful, use a Telnet program and attempt to access the server using port 1352. If the server will not allow access via this port, a firewall may be blocking access.

Domino server uses standard HTTP authentication as the basis for Web services. Based on this structure, the server will assume that users who authenticate to the highest level of the server will have access to the existing subdirectories. Assuming that your server name is www.test.com, giving users access to the server at the top level will allow access to the server and will only require the user to authenticate one time. If you provide access at a level below the top level—www.test.com/files for instance—a user who enters the server at the /files level and attempts to access www.test.com/pictures, will be required to authenticate to the server again. To minimize the number of times a user has to supply a user name and password, define your server so that users access the server at the highest level in the directory structure.

To display a home page on the Domino Web server, the server document must be modified to allow users to access the page. The field default home page, or the field Home URL on the HTTP tab of the server document must be populated with the name of the home page to permit access. If the field is not completed, users attempting to access the server will receive the error Error 403 - Directory Browsing Error - Access Forbidden.

Web pages may be designed with a URL that allows users to send mail via a mailto link. To enable users to send mail with the link, make sure mail routing to the Internet is enabled.

Proper definitions of communications links on the server are vital to ensuring reliable communications. If users are experiencing the errors TCP/IP host unknown or Remote System Not Responding, then the problem may be resolved by verifying that the Web Navigator is running. If the Web Navigator is running, then make sure the communications settings are correct in the server document. If the server document is populated with host names rather than IP addresses, DNS should be enabled or the Hosts file on the server should be populated with valid addresses.

If a user attempts to access a Web page and the Web task is not running, users will receive the error The Web Navigator Retrieval Process Is Not Running. To fix this problem, start the Web process. If the Web process is running and users are still getting the error, make sure the server name in the users' location document is defined correctly.

Activity on the Web site can be tracked in various ways. The Domino Web server log (DOMLOG.NSF) logs all activity on the Web site and logs information about http requests. This information includes the following:

- IP address of the user
- The name of the user, assuming that a name and password were use to log in to the Web site
- The date and time the Web site was accessed
- Identification of the type of browser used
- Program errors

- Processing time for each request

- Defined data types accessed by the client

- Successful or unsuccessful server access requests

- Communication traffic between the server and the client

- IP address of the server or its DNS name

Domino is a complete product in that, in addition to the preceding information, other log files exist to assist in the maintenance of the server. These log files include the Agent log, CGI Error log, and the Access log.

The Agent log is used to monitor the status of Agents on the server to determine if problems occurred while they were executing.

The CGI Error log displays problems encountered while CGI programs were executing so that the Domino Administrator can troubleshoot these problems.

The Access log is used by the Administrator to monitor client and server access to the server.

MONITORING/MAINTAINING/MODIFYING SERVER ACCESS CONTROL

Server access control is defined in the server document located in the Domino Directory. The following list explains the various fields in the server document regarding access control:

- **Server Access List.** The Server Access list dictates what resources users and servers can access on the server. Using a Server Access list will require additional authentication and may slow down access to the server.

- **Deny Access List**. The Deny Access list is used to define users whose security level requires that they do not have access to the server. This typically is the case when users leave the company, but may also be required to deny access to one server while the user is moved to another domain or server.

- **Notes ID Lockout.** Similar to the Deny Access list, Notes ID Lockout is used in instances where users may still have access to their Notes ID file. In addition to locking out the user ID, enable password checking so that the user will be required to enter a password that matches the password defined in the Domino Directory. Notes ID Lockout will also deny users access to the system, but not allow users to examine users who are in the Deny Access list to determine employees who have left the company.

- **Anonymous Access.** Anonymous Access permits users and servers to gain access to the server while not requiring validation and authentication. This will allow access to the server without having a common cross certificate. After a server has been defined for Anonymous Access and a user attempts to validate to the server while not having a common certificate, a message will be generated for the user informing them that validation was not possible and Anonymous Access has been granted.

- **Network Port Access.** Network Port Access is used to deny access to users while using a specific communications port. Instances may occur where a user may be restricted from using a dial-up connection, but may be permitted to use a LAN connection via the SPX or TCP/IP ports defined on the server.

- **Server Access.** Server access can be monitored by examining the LOG.NSF and DONLOG.NSF files. These databases will display date and time of access by the user.

- **Secure Socket Layer Authentication.** Server access control can also be established by using session Secure Socket Layer (SSL) authentication. Additional methods of control include session based authentication and name and password authentication.

RECONFIGURING/REMAPPING DIRECTORIES AND LINKS

Domino provides administrators the capability to remap the location of the resources assigned in the Domino Directory without affecting access by the users. To remap a resource, follow these steps:

1. Start the Domino Administrator and select the Configuration tab. Select the server and open the server document to be modified.

2. In the View pane click the Web button. This will display four available options. Select Create URL Mapping/Redirection.

   Five new sets of tabbed documents will appear. The following fields should be completed for each tab:

   - The Basic tab requires you to define what type of mapping you want to define. The choices are URL to directory, URL to Redirection URL, and URL to URL. Using this tool will allow an administrator to keep files in various locations without generating broken links or being forced to make changes in the Domino Directory.

   - The Site Information tab has two fields. The first field is used to assign IP addresses for virtual servers. The second field is used for comments regarding the link. A *virtual server* is a tool that provides the capability to host more than one Web site with a distinct DNS name on the same machine.

   - The Mapping tab has two fields. The Incoming URL String is used to define the URL string provided by the incoming browser. The Target Server Directory is used to define the location of the resource being reassigned.

   - The Access tab has one field. The two options for this field are Read or Execute. Read provides read-only access, and execute allows for changes to occur.

   - The Administration tab has two fields: Owners and Administrator. These options can be completed by defined users in the Domino Directory via the Access tab, or by typing the users' names in the provided fields.

3. Pressing the Esc key will prompt you to save the new document. Click Yes to continue. To enable the changes, type **Load HTTP Restart** at the server console.

RUNNING PROGRAM DOCUMENTS

Program documents permit administrators to automate tasks to execute at scheduled times for a number of instances.

To define a program document, follow these steps:

1. Start the administrator program and open the Domino Directory.

2. Select the Server tab and click Programs. In the View pane created programs will be displayed. To add a new program, select Add Program.

3. The Administrator client will now display three tabs: Basic, Schedule, and Administration. The fields you see will be dynamic, based on the requirements, and you should adjust your entries accordingly.

   ◆ The Basic tab displays the following fields:

   Program Name. The name of the program to be executed.

   Command Line. Optional parameters or software switches to run with the program. The complete path of the program to execute.

   Server to Run On. The server to execute the program.

   Comments. Used to document program purpose.

   ◆ The Schedule tab displays the following fields:

   Enabled/Disabled. Sets the state of the program.

   Run at Times. The executable time of the program. Notes will convert Military time to standard time as the program is saved.

   Repeat Interval. Number of times to repeat the program. The default interval is 0, which will execute the program one time only.

   Days of the Week. Select the days on which to run the program.

   ◆ The Administration tab displays the following two fields:

   Owners. The Program Document owner, typically the Notes administrator by default.

   Administrators. The names of the Notes administrators, typically the creators of the documents on the server.

TROUBLESHOOTING ADMINISTRATION PROCESS PROBLEMS

The Administration Process executes commands submitted by the administrator from the Administration Requests database.

The first item to check when the Administration Process is not running correctly is system resources. If memory is plentiful and adequate disk space exists, follow these steps to verify that things are configured correctly.

1. If a server exists that does not have a replica of the Domino Directory, execute the Administration Process and verify that it runs correctly.

2. At the server console, type **Show Tasks** and verify that the Administration Process is running. If AdminP is not displayed as an active task, type **Load Adminp** to start the process.

3. Using the Administration client, open the Domino Directory. Select File, Database, Access Control and select the Advanced Icon. Verify that the Administration Server has been selected with the correct server name.

4. Verify that replication is occurring properly between the Domino Directory, and the Administration Requests Databases between the servers. The default name for the Domino Directory is NAMES.NSF and ADMINS4.NSF for the Administration requests database.

5. After a successful Administration Process has been completed, a response document will be generated. Inspect the Administration Process database for response documents to troubleshoot problems in the database. Mismatched public keys between the certificate documents and the CERT.ID file will stop Administration requests from operating correctly.

Administration Process errors, when they occur, will appear in the Certification Log file or on the Server Console screen. Some messages may appear in both. Messages vary in nature.

Messages will appear that are status messages only and require no action on the part of the administrator. Examples of these messages are as follows:

- Administration Process: Retrying a request that could not be performed previously because another process was modifying the document.

- Removing *viewname* view notes in the Address Book.

- Reporter: Could not locate view *viewname*.

- The Administration Process cannot delete the database *database-name* at this time because it is in use by someone else; will try again.

- The Administration Process could not change or delete the name from the document because another process was modifying it.

- The Administration Process is retrying a name change or deletion from the document.

- The replica of the database moved by the Administration Process has not been initialized by the replicator.

Status messages will appear that require the server or Administration Process to be restarted. Examples of these messages are as follows:

- Administration Process: Unable to access transfer context information.

- Administration Process: Unable to create entry thread.

- No Address book is present on this server; the Admin Process cannot continue without one.

Status messages will appear that can be corrected only by restarting the server. Examples of these messages are as follows:

- Insufficient memory: Admin's request queue pool is full.

- The Administration Process does not have enough memory to compute the formulas required for request processing.

Status messages will appear that are related to problems related to certificate issues. Examples of these messages are as follows:

- The certificate contained in the note was not issued by the selected certifier.

- The selected certifier isn't an ancestor of the entity to be updated.
- The selected certifier isn't the target certifier in the move request.

TROUBLESHOOTING CLUSTER PROBLEMS

A Domino cluster is made up of servers that are grouped together to provide data redundancy, distribution of workload, and improvement of server performance. Domino clusters range in size from a minimum of two servers to a maximum of six. Database synchronization occurs continuously on the clustered servers; if a database is unavailable on a server in the cluster, the next available instance of the database in the cluster is presented to the user with the most current data intact.

The Domino cluster should be monitored to ensure error-free operation. Although redundancy is inherited by design in the cluster environment, it is not without flaws. The following errors may occur during cluster operation:

- **Databases are not consistent within the cluster.** If you get this error, do the following:

    1. Verify that the cluster replicator is running.

    2. Verify that the databases are listed in the Cluster Database directories.

    3. Verify that all databases have common replica IDs.

    4. Verify that replication between the servers is not encountering error by examining the replication events in the Domino log database.

    5. Verify that replication is enabled for the database and all of its replicas in the cluster.

    6. Verify that the database does not have quota restrictions enabled. Databases will not replicate between servers with quota restrictions exceeded.

- **Client access to databases does not take place automatically between servers.** The Domino Cluster Manager accesses the databases within the cluster by using a process called fail over. Fail over works by using defined database paths, not by replica ID. Based on this process, multiple replicas of the same database on the server will cause the replicator to not function.

- **Databases defined as Out of Service are still accessible.** Databases that are marked Out of Service are defined as Out of Service only as long as they are within the Domino cluster. Verify that the database users are accessing is in the defined cluster and that the database attributes are defined correctly.

- **Duplicate copies of documents exist in the cluster database directory.** The Cluster Database Directory Manager monitors the servers in the cluster and verifies that the Cluster Database Directory is deployed on each server. When the manager discovers that a directory does not exist, the manager re-creates the database complete with documents representing all databases on the server. The manager then replicates the database to all servers in the cluster, generating duplicate documents in the existing databases. Unlike the Domino Directory, however, save and replication conflict documents are not created and the cluster operates normally. The next manager starts, and the databases are scanned and automatically corrected.

- **Cluster Replicator was unable to configure using Cluster Database Directory CLDBDIR.NSF: File does not exist.** Deployment strategy of the cluster is important. If a server is added to the Domino cluster and the cluster replicator is engaged before the Directory Manager has started, the CLDBIR.NSF will not be available and the error will be generated. The error will also be generated if the Cluster database directory has been deleted. Re-create the Database Directory by creating a new replica to correct the problem. Entering **Load Clbdir** at the server console will also cause the database to be re-created.

- **Cluster Replicator was unable to configure using Cluster Database Directory CLDBDIR.NSF: Invalid replica ID for cluster database directory. If cluster name changed, delete cluster database directory and restart CLDBDIR task.** If the CLRepID in the server document of the Domino database and replica ID in the Cluster Database Directory do not match, delete the Cluster Database Directory and regenerate it by typing **Load**

C1bdir at the server console. If re-creating the directory does not correct the problem, remove the server from the cluster, verify that the setup is correct, and add the server to the cluster.

- **Private folders do not replicate from one clustered database to another.** Incorrectly defined ACLs will prevent databases from replicating in a cluster in the same way that replications take place in a regular Notes network. Verify that ACLs are set for Server or Server Group to correct this problem.

- **HTTP Server Initialization error. Could not bind port 80. Port may be in use.** If the Domino ICM is running and selects port 80 as its default port, this message will appear after the HTTP server task is started. This is not a problem if the ICM and the HTTP tasks are defined with unique IP addresses in the server document and the option to Bind to Host Name field on Internet Protocols on the HTTP tab is enabled.

Troubleshooting Partition Problems

Problems may occur when you are running a partitioned server. Some of these errors include the following:

- **Server crashes.** When running a partitioned server, all processes on the server share name space for basic server operations. When a partitioned server crashes, the first step for an administrator is to stop all processes that are associated with the server. Stopping all processes will ensure that when the server is restarted there will not be a conflict from a previous crash causing a memory corruption. Adding the parameter Kill Process=1 in the NOTES.INI file will automatically clean up previous memory conflicts and allow the server to start without error.

- **Server exiting. Partition number *xx* is already in use.** If a Domino server is running in a partition and an attempt is made to start another server in the same partition, this error will be generated. If this occurs, stop all processes in the conflicting partition. If the problem is not corrected, the server will need to be restarted.

- **When connecting to a server the error message Server Not Responding is generated.** This is a message that may be related to problems with TCP/IP port mapping on the server. Verify that the

TCP/IP port mapper is running on the server. If the mapper is running, verify that the NOTES.INI file has the correct mapper entries.

For further information on problems related to server operations check the lotus Web site for further information at www.Lotus.com.

TROUBLESHOOTING SERVER ACCESS PROBLEMS

Server access problems prohibit users and administrators from accessing the Domino Server. Following are typical examples of these errors:

- **Access at the server is not available.** If server access is not available using the Domino client at the server, or administrative utilities, such as Load, Tell, or Set Config commands are not executable, the password-protection option of the server has been enabled. Using the Domino Administrator or at the console, issue the Set Secure command to clear the password.

- **New servers are not available in the server list.** Servers will not be available to users unless the administrator properly defines them. Make sure that each server has a properly configured server document. After configuring the server document, replicate the document to all servers in the domain. If the server documents are defined correctly, verify that users have proper communication access to the servers.

- **The message Server Not Responding appears while attempting to access the server.** The most obvious reason to receive this message is that the Domino server is not running. If the server has been verified as being active, check the following:
  - Verify that the server's name has not been changed. If the server's name was changed, notify users of the new name to provide access.
  - If the server is configured to use a proxy server and one does not exist, Domino will still attempt to route traffic through the defined port. Additional errors that may appear are No Path

Found to Server or Proxy Reports the Connection Request Failed.
Check the Configuration tab in the Domino Administrator and
click the Ports – Proxies tab to disable the Proxy port.

- NetBIOS will not operate properly if not set up correctly. Make
  sure that both the server and the workstation experiencing
  connection problems are using the same versions of NetBIOS.
  If the numbers of sessions defined on the server are not sufficient to handle the communications traffic the client will not
  be able to access the server. Ensure that the correct number of
  NetBIOS sessions have been defined. NetBIOS requires
  broadcast defined on bridges and routers to operate. If problems persist, check the setup of routers and bridges in the infrastructure to determine whether they are filtering broadcast
  traffic.

- **Users are receiving You Are Not Authorized to Access the
  Server.** The first thing to verify is that the server is running and
  that the network connections are in place. If the server is operating
  properly, check the following items:

  - Check the server document in the Domino Directory. On the
    Network Configuration tab, make sure the server name and
    domain name are defined correctly. Com ports are only con-
    figured in the ports configuration section, so if a Com port is
    defined, remove it. Verify that the Notes Network is defined
    correctly.

  - Also in the server document, check the Restrictions tab to ver-
    ify that the Access Server field is blank. The Not Access Server
    field should also be blank.

  - It is possible that the Server document is defined correctly, but
    may be corrupt. Create a new server document; if the problem
    is corrected, the previous document was corrupt.

  - Make sure that the ID file in the server's ID file matches the
    public key.

  - Verify that groups are defined to provide correct access for
    users and servers.

- Check the Group and People views for Save or Replication conflicts and resolve.

- The views in the Domino Directory may be corrupted. At the server console type `Load Updall names.nsf -r`.

- The design of the database may be corrupt. Replace the design of the Domino database.

- Ensure passthru is set up correctly.

- The server ID may be damaged. Replace the ID with a backup copy and see if the problem is corrected. Make sure that the server ID contains all the proper certificates and that the public key is not corrupt. If necessary, restore the public key Server document.

WHAT IS IMPORTANT TO KNOW

- To re-certify a server ID, the administrator will require Author access and the ability to create documents as well as the role of ServerModifier.

- The Administrator client provides server resource monitoring in real-time and on-demand modes. Disk space, memory, and status of servers can be checked for availability.

- New to Domino Release 5 is the ability to run HTTP services using Microsoft IIS server.

- Domino server uses standard HTTP authentication as the basis for Web services.

- Server access control is defined in the server document located in the Domino Directory.

- Typical examples of server access problems are as follows:

Access at the server is not available.

If server access is not available using the Domino client at the server, or administrative utilities, such as Load, Tell, or Set Config commands are not executable, the password-protection option of the server has been enabled. Using the Domino Administrator or at the console, issue the Set Secure command to clear the password.

New servers are not available in the server list.

Servers will not be available to users unless the administrator properly defines them. Make sure that each server has a properly configured server document. After configuring the server document, replicate the document to all servers in the domain. If the server documents are defined correctly, verify that users have proper communication access to the servers.

The message `Server Not Responding` appears while attempting to access the server.

The most obvious reason to receive this message is that the Domino server is not running. If the server has been verified as being active, check the following:

Verify that the server's name has not been changed. If the server's name was changed, notify users of the new name to provide access.

If the server is configured to use a proxy server and one does not exist, Domino will still attempt to route traffic through the defined port. Additional errors that may appear are `No Path Found to`

`Server` or `Proxy` `Reports` `the` `Connection` `Request` `Failed`. Check the Configuration tab in the Domino Administrator and click the Ports – Proxies tab to disable the Proxy port.

NetBIOS will not operate properly if not set up correctly. Make sure that both the server and the workstation experiencing connection problems are using the same versions of NetBIOS. If the numbers of sessions defined on the server are not sufficient to handle the communications traffic, the client will not be able to access the server. Ensure that the correct number of NetBIOS sessions have been defined. NetBIOS requires broadcast defined on bridges and routers to operate. If problems persist, check the setup of routers and bridges in the infrastructure to determine if they are filtering broadcast traffic.

▶ Maintain Domino Certifier IDs

▶ Modify/Maintain Domino Connectivity

▶ Monitor/Maintain Connectivity

▶ Monitor/Maintain Domain Access

▶ Monitor/Maintain Domains

▶ Monitor/Maintain the Domino System

▶ Troubleshoot Domain Access Problems

▶ Troubleshoot Network/Protocol Problems

▶ Troubleshoot Port (Modem) Problems

C H A P T E R **5**

Monitoring, Maintaining, and Troubleshooting Domino Systems

MAINTENANCE OF DOMINO CERTIFIER IDs

Lotus Notes and Domino authentication is based upon the trust rela-
tionship established by the electronic stamp of a Certifier ID. Each
Notes ID contains certificates, which are electronically stamped by a
Certifier ID.

Users and servers may authenticate with each other provided they share
at least one common certificate. Certifier IDs are not used for access to
a resource but only to stamp other Notes IDs.

These certifiers and their passwords should be stored in a secure location
on a floppy disk or other secure media, not left on a server hard disk. The
top-level certifier is the Organizational Certifier. The second level is the
Organizational Unit Certifier. Certifier IDs are created based upon an
organization's hierarchical naming scheme.

Certifier ID Location

By default, R5 Certifier IDs are stored in Lotus\Notes\Data\ids\certs\.

Specify a different location through the Administration Preferences
interface. During the registration process, the system administrator may
also specify a different location for the creation of an ID file.

Password quality may also be altered at this location.

From the Domino Administrator, select File, Preferences, Administration Preferences, Registration, ID File Settings, Certifier ID Folder.

Certifier ID Properties

Examine the properties of the Certifier ID through the Certification tab
in the Domino Administrator by executing the following steps:

1. Select Configuration, Certification, ID Properties.

2. Select the Certifier ID file and click Open.

3. Enter the password when prompted. Click OK.

Change Certifier ID Password

To change the Certifier ID password, you must go to the Certifier ID Properties screen and execute the following steps:

1. Select Basics.

2. Set Password.

3. Enter the new password; click OK.

4. Reconfirm the new password; click OK.

Recertifying the Certifier ID

By default, a Certifier ID is valid for 100 years. Certain organizations may elect to use a shorter period for security reasons. Recertify Certifier ID if you want to do the following:

- Add a new alternate name or language. R5 supports two names for user IDs: a primary and an alternate. Before an alternate name can be assigned to a user, you must add an alternate language and name to the Certifier ID.

- Change the minimum password quality.

The Organization Certifier is used to recertify itself. Organizational Unit IDs are recertified using the appropriate Certifier ID.

From the Domino Administrator, execute the following steps to recertify the Certifier ID:

1. Click Configuration.

2. Select Tools, Certification, Certify.

3. Choose the Certifier ID to be recertified.

4. Enter the password and click OK.

5. Choose the same Certifier ID in the Choose ID to Certify infobox.

6. Click Open.

7. Enter the password and click OK.

Editable fields include the following:

- **Server.** Allows a different registration server to be chosen.

- **Expiration Date.** Enter a new expiration date.

- **Subject Name List.** Click Add to add alternate language support.

- **Password Quality.** A value from Weak (password optional) to Strong (16 characters) may be chosen.

8. Click Certify.

9. To certify another Certifier ID, click Yes. Otherwise, click No.

Add Multiple Passwords to the Certifier ID

The main purpose of adding multiple passwords to any Certifier ID is security. Requiring multiple administrators to act in concert, theoretically, protects against unauthorized usage of a Certifier ID by a single administrator.

If you need to add multiple passwords to the certifier ID, go to the Domino Administrator and execute the following steps:

1. Click Configuration.

2. Select Tools, Certification, Edit Multiple Passwords.

3. Choose the Certifier ID.

4. Enter the password and click OK.

5. Have each person who will be required to access the ID file enter his or her user name and new password and then confirm the password.

6. Click Add.

7. Enter the number of passwords that will be required to access the Certifier ID file. Enter a number that is less than or equal to the number of administrators entered.

8. Click OK.

Note that passwords previously assigned to this ID are no longer valid.

Editing Multiple Passwords on the Certifier ID

An administrator may desire to change his password if it has been compromised in any way. To edit multiple passwords, go back to the Domino Administrator and execute the following steps:

1. Click Configuration.

2. Select Tools, Certification, Edit Multiple Passwords.

3. Choose the Certifier ID.

4. Enter the password and click OK.

5. Have each person who will be required to access the ID file enter his or her user name and new password, and then confirm the password.

6. Select the user name to be edited.

7. In the New Password field, enter a new password and then confirm it by retyping the password into the Confirm Password field.

8. Click Modify.

9. Click OK.

Deleting Multiple Passwords on the Certifier ID

If, for example, an administrator leaves the company, security policy should mandate the removal of that person's name and the associated password from the Certifier ID to prevent improper use. From the Domino Administrator, follow these steps:

1. Click Configuration.

2. Select Tools, Certification, Edit Multiple Passwords.

3. Choose the Certifier ID.

4. Enter the password and click OK.

5. Have each person who will be required to access the ID file enter his or her user name and new password, and then confirm the password.

6. Select the user name to be deleted and click Remove. If necessary, follow the steps to add a new user to the list or change the number of passwords required to access the Certifier ID in the future.

7. Click OK.

Recovery Information

Newly created Certifier IDs do not contain password recovery information. In R5 the Escrow Agent functionality is no longer supported; therefore, Certifier IDs on upgraded servers must also have recovery information configured to support password recovery. During this process, a backup copy of the ID file is encrypted and mailed to the database designated during setup of the password recovery process. Execute the following steps (from the Domino Administrator) to enable password recovery:

1. Click on Configuration, Tools, Edit Recovery Information.

2. Choose the Certifier ID.

3. Enter the password and click OK.

4. Use the Edit Master Authority List infobox to add or edit the number of Recovery Authorities required to recover IDs and passwords from this certifier. Lotus recommends at least three. Enter a number less than or equal to the number of Recovery Authorities. As administrators join or leave the company, it may become necessary to edit the recovery information.

5. Click Add.

6. Select the names of users who will act as recovery administrators.

7. Click on Address to specify the name of the centralized database that will hold encrypted copies of passwords created with this Certifier ID.

8. Click OK.

The Export button is used to send a memo to existing users whose ID files were created prior to recovery information being added to the Certifier.

Users created after recovery information is added will already have the recovery information in their IDs. There is no method to force a user to add recovery information to their IDs.

MODIFICATION AND MAINTENANCE OF CONNECTIVITY

After Domino server code is installed or upgraded, it may be necessary to update connectivity information due to addition or deletion of modems or interface cards. Enabling certain services may also necessitate modifying the connectivity environment. For example, TCP/IP must be enabled to run POP3, IMAP, LDAP, NNTP, or the SMTP Internet client.

Configure Port Information from Domino Administrator

The Server, Status Tab in the Domino Administrator displays an inventory of the tasks, ports and users currently on the selected server. The Tasks screen is divided into two parts. The top half displays the total number of tasks, configured ports, and current activity. The bottom half of the screen displays information about users and session activity. The following list summarizes the available options. Options are available either through the menu or by right-clicking on a server task, port, or user. Options are also available to replicate, route mail, or shut down a server.

- **Port.** Right-click on a port entry for the following options:

    Stop the selected port or set up communication ports.

- **Server Task.** Right-click on a server task for the following options:

    Issue a Tell command with selectable options for the specified task. The dialog box also provides an explanation of each available option.

    Stop the task.

    Start a new task.

- **User.** Right-click on a user name for the following options:

    Broadcast a message to all or a selected user.

    Drop the selected user session.

- **Server.** Right-click on a server entry for the following options:

    Replicate, route mail, secure server console, or shut down the selected server.

New server ports may be configured via the Status tab in the Domino Administrator. Prior to adding a new network port or modem, ensure that the appropriate hardware and software have been installed.

After the new components have been installed and properly configured, execute the following steps from the Domino Administrator to add a new port to the server:

1. Click on Server, Status, Tools, Setup Ports.

    The Port Setup for the selected server is displayed.

2. Enter a name for the port.

3. Select a communications driver.

4. Select the locations at which to use this port.

5. Select any port options.

If the port being added is a TCP/IP port, note the option for a connection timeout option. This setting is used only the first time that the workstation or server establishes a connection with a Domino server.

If the port being added is connected to a modem, the following options may be configured:

- **Modem Type.** Select the type of modem installed using the drop-down menu. If the exact modem is not listed, choose the closest match by brand and speed. For Hayes-compatible modems, you can use Auto Configure. If the installed modem is not Hayes compatible, you may need to create or edit a modem command file. The default is .AutoConfigure.

- **Maximum Port Speed.** Enter the maximum speed of the installed modem. If the modem encounters trouble connecting, try a lower speed. The Notes modem file or the OS port settings may also limit port speed. The default is 19200.

- **Speaker Volume.** Select Low, Medium, or High at first so you can hear the modem. The default is Off.

- **Dial Mode.** Select Tone or Pulse dialing. Tone is the default.

- **Log Modem I/O and Log Script I/O.** Selecting this option enables recording of modem commands and responses in the Miscellaneous Events view of the Notes log. The option is deselected by default.

- **Hardware Flow Control.** Deselect this option if using a modem or external serial port that does not support flow control. This option is selected by default, except on UNIX systems.

- **Dial Timeout.** Set the number of seconds Notes will wait before canceling the connection attempt. The default is 60 seconds.

- **Hangup If Idle.** Set the number of minutes of inactivity allowed before the connection terminates. The default is 15 minutes.

- **Port Number.** Enter the port on which the modem is connected.

- **Modem File.** View or edit the modem command (.mdm) file associated with the modem.

- **Acquire Script.** Select or edit a communications script file.

- **Modem File Directory.** Specify the location of modem command files. The default is the \MODEMS subdirectory, under the Notes data directory.

Existing ports may be modified from this screen as well. Additional options are as follows:

- Rename, Delete, or Reorder Ports

- Enable/Disable Ports

- Encrypt Port Data

MONITOR CONNECTIVITY

Probes are a new feature in R5 monitoring that allows you to monitor connectivity. The following sections describe the three different types of Probes available and their function.

Probes

Probes check for the availability of a resource for a specified timeframe. If the resource does not respond within the specified timeframe, an event is generated and the associated action performed. Note that you can disable probes by selecting the Disable This Probe option on the Other tab of each probe configuration document. The three types of probes in Domino R5 are summarized in the following list.

- **Domino Server Probe.** Tests for the availability of target servers using a specified port or any available port. Any network port configured on the testing server may be specified.

   There is also an option to check for the ability to access the server and open a specified database.

   If the probe fails, the statistic has a value of –1.

- **TCP Server Probe.** Tests for the availability of TCP or Internet services on all or specific target servers in the domain. The probe measures response time, in milliseconds. If the probe fails, the statistic has a value of –1.

   Services that may be monitored are as follows:

   DNS. Failures generate a Network event type.

   FTP. Failures generate an FTP event type.

   HTTP. Probes for the availability of the assigned port. Optionally, the ability to open a specified URL may be tested. Failures generate a Web (HTTP/HTTPS) event type.

   IMAP. Failures generate a Mail event type.

   LDAP. Failures generate a Directory (LDAP) event type.

   NNTP. Failures generate a News (NNTP) event type.

POP3. Failures generate a Mail event type.

SMTP. Failures generate a Mail event type.

Other. Allows for creation of a new probe event. A severity level must be specified.

In addition, there is a button that will start the Event Notification Wizard.

♦ **Mail Probe.** A test message is sent to a user on the target server. This message generates a confirmation from the recipient. Completion of these events, within a specified number of minutes, signifies successful completion. Probe intervals and timeouts are configurable. If the probe fails, the statistic has a value of –1.

The Other option allows for creation of a new Mail event. A severity level must be specified. In addition, there is a button that will start the Event Notification Wizard.

ISpy Server Task

This server task is used to send server and mail probes. The results are recorded as events in the Statistics Reporting database (STATREP.NSF). The ISpy task must be started before creating server or mail probes. Note that the command syntax is case sensitive.

♦ To enable ISpy from the NOTES.INI file, type `RunJava ISpy` into the ServerTasks line.

♦ To start ISpy from the server console, type `load runjava ISpy` and press Enter.

♦ To stop the ISpy task from the server console, enter either `tell runjava ISpy quit` or `tell runjava quit`.

The first time this server task starts, a mail-in database record is created in the Domino Directory via the Administration Process.

MONITORING AND MAINTENANCE OF DOMAIN ACCESS

Maintaining domain access is synonymous with controlling access to those resources. There are two general aspects involved. The first is keeping unauthorized users out. The second aspect is keeping authorized users connected. The discussions on monitoring access provide the tools to monitor both authorized and unauthorized access through native Notes features.

Physical Security

Precautions should be taken to physically secure every Domino server in the domain. In most cases, this means placing servers behind locked doors with limited access. Other precautions may be taken to prevent unauthorized usage of the server from within the server room. These precautions include, but are not limited to, the following:

- Certifier ID files should be stored in a physically secure location or in an encrypted database. There is no operational reason to leave Certifier IDs in an unsecured subdirectory on your server.

- Depending upon your needs, consider using alarms, motion sensors, or cameras to ensure that physical access to the server room is not breached. Key-card access to a server room is relatively common today.

- Use server racks with lockable doors.

- Disable the server's mouse, keyboard, and monitor.

- Use the Set Secure command at the Domino Console; the syntax for this command is Set Secure <password>

  This command does not block all access to the console. Most console commands may be issued at the console or remotely. Set Secure does prevent the Domino servers from being shut down by someone typing **quit** or **end** at the console or via the Domino Administration client. To reverse the command, an administrator is required to enter the command again, using the correct password at the console.

Operating System Level Security

Following are a few general items regarding operating system-level security for a Domino server:

- Screen-saver password protection. Screen savers using elaborate graphics use large amounts of system resources. A simple screen blanker is preferred.

- Programs allowing access to database files via methods other than through the Domino server (such as NFS or FTP) can be disabled. If such programs are necessary for application function, ensure that they are properly configured.

- Users should not have higher access to files via the operating system than those granted through a Notes client.

- On UNIX systems, the account designated to run the server process must be secured. Consider using an account name other than the default "notes" account.

Controlling Access to the Domino Server

There are several fields on the Security tab on each Server document, in the Domino Directory, which can enable tighter security requirements for the Domino server. Enabling some of these features may increase the time necessary to authenticate with the server. The following sections summarize the purpose and options for each field on the Security Tab governing domain access.

Security Settings

The following options exist on the Security Settings tab:

- **Compare Notes Public Keys Against Those Stored in the Directory.** Choices are Yes or No. The default is No. When this field is set to Yes, the public key of the ID file being used to access the server is compared to the correlating public key stored in the user's person document in the Domino Directory.

- **Allow Anonymous Notes Connections.** Choices are Yes or No. The default is No. When this field is set to Yes, users will not be required to authenticate with the server before gaining access. The administrator should also ensure that proper access levels are set in database ACLs for a user named Anonymous; otherwise, the access granted to Default will apply.

- **Check Passwords on Notes IDs.** Choices are Enabled or Disabled. The default is Disabled. When this feature is enabled, the server will compare the password in the ID attempting to access the server to that stored in the user's person document. When this feature is selected, password-checking must also be enabled on the user's person document.

Web Server Access

The Web Server authentication choices are as follows:

- **More Name Variations with Lower Security.** This is the default choice. Valid usernames are a full hierarchical name, common name, or alias contained in the User Name field of the person document. Alternatively, a user may enter only his or her last name or first name, or an equivalent Soundex value.

- **Fewer Name Variations with Higher Security.** Valid usernames are a full hierarchical name, common name, or alias contained in the User Name field of their person document. Note that servers must be using the R5 Domino Directory template.

Server Access

Only allow server access to users listed in this directory: Choices are Yes or No. The default is No. When this feature is enabled, access is granted only to users with a person document in the Domino Directory. If servers are not listed in the Access Server field, they will be denied access to this server.

- **Access Server.** Choices are either blank or a valid user or group name. The default choice is blank. Use of wildcards is allowed. Note that if there is any entry in this field, and the Allow Anonymous Notes Connections feature listed earlier in this section, is set to Yes, you will need to enter **Anonymous** in this field.

- **Not Access Server.** Choices are either blank or a valid user or group name. The default choice is blank, which denies access to any listed user, group, or server. This group should be of the Deny List Only type.

- **Create New Databases.** Choices are either blank or a valid user or group name. The default choice is blank, which allows any user or server with proper credentials to create a new database on this server. Use of wildcards in this field is allowed.

- **Create Replica Databases.** Choices are either blank or a valid user or group name. The default choice is blank, which allows any user or server with proper credentials to create a replica of an existing database on this server. Use of wildcards in this field is allowed.

- **Allowed to Use Monitors.** Choices are either blank or a valid user or group name. The default choice is an asterisk (*), which allows everyone to use database monitors.

- **Not Allowed to Use Monitors.** Choices are either blank or a valid user or group name. The default choice is blank, which allows everyone to use database monitors.

- **Administer the Server from a Browser.** Choices are either blank or a valid user or group name. The default choice is blank, which prevents anyone from using the Web Administration application to administer this server.

Passthru Use

The following list details the options available on the Passthru Use tab:

- **Access This Server.** Choices are either blank or a valid user or group name. The default choice is blank, which prevents anyone from accessing this server via Passthru. Wildcards are acceptable in this field.

- **Route Through.** Choices are either blank or a valid user or group name. The default choice is blank, which prevents anyone from routing through this server via Passthru to another server. Wildcards are acceptable in this field.

- **Cause Calling.** Choices are either blank or a valid user or group name. The default choice is blank, which prevents anyone from causing this server to call another server for purposes of routing through this server via Passthru to another server. Wildcards are acceptable in this field. This field is used in conjunction with the Route Through field discussed earlier.

+ **Destinations Allowed.** Choices are either blank or a valid server name. The default choice is blank, which allows users to reach any server that is configured as a valid Passthru destination. This field is used in conjunction with the Route Through field discussed earlier.

User and Group Types

Enforcing correct usage of User and Group types in both the Domino Directory and database ACLs will assist the administrator in maintaining appropriate access to their domain. Improper usage may inadvertently grant higher access than intended, or worse—allow access to the very users you are trying to keep out.

Group Types in the Domino Directory

Groups are created, edited, or deleted in the Group view of the Domino Directory. Every group has one of four group types associated with it. The following list summarizes each of the group types and its purpose:

+ **Multi-Purpose.** Groups of this type can be used for any purpose, including access control or mailing. Do not use a Multi-Purpose group in place of a Deny Access List group type. The Administration Process will search such groups and delete user names that are correctly being removed from other groups that grant access. This can have the effect of unintentionally granting server access to a terminated employee.

+ **Access Control List Only.** Groups of this type are used to control database access. Groups of this type are not displayed when a user selects the Address button when sending mail from within the Notes client.

+ **Mail Only.** Groups of this type are used for mail distribution only. If a Mail Only group is used in a database ACL, its members will receive the same level of access given to users with Default access.

◆ **Deny Access List.** Groups of this type contain members to whom server access is denied. These are typically users who have left the company and should no longer have access to server resources.

User Types in Database ACL

A User Type is assigned to each entry in a database ACL. These designate the type of ID file required to open the database by a user with the associated server, user, or group name. The five user types that may be designated in a database ACL are summarized here:

◆ **Unspecified.** This is the default user type. Using this user type effectively disables this feature, and may hamper security auditing.

◆ **Person.** When each user authenticates with a Domino server, a list is generated of the various names each user may be known by. Both common names and group memberships are tracked. The server is able to identify the type of ID being presented by a user and compares that ID type to the user type in the database ACL. This method disallows access by users who may be attempting to gain inappropriate access by creating a user ID with the same name as a group.

◆ **Server.** Designating an ACL entry to be of this type denies access to a user of this name from the Notes client. This feature was introduced to ensure a better audit trail for security personnel.

◆ **Mixed Group.** A group with this user type designation usually contains a combination of server and user names. The server will allow members of this group to access the database, at the designated ACL level, using either a server or user ID.

◆ **Person Group.** Designating an ACL entry to be of this type signifies that the member list contains only users, as opposed to servers.

◆ **Server Group.** Designating an ACL entry to be of this type signifies that the member list contains only servers. Examples: The default entries for LocalDomainServers and OtherDomainServers.

Assigning Default Access in Database ACLs

During Domino installation there are options allowing you to create a user named Anonymous and assign its ACL access to No Access in every database. The Anonymous entry helps to protect databases against unauthenticated users.

You can also designate a group name for an administrator group that is placed into every database ACL. Having an administrator group in every database ACL ensures that administrators are able to appropriately manage databases on their servers.

Monitoring Domain Access

The last section of this test objective discusses monitoring domain access. The two test objectives that follow, Monitor/Maintain Domains and Monitor/Maintain the Domino System, require a good understanding of monitoring concepts. To effectively monitor the domain, Domino server, and Notes client, administrators must understand Statistics and Events.

Statistics Versus Events

Many administrators, especially those new to Domino and Notes, seem to confuse statistics with events, hampering effective monitoring. While statistics and events share similar concepts, there are significant distinctions:

- The Domino server is constantly generating statistics. They are the measure of resources or processes available on a given server at a particular point in time.

- Configuring system monitoring enables the administrator to track statistics generated by servers.

- Two databases are used in the collection and monitoring of statistics. Statistics are collected in the Statistics database (STATREP.NSF). Statistic Monitor documents, created in the Statistics & Events database (EVENTS4.NSF), are used to set a threshold for a statistic.

- When a threshold is crossed, an alarm is created in the Statistics database. If an Event Notification document (EVENTS4.NSF) has been created to monitor for that statistic, an event is generated.

- Other types of occurrences besides statistics can be configured to generate Events. For example, if an important database fails to replicate within a given period, a Replication event may be generated.

- Creating an Event Notification document allows Notes to respond when any event with a predetermined severity level is created. When an event takes place, Notes can be programmed to carry out an action specified in an Event Notification document. For example, administrators may be notified via mail or pager, or perhaps a program is launched in an attempt to automatically correct the situation.

- Simply stated, statistics and events have a cause-and-effect relationship. For additional explanation and the specific steps necessary to configure server monitoring, read the sections that follow.

Tools to Monitor Domain Access

Some monitoring tools are passive and others are active. A passive tool simply tracks information but does not take any action. Active monitoring involves a programmed response to a specific situation.

Examples of passive monitoring tools in Notes are as follows:

- Domino Server Monitor
- Statistics Reports
- Notes Log
- Statistics tab in the Administration client

Examples of Active monitoring tools in Domino are as follows:

- Events
- Monitors
- Probes

MONITORING AND MAINTAINING DOMAINS

The Domino Administration client is the primary tool administrators use to monitor and maintain the overall health of the domain. Setup for the Administration Client is relatively minimal.

Administration Preferences

Defaults for domain and server monitoring via the Domino Server Monitor are set through the Administration Preferences dialog box, located under the File menu. Select the Monitoring button in the Administration Preferences dialog box to do the following:

- **Choose which Domino Domains are to be monitored.** The servers in an added domain do not appear in the Server Monitor. After adding a new entry to the list of domains to be monitored, it is necessary to choose Administration, Refresh, Server List, All Domains in the Administration Client.

- **Limit the amount of virtual memory reserved for monitoring.** Valid choices are between 4MB and 99MB.

- **Automatically monitor all new servers in the domain.**

- **Specify where statistics are collected for any of the user's locations.** Choices include the current computer or a remote server running the Collect server task.

- **Specify the default-polling interval of monitored servers.**

- **Specify whether servers are monitored when the Administrator Client is started.**

NOTE
There is a shortcut to reach the Administration Preferences dialog box. From the Administration Client, right-click on the server icon located on the icon bar and select Preferences.

Domino Administrator Database

This database provides the opening screen for the Administration Client and caches information, such as the monitored servers displayed in the Server-Monitoring tab. Normally maintenance is not required. When something goes wrong with the database, such as a corrupted index, the administrator can simply rename the database and Notes will generate a new copy.

Administration Execution Control List

Workstation and Administration Execution Control Lists are not new features in R5. Beginning with Notes Release 5.0.2, the default permissions for the No Signature and Default entries have been changed to enforce ECL security.

The Administration Execution Control List sets domain-wide default security for the formulas and scripts created by other users. Users inherit their ECL from the Domino Directory when they are created. The Administration ECL dialog box allows access levels for Workstation, JavaScript, and Java applet security to be set. Deselecting the check box Allow Users to Modify is preferable.

The ECL default settings for users created with versions prior to 5.0.2 will not be protected by the domain's ECL default settings. After making changes to the Administration ECL, Workstation ECL's may be updated through use of the @Command @RefreshECL. The targeted users can execute the command from a button on a mail message, for example. At this time there is no way to force a user to accept the changes automatically.

The Administration ECL is located in the Domino Directory. To reach it, click on Actions, Edit Administration ECL.

> **NOTE**
> This paper describing various aspects of the ECL is available on Lotus' Notes.net Web site. The URL is
>
> `http://notes.net/today.nsf/62f62847467a8f78052568a80055b380/`
> `3a9da544637a69b2852568310078b649?OpenDocument`

Signing Design Elements

A concept related to Execution Control Lists is that of signing database elements. Each design element in a database created with version 4.5 and above has an electronic signature associated with it. Administrators may see error messages such as Error validating user's agent execution access. These may appear in the Notes log or on the browser, depending upon the location and type of code the agent is attempting to execute.

Administrators are most likely to encounter problems when the user associated with an agent signature lacks sufficient authority to execute the code in the production environment. When this sort of mismatch occurs, errors similar to the one mentioned previously are encountered. The default Execution Control List created during the installation of the first server in a domain.

To view the signature associated with a particular agent, open the database with the Design Client, highlight the agent, and view its properties. On the Design tab of the Agent Properties infobox, you can see who last modified the agent. This person is the current Agent Owner. It may also be necessary to enter the user's running code accessing the OS, for example, to be entered in the Run Restricted LotusScript/Java Agents field of the Server document.

Data Backup

Significant changes have been made to Notes databases and the backup methodology. There are two basic choices when formulating a backup policy for your domain. The first is to shut down the Domino sever while completing a backup with a traditional backup package. If the server is not down, Notes system databases (NAMES.NSF, LOG.NSF, and MAIL.BOX, for example) remain open. User mail and other critical database files may also be open while backups are run. Backup agents meant for use with earlier versions of Notes are not guaranteed to work with R5.

The second option involves the use of an R5-compliant software package. Check with your vendors for R5-compliant products. R5-compliant backup software requires that Transaction Logging be enabled.

Transaction Logging

Transaction logging may require reconfiguration of server architecture in existing implementations as Lotus recommends putting the transaction log on a separate hard drive, optionally connected to a separate disk controller. The device used for transaction logging may also be mirrored for additional safety.

Transaction logs are written sequentially, as opposed to the random method used by most applications. Sequential writes allow faster data access but also require hardware to switch between modes if transaction-logging data is saved on a disk with other data.

The transaction log captures any changes made to databases that have logging enabled. R5-compliant backup packages use the transaction log to restore databases in the event of corruption or media failure. The time necessary to restart a server, for example, is reduced because the automatic Fixup routine that otherwise occurs is not necessary. Only changes not written to disk when the shut down occurred are removed. Without transaction logging in place, Fixup checks each document in every database that was open on the server when an unexpected shutdown occurred.

To use transaction logging effectively, all databases should use the R5 ODS (On Disk Structure) format. In the Domino Administration client, click on the Files tab and check the entries under the File Format column to identify any database using an earlier format. Databases in the R5 format will display R5 (41:0) in this column.

The following sections identify additional concepts you should be familiar with prior to enabling transaction logging.

Database Instance ID

When transaction logging is enabled for the first time on a Domino server, or when databases are moved from one server to another, each database using the R5 ODS is assigned a database instance ID number (DBIID). The DBIID is used to correlate transactions recorded into the log with the appropriate database on the server.

Some actions that administrators routinely initiated will now require a full backup of at least one database. An action such as running Fixup changes the databases DBIID. Once this happens, the transaction log and database are out of synch. Any new transactions recorded for that database will use the new DBIID, whereas old transactions still have the old DBIID and no longer match the database's new DBIID. As a result, Domino cannot restore transactions made prior to the new DBIID assignment.

Lotus recommends performing a full backup of any database as soon after the DBIID change as possible. A full backup captures all of the transactions up to that point. Afterward, Notes requires only the transactions associated with the new DBIID to properly restore a database.

Actions Affecting Transaction Logging

There are several actions that result in a new DBIID being issued to a database. The next few sections identify potential pitfalls associated with enabling transaction logging.

Fixup

Domino versions prior to R5 used Fixup to check each database that was open when the server was shut down unexpectedly. With transaction logging enabled on an R5 server, this process is much faster. The transaction log information is used to correct problems with any logged database using the R5 ODS. If there are any databases in formats prior to R5, Fixup still runs against these.

Administrators also ran Fixup manually to correct corrupted database elements. Lotus states that Fixup generally doesn't run against databases with transaction logging enabled. Running Fixup with the –J option (Fixup –J) allows Fixup to run against a database with transaction logging enabled.

Compact

Another task used to fix database problems and reclaim disk space is Compact. Administrators use this task to remove unused or white space in a database. A copy of the database is made in memory and replaces the original on the hard drive. In R5 this is referred to as Copy style Compact. When Compact is run this way, a new DBIID is assigned to the database.

R5 introduces two new methods of running Compact. In-place compacting with space recovery and reduction in file size also changes the database DBIID requiring a full backup of the affected databases after Compact finishes.

The only style of Compact that retains the DBIID is In-place compacting with space recovery only. This is the default style that will run if you enter Compact with no options.

Advanced Database Properties and DBIID

Changing the Advanced properties of a database may change the DBIID, requiring a full backup of the database to maintain logging integrity. Select a database icon; click on File, Database, Properties, Advanced tab to access the Advanced database properties.

Document Table Bitmap Optimization

When Notes updates a view, it refers to document information tables to determine which documents to display in that view. Selecting Document Table Bitmap Optimization will cause Notes to associate tables with forms used by each document. Domino will then search only the tables associated with the forms used by documents in the view that is being updated. After changing this property, you must compact the database for the change to take effect. If transaction logging is enabled for this database, Lotus recommends a full backup as soon as possible after making this change.

Disable Transaction Logging

Selecting this option will turn off transaction logging for this database. Execute the following steps to disable transaction logging:

1. Ensure that no users have the database open before proceeding.

2. Select Disable Transaction Logging in the database Advanced Properties. Close the database.

3. Run Compact with the –t option (Compact –t <database name>) to disable transaction logging. Note that the Compact option is case sensitive.

4. Run the Dbcache flush Server command (Dbcache flush) to close any databases within the database cache.

5. Open the database.

A similar process is used to restart transaction logging for a database.

Re-enable Transaction Logging

1. Ensure that no users have the database open before proceeding.

2. Deselect Disable Transaction Logging in the database Advanced Properties. Close the database.

3. Run Compact with the –T option (Compact –T <database name>) to disable transaction logging. Note that the Compact option is case sensitive.

4. Run the Dbcache flush Server command (Dbcache flush) to close any databases within the database cache.

5. Open the database.

Don't Support Specialized Response Hierarchy

Notes documents track information about child and response documents. This information is used only if the @functions @AllChildren and @AllDescendents are used a view selection formulas. If these @functions aren't used, you may choose to select the Don't Support Specialized Response Hierarchy option. If transaction logging is enabled for this database, Lotus recommends a full backup as soon as possible after enabling or disabling this option.

Editing the Transaction Logging Tab

After transaction logging is enabled, changing the values in any of the following fields on the Transaction Logging tab in the Domino Directory will result in the assignment of a new DBIID to all databases that have transaction logging enabled.

- Transaction Logging

- Log Path

- Maximum Log Space

A full backup of that server's databases is necessary to maintain the integrity of logging. A full backup of the databases ensures that you have a record of all changes made, and a recovery point for the database. The procedure is simple, but it is crucial that it be followed.

1. Do a full backup of all the databases on the affected server.

2. Edit the Transaction Logging fields in the Server document. Check for misspellings! Save and close the Server document.

3. Shut the Domino server down, make any physical or logical configuration changes.

4. Restart the Domino server and immediately perform a full backup.

Setting Up Transaction Logging

Changes to the values in any of the following fields on the Transaction Logging tab in the Domino Directory do not cause a new DBIID to be assigned. Note that changes to the Logging Style field require a full backup and restart of the Domino server for the change to take effect.

Changes to the Automatic Fixup of Corrupt Databases field or the Runtime/Restart performance field do not require that the Domino server be restarted to take effect.

After installing any additional devices to store transaction logs, ensure that every database you want to log is in the correct ODS format. In the Administration client, click on the Transaction Logging tab and enter the edit mode. There are seven fields on this page. The choices for each are summarized:

- **Transaction Logging.** Choices are either Enabled or Disabled. The default is Disabled.

- **Log Path.** Enter the path to the logical location of the log files. Enter either the absolute path to the device location (such as l:\logs\) or a path relative to the domino data directory (such as \logdir).

- **Use All Available Space on Log Device.** Choices are Yes or No. The default is No. If the device capturing the logs is dedicated solely to transaction logging, choose Yes.

- **Maximum Log Space.** If you choose Yes in the Use All Available Space on Log Device field, no entry is necessary in this field. If you choose No in that field, enter the number of bytes you want to use here. Transaction logs may be up to 4GB in size.

- **Automatic Fixup of Corrupt Databases.** Choices are Enabled or Disabled. The default is Enabled. When enabled, Fixup will automatically be run on a corrupted database that cannot be restored via the transaction log. Fixup will change the database DBIID, requiring that the database be backed up. If disabled, a message is sent to the administrator that Fixup –J should be run.

- **Runtime/Restart Performance.** Choices are Standard, Favor Restart Recovery Time, or Favor Runtime. The default is Standard, a compromise between the other choices and is the recommended value.

  This field determines how often a recovery checkpoint is created in the transaction log. The frequency of recovery checkpoints determines how many transactions are kept in memory versus written to disk.

  Favor Runtime means fewer checkpoints are created. Because fewer system resources are used, runtime performance is better.

  Favor Restart recovery time means more checkpoints are created so fewer transactions need to be recovered at server startup.

- **Logging style.** Choices are Circular and Archived. The default is Circular, which overwrites the oldest transactions with new ones when the file reaches its maximum size. Restore ability is limited because only transactions currently in the log may be restored. Choose Archived to create sequential backups of the log file.

Translog_Status Notes.ini Setting

This notes.ini setting is used to enable or disable transaction logging for all R5 databases on the server. The default setting for Translog_Status is 0 (disabled). This parameter is set through selections on the Transaction Logging tab in the Server document.

Establish Backup Policy

A comprehensive strategy will involve an R5-compliant backup solution allowing daily incremental backup of the transaction logs, as well as any other critical files that support database applications on each server. Perform a full backup of all databases on a weekly basis. Reclaim disk space by running Compact with the option to reduce file size (Compact –B).

MONITORING AND MAINTENANCE OF THE DOMINO SYSTEM

To successfully monitor Domino Systems, the administrator should have some familiarity with the monitoring tools available at the operating system level as well as in Domino.

Domino Integration with the NT Operating System

Domino system monitoring may be integrated with NT Performance Monitor utility allowing administrators to more effectively gauge the health of both the operating system and Domino server. Lotus has provided a batch file (NOTESREG.BAT) that adds Lotus Notes object and Domino-specific counters to Performance Monitor. NOTESREG.BAT is copied to the Domino Program directory (D:\lotus\domino) during installation if the Notes Performance Monitor option is checked. Execute the batch file from the operating system command line, adding a parameter indicating the full path to the Domino server's program directory (such as notesreg.bat D:\Lotus\Domino).

The NT Registry is updated and Domino monitors become available through Performance Monitor. After installing the Notes counters, restart the Domino server. The next time Performance Monitor is opened, the Lotus Notes object will be available.

Statistics gathered natively within Domino are constantly updating while the server is running. Performance Monitor has to be started separately. Also, additional information such as Domino server uptime is available only through Domino.

Basic System Monitoring Using Native Notes Tools

Entering commands either at the console or through a remote session from a Notes Administration client allows basic server monitoring. The Show Statistic command provides a current listing including all the counters available through the NT Performance Monitor, plus a few additional ones.

Information that is returned to the graphical Domino Administration client is the result of the remote issuance of a console command. For example, using the Domino Administration client to issue the show users command causes a command similar to show users >C:\WINDOWS\ TEMP\81916467.TMP to be executed on the server. It is the contents of that .TMP file that are displayed to the user in the Administration Client.

The following list of console commands is related to system monitoring. Most, but not all, are shown in Appendix B of the Notes Administrator's Guide that ships with Notes.

- **Dbcache Disable.** Disables the database cache.

- **Dbcache Flush.** Clears the database cache contents.

- **Dbcache Show.** Shows the current contents of the database cache.

- **Show Allports.** Displays configuration information for all active and disabled ports.

- **Show Cluster.** Displays clustering configuration for this server.

- **Show Configuration <variable name>.** Displays current values for the specific Notes.ini variable.

- **Show Database <file name>.** Displays view and document information for the specified database.

- **Show DBS.** Displays a listing of information used to monitor database performance.

- **Show Directory.** Displays a list of all database files in the Domino server's data directory and whether multiple replicas exist.

- **Show DriveSpace <drive letter>.** Displays the amount of available space on the specified drive. Note that this statistic may be reported differently on the various operating systems supported by Domino.

- **Show Memory.** Displays amount of memory available to the Domino server.

- **Show Port <port name>.** Displays information associated with a specified port.

- **Show Schedule.** Displays a listing of scheduled tasks.

- **Show Server.** Displays a summary of this server's vital information.

- **Show Statistic <variable>.** Displays the current value for a statistic. Omitting the <variable name> argument will result in a display of all current statistics.

- **Show Tasks.** Displays a listing of server tasks currently running.

- **Show Users.** Displays a listing of users with a session established with the server.

- **Trace <server name>.** Traces a connection to the specified server.

Log Analysis

The Miscellaneous view in the server log (LOG.NSF) provides an unfiltered list of events over time. The Log Analysis (Server, Analysis, Tools, Analyze, Log) tool will search the Miscellaneous view on the specified server and place the output into the specified database. The default output location is the Log Analysis (LOGA4.NSF) database on the local drive.

Server Properties

Server properties are viewable through the Domino Administration Client by right-clicking on an individual server icon and selecting Properties. The information reported is categorized into five tabs:

- **Basics**. Displays the Domino software version, platform, license, current time, and date. Note the similarity to the information returned from the Show tasks command at the server console.

- **Disks**. Displays information about installed hard disks. Displayed information is organized by drive letters, percent free space, free megabytes, and total size.

- **Cluster**. If the server is configured as part of a cluster, statistics include cluster name, availability threshold, availability index, cluster network port, probe time out and count values, and cluster members.

- **Ports**. Provides access to port configuration dialog box.

- **Advanced**. Displays statistics including the number of total transactions, peak transactions, and number of transactions in the last hour and minute. Users statistics include the number of current users, peak number, and the date and time that peak occurred. Memory statistics included are availability, allocated memory, and available memory.

Domino Server Monitor

Task information is shown using one of six symbols, indicating the status of each task on monitored servers. Monitored statistics display a value. At the top of the display of the By Timeline view is a user-adjustable time scale indicating the update interval. This scale is used to set the frequency of status updates. Valid choices are between 1 and 60 minutes. Monitoring is initiated by clicking on the Start button at the top of the display or automatically by selecting Automatically Monitor Servers at Startup in the Administration Preferences menu.

Clicking on a server name shows the status of any monitored task or statistic on the server. Additional tasks, statistics, or servers can be added or deleted on individual servers through the Monitoring menu. Tasks or statistics can be added or deleted by right-clicking on the Server-Monitoring tab and choosing from the list.

The second view, By State, uses the same symbolic reporting presentation but the server information is expanded, making detailed viewing easier.

> **NOTE**   In order for the indicator icons to function properly, the monitored tasks must be running on a Domino R5 server, with the Event server task started.

The following list summarizes the status icons on the Domino Server Monitor:

- **Fatal**. Fatal errors are being generated but the task is running.

- **Failure**. Failure errors are being generated but the task is running.

- **Warning**. Warning errors are being generated but the task is running.

- **Not responding.** The task is responding slowly.

- **Not running.** The task has not been running since the Server Monitor was started.

- **Running.** The task is running properly.

The Administration Client Server, Statistics Tab

The Statistics tab—available from within the Administration Client by clicking on Server, Statistics tab—displays the same output as a Show statistic command, entered at the server console. Statistics in the Administration Client are organized by type and presented graphically. Right-clicking on the Statistics tab gives the option of either expanding or collapsing all of the categories or copying the selected information.

COMPONENTS OF ACTIVE SYSTEM MONITORING

The native monitoring tools discussed thus far require little administrator configuration. They also provide little opportunity for convenient, meaningful analysis.

Running the Event Monitor and Statistics Collector server tasks enables statistics and Event reporting. Each reports different types of information. Either server task may be loaded at the console manually or added to the NOTES.INI file to ensure the tasks start each time the server starts. Basic monitoring involves four components:

- Statistic Collector (Collect) server task
- Event Monitor server task
- Statistics & Events database
- Statistics database

Statistic Collector Task

The Statistic Collector (Collect) task gathers system statistics on one or multiple servers in the domain. It is only necessary to run this task on a single server.

Create a Statistic Collection document in the Statistics & Events database to specify the servers for which statistics are to be collected and where these statistics are stored. The Statistics database (STATREP.NSF) is the default location for collection and summary of statistics in the domain.

Starting the Collect or Event task creates the Statistics & Events database if it does not already exist. Statistics collection must be configured manually.

To start the Statistics Collector via the Administrator client, follow these steps:

1. Open the Domino Administrator client.
2. Click on the Server, then Status tab.

3. Click on Tools, Task and select Start.

4. Select Collector from the list when the Start New Task box appears.

5. Click on the Start Task button.

6. Click Done to close the New Task box.

Remove the Report Task on Upgraded Servers

The Collect task now incorporates functions previously handled by the Reporter task. The Reporter task (Report) should be removed from upgraded servers to avoid receiving the `Error attempting to load or run report.exe. Unable to invoke program` error message during server startup.

Event Monitor Task

The Event Monitor (Event) task is used to monitor system activity on a Domino server. Unlike the Collect task discussed in the previous section, the Event Monitor task must be started on every server you want to monitor. Event is not placed on the ServerTasks line of the notes.ini file by default. It must be added manually in new installations. Running the Event or Collect task automatically creates the Statistics and Events database if it does not already exist.

To start the Event task using the Domino Administration client, follow these steps:

1. Open the Domino Administration client.

2. Click on the Server, Status tab.

3. Click on Task, Start.

4. When the Start New Task box appears, select Event Monitor from the list.

5. Click the Start Task button, then click Done.

When a monitored event occurs, a specified action is triggered. Following is a list of available actions in response to an event:

+ Broadcast a message to a specified or all server users.

+ Mail a notification to an administrator, user, group, or another database.

- Log the event to a local database or remote server, usually the Statistics Reporting database.

- Report the event to the Windows NT Event Viewer or the UNIX System log.

- Send a pager message with a modified description of the event.

- Generate an SNMP trap.

- Run a program, either on the local or reporting server.

- Relay the event to another server in the domain.

Additional options are available if server management programs are installed on the system.

Events have two main components: Type and Severity. Event reporting is categorized events by functional area. A list of events, their type, and severity can be viewed through the Domino Administration client.

1. Click on the Configuration tab.

2. Select Event Messages.

Events have a default severity level and type viewable on the Basics tab of the Message form. The Severity or Type field may be edited to reflect values appropriate for a specific environment.

Event types native to Domino are as follows:

- Add-in

- AdminP

- Agent

- Client

- Comm/Net

- Compiler

- Database

- Directory (LDAP)

- FTP

- Mail

- Misc

- Network

- News (NNTP)

- Replica

- Resource

- Router

- Security

- Server

- Statistic

- Unknown

- Update

- Web (HTTP/HTTPS)

Available severity levels are as follows:

- **Normal.** Informational message.

- **Warning (Low).** May cause some performance degradation.

- **Warning (High).** Intervention probably required.

- **Failure.** Severe failure in the associated component.

- **Fatal.** System crash is probable.

The Advanced tab provides fields to note probable causes, possible solutions, and additional comments for each event message.

CONFIGURING ACTIVE SYSTEM MONITORING

The previous section described the components of active monitoring. This section describes the configuration options for thresholds and responses to be taken in response to Events. Options for server monitoring are configured via the Server, Configuration tab in the Domino Administrator.

Configuring the Statistic Collector

A Server Statistic Collection document configures the Statistic Collector (Collect) task. Unless a Statistic Collection document is configured, statistics will be collected only for the server running the Collect task. Server Statistics Collection documents are accessed via the Administration Client. To configure a Statistic Collection document from the Domino Administration client, follow these steps:

1. Click on the Configuration tab.

2. Click on Statistics & Events.

3. Click on Server Statistic Collection.

4. If a document already exists for the target server, edit that document. Otherwise, select New Server Statistic Collection. Choices for filling in the document are summarized here:

   - **Collecting Server.** Enter the name of a server running the Collect task.

   - **All Servers in This Domain.** Statistics will be collected from all of the servers in the domain.

   - **All Servers That Are Not Explicitly Listed to Be Collected.** Statistics will be collected from servers in the domain on which statistics are not currently collected.

   - **From the Following Servers.** Designate specific servers to collect from.

   - **Database to Receive Reports.** Selecting this option enables statistics logging to a specific database.

   - **Database to Receive Reports.** Normally statrep.nsf, the Statistics Reporting database.

   - **Collection Report Interval.** The number of minutes between generation of statistics reports. The minimum value is 15 minutes. The default is every 60 minutes.

   - **Collection Alarm Interval.** The number of minutes between generation of alarms. The minimum value is every 15 minutes. The default is every 60 minutes.

5. Click OK to exit.

Statistic Thresholds

Review and edit statistic thresholds in the Administration client to ensure that default thresholds are appropriate for the environment.

1. Open the Administration client.

2. Click on the Configuration tab, then select Statistics & Events.

3. Select Default Statistic Thresholds.

Each Statistic Description document contains the following information of interest for editing statistics:

- Statistic name

- Data type

- Statistic unit

- Statistic description

- Normal value

- Threshold operator

- Threshold percentage

- Event severity

These additional views are also available through the Administration-Statistics & Events:

- Statistic names by description

- Statistic names

Configuring Event Notification Documents

Event Notification documents are accessed through the Administration client and stored in the Statistics & Events database. Event Notification documents configure event reporting and triggered actions. Follow these steps to create an Event Notification document:

1. Open the Administration client.

2. Click on the Configuration tab.

3. Select Event Notification.

4. Create new or edit existing Event Notification documents as appropriate.

The options in an Event Configuration document are summarized as follows:

- **Basics tab, Notification Trigger.** The choice selected determines what is displayed on the Event and Action tabs. Choices are:

    - Any event that matches a criteria

    - A built-in or add-in task event

- **Basics tab, Servers to Monitor.** Select either Notify of the Event on Any Server in the Domain or Notify of the Event Only in the Following Servers to specify servers running the Event task you want to monitor.

    After appropriate choices are configured, proceed to the Event tab.

- **Event tab, Criteria to Match.** If Any Event That Matches a Criteria is selected on the Basics tab, the following choices are available. Choose one from each of the following pairs:

    - Events Can Be Any Type or Events Must Be This Type

    - Events Can Be Any Severity or Events Must Be One of These Severities

    - Events Can Have Any Message or Events Must Have This Text in the Event Message

    If A Built-In or Add-In Task Event is selected on the Basics tab, the following choices are available. Choose one from the following pair:

    - Events Can Have Any Message or Events Must Have This Text in the Event Message.

    Click on the Select Event button to open a list of available error messages and their types. Select the desired event message text. The type, severity, and message text are then displayed on the Event tab.

    After appropriate choices are configured, proceed to the Action tab.

◆ **Action tab, Notification Method.** Actions taken in response to an event are selected on the Action tab. A summary of the available actions is presented earlier in the section.

The administrator may also choose to enable or disable monitoring of this action. A time period for monitoring of this action can also be specified.

Monitors

Monitors track server resources as well as network or system activity. Monitors differ from events in that monitors do not have any actions associated with them. If the specified threshold is crossed, a monitor triggers an event, which in turn performs an associated action.

The following sections describe each type of monitor and their use. There are two types of monitors: database (ACL Change, File, and Replication) and statistic monitors.

ACL Change Monitor

Track ACL changes in a database on all or specified servers in the domain.

Use the Other field to specify the severity level of the security event generated by this monitor. In addition, there is a check box that allows the monitor to be disabled.

File Monitors

Track the amount of unused space in a specified file on all or specific servers in the domain. After the threshold is crossed, an event is triggered. Optionally, the file may be automatically compacted.

Track whether a specified minimum number of user sessions have been established with the specified database. Otherwise, an event is triggered.

Use the Other field to specify the severity level of the security event generated by this monitor. In addition, there is a check box that allows the monitor to be disabled.

Replication Monitors

Track replication activity for a specified file between either all or specified servers in the domain.

Use the Other field to specify the severity level of the security event generated by this monitor. In addition, there is a check box that allows the monitor to be disabled.

Statistic Monitors

Track a specific statistic on all or specific servers in the domain. Click the Change button to select from a list of all available statistics which can be monitored.

Use the Other field to specify the severity level of the security event generated by this monitor. In addition, there is a check box that allows the monitor to be disabled.

Web Administrator

The Domino Web Administrator provides many of the functions available from the Domino Administrator client via an http session using a browser.

Setting Up Web Administrator

The target server must be running the http task to be accessed by a browser. Ensure that the user name is entered into these three fields in the Server Document:

- Administrators
- Run Unrestricted LotusScript and Java Agents on the Server
- Administer the Server from a Browser

The Web Administration database is automatically set up the first time that the http task is loaded on the server.

Using the Web Administrator to Monitor Domino Servers

To access the Web Administrator with a browser, enter the URL in this format:

http://hostname/webadmin.nsf

The opening screen of the Web Administrator is an informational display of the server name and the name of the host computer. Operating system, Domino Release and Build information are also displayed. The functions available through the Web Administrator are largely the same as those available via the Notes Administration Client. Note, however, that although Person and Server documents can be created manually, servers and users cannot be registered with ID files from the Web Administration client.

TROUBLESHOOTING DOMAIN ACCESS PROBLEMS

One of the most common errors Notes users see is You are not authorized to access this server. If the error is received on a new installation, as opposed to an upgraded server, begin by checking the information and spelling of the fields (see step 2 below) in the Server Document.

Begin troubleshooting in the Domino Administrator by following these steps:

1. Select the desired server and click on the Configuration tab, Server, Current Server Document.

2. Review the following fields on the Basics tab for errors:

   ◆ **Server Name.** Ensure that the full hierarchical server name is entered and spelled correctly.

   ◆ **Domain Name.** Ensure that the name is spelled correctly.

   Review the following fields on the Security tab for errors:

   ◆ **Access Server.** Delete the contents of this field if it contains any information. Only those names or groups listed in the field are allowed to access the server.

- **Not Access Server.** Delete the contents of this field if it contains any information. The users or groups listed in the field are not allowed to access the server.

Review the following field on the Ports tab for errors:

- **Notes Network.** Make sure that at least one Notes network is enabled and has a unique Notes network name.

3. If, after correcting errors in the previous fields the problem persists, check for corruption of the server document by creating a new Server document and using it to connect users instead of the old one. To preserve any needed information in the original, create a backup copy of the original Server document. Cut and paste the original into another database or back up the database, then delete the original in the active Domino Directory. This also enables you to be sure that the newly created document is the one the system uses to attempt the connection.

4. If this fails, try rebuilding the hidden views used in client authentication. These are the $ServerAccess and $People views. To rebuild an individual index while the server is running, enter the following command at the server console:

```
Load updall names.nsf -t <view name> -r
```

> **NOTE**
>
> Other hidden views—$Groups, for example—determine access to resources, such as membership to groups, and are therefore valuable for troubleshooting access problems in other areas. If users who are recently added to a group cannot gain access to resources controlled by group membership, rebuilding $Groups may correct the problem.

5. An alternative is to rebuild every view in the Domino Directory. Lotus recommends that the Domino server be stopped beforehand to prevent any further updates during this process. At the operating system prompt, enter `updall names.nsf -r`.

6. If database corruption is suspected, consider running the Fixup task. Complete a backup of databases prior to running Fixup. Review options available for Fixup prior to running the task.

7. Check for and resolve Replication or Save conflict documents in the Group and People views of the Domino Directory.

8. Try using a backup copy of the Server ID file. If the Server ID was recertified as part of a recent upgrade, it is possible that it was damaged.

9. Review the certificates stored in the Server ID to ensure that it contains all appropriate certificates. Perform the following steps to accomplish this from the Domino Administration client:

1. Click on Configuration, Tools, ID Properties.

2. Select the desired Server ID file and click Open.

3. Click Certificates.

4. If all appropriate certificates are not listed, consider recertifying the Server ID.

5. Replace the design of the Domino Directory to ensure that the correct template (PUBNAMES.NTF) is being used.

TROUBLESHOOTING NETWORK AND PROTOCOL PROBLEMS

When a Notes user or server cannot successfully establish communications, an error message similar to `Server not responding` is displayed. First, determine whether it is a problem within Notes, the protocol stack, or the network. Review the Notes log for error messages. Consider using the Log Analysis tool to search for error messages. Pinpointing the time the errors began occurring can provide vital clues.

Following are two ways to establish whether network communications are functioning correctly on a Windows 95, 98, or NT client computer running TCP/IP. The first method is used to test connectivity via the OS. The second method is used to test connectivity from a Notes client.

Testing OS Connectivity

To begin, the administrator needs to know basic configuration information, such as the IP address and DNS alias of the workstation and the server. If DNS is not used on the network, check for a local HOSTS or LMHOSTS file. These ASCII files are used for numeric address to name resolution.

Using the PING utility is the traditional method used to find out if a client workstation can communicate with the rest of the network. To use this method, execute the following steps:

1. Ping the network adapter's loopback address of 127.0.0.1. If this is successful, the adapter is responding properly. If this fails, check the network adapter card for problems.

2. Ping the network address of the workstation. This will establish that TCP/IP is configured correctly. It will also indicate whether there is another computer on the network configured with the same network address. This may be the cause in the case of inter-mittent connection problems, because the first machine that connects has rights to that address.

3. Ping the numeric IP address of the server you want to reach. A successful reply means that IP–level connectivity is available between this client and the intended server.

4. Ping the fully qualified domain name of the Domino server you are trying to reach (for example, ping orion.ibm.com). The Notes client communicates with the Domino server by name, as opposed to numeric IP address. Success here verifies that the workstation is able to resolve the server name. If pinging by the numeric IP address is successful, but using the host name fails, the problem is likely with name resolution.

5. Ping the alias name of the Domino server (for example, OrionDomino). An alias would be used if the fully qualified domain name is different from that of the Domino server. This establishes that the alias is entered correctly in the DNS or hosts file. Failure here indicates that the alias is missing or incorrect in the DNS or HOSTS file.

If the administrator successfully completes the preceding routine and the workstation still cannot connect to the server, consider whether the client is functioning correctly.

Note that this process will fail if the Domino server name contains illegal characters (such as a space or ampersand) in a TCP/IP host name.

Testing Connectivity from Within an R5 Client

The previous section described steps to check connectivity at the Operating System level. In this section, the method of testing for connectivity from within the Notes client is discussed.

Occasionally, users having difficulty connecting to a target server have inadvertently switched to an inappropriate location document. The R5 client includes several default location documents that may be edited by the user. Because location documents define connectivity parameters, such as the port and connection type, it is possible that simply switching to an appropriate location document may solve the problem.

If after confirming that the current Location Document contains appropriate entries for the desired connection, proceed to the next step.

To begin, navigate to the Ports section within User Preferences:

1. Go to the Ports dialog box at File, Preferences, User Preferences, Ports.

2. Click on the Trace button.

3. In the Trace Connections infobox, select the name of the destination server from the drop-down list.

4. Click on the Trace button.

Notes will attempt to establish a connection to the specified server. If this client has connected to the server previously, Notes will use the IP address stored in the client's Personal Address Book. The address is stored in the client's location document in a hidden field named $SavedAddresses. Notes will always attempt to connect to the server using the address stored in this field. Caching the address is meant to save time when connecting to a server. This setting may create problems if the server's address has changed.

Connectivity Problems Caused by Switching Server IP Address

Changing the network address of a server running Domino may cause connectivity problems. The following scenario illustrates a practical example of a problem experienced by users.

Suppose that the IP address of a server called EagleMountain/Eagle was changed from 169.254.90.26 to 169.254.90.12. The changes have been made on the network DNS servers. I have connected to EagleMountain/Eagle in the past. I also have checked that the server is running.

When I try to establish a connection, I get the error message Unable to find path to server. I ping the server by numeric IP address and host name, and both report that the server is available. The Notes client, however, cannot connect. By tracing the connection from within the Notes client, I learn that the Notes client is still using 169.254.90.26 when attempting to connect.

To fix this problem, I could delete the current location document from my Personal Address Book and create a new one. This forces a new lookup of the address. Alternatively, I could place the parameter dont_use_remembered_addresses=1 in the NOTES.INI file.

There are actually four fields involved in the previous scenario. These fields cache information about the servers that the client has connected to in the past to improve performance on future connections. To view these fields, look at the Document Properties for a location document in the Personal Address Book. The $SavedAddresses field contains only one entry per location document. The other fields are multi-value fields. However, only the first entry in each is visible through the Document Properties. Each of the four hidden fields and its purpose is listed here:

- **$SavedAddresses.** May contain the target server's DNS name, numeric IP address, or alias.

- **$SavedPorts.** Saves the port over which connections were established, with each server stored in $SavedServers.

- **$SavedDate.** Saves the date of the last connection for each server in the $SavedServer field.

- **$SavedServers.** Saves the names of servers to which the client has connected.

TROUBLESHOOTING MODEM PROBLEMS

The first step in troubleshooting modem problems is to physically check the hardware, cable connections, software settings, and so on. If this is a new installation, try replacing components with ones known to work. Check with the administrator of the target server to ensure that the server is available. Troubleshooting a modem problem often requires examining conditions on both sides of the connection.

Ensure that the telephone line is functioning properly. Using an analog telephone, check for dial tone. Manually dial the telephone number of the target server. If necessary, contact the Telephone Company to check the line. If the modem is external, it may be helpful to turn the modem off and back on. If you are able, cycle the server.

Enable logging of modem I/O to the Notes log (log.nsf). From the Notes Administrator, execute the following steps:

1. Click on Server, Status, Tools, Setup Ports.

2. Select the target modem port.

3. Select <portname> Options (such as Com2 Options). The Additional Setup screen is displayed.

4. Select Log Modem I/O.

5. Optionally, increase the value in the Speaker Volume field. Listen for errors as the modem attempts to make the connection.

6. Click OK twice.

Following are some additional troubleshooting steps that might be done with modem logging either on or off:

- Check the Miscellaneous view of the Notes log for messages indicating modem or port errors.

- If normal responses are not recorded in the Miscellaneous view of the Notes log, it may be necessary to review the modem command file. Look at the command string being sent to the modem. Sometimes AT commands sent in mixed-case characters may cause errors. Enter the AT setup string at the command line and review the responses. Review modem documentation for help with commands for the particular modem.

- Check the Phone Calls view in the log. Numerous CRC or retransmission errors indicate that one or both modems detect transmission errors.

- Check that the telephone number is correct and in the correct format. Some locations require that call waiting be disabled, or a prefix may be necessary to reach an outside line.

- Review the fields in the Connection document to ensure that there are no misspellings, and so on.

WHAT IS IMPORTANT TO KNOW

- Objects defined in a shared Domino Directory define a domain. Prompt maintenance and troubleshooting ensure both security and access.

- Security and management of Certifier IDs are crucial for domain security. Multiple passwords provide greater security but require maintenance and planning.

- ID file recovery has replaced the Escrow process in prior versions of Notes. Recovery information is stored in the user's ID files and an encrypted copy of the ID file is stored in a designated database allowing recovery of a damaged ID or forgotten password.

- ID recovery should be configured before creating new ID files. Users without recovery information should be identified and must accept recovery information into their ID manually. There currently is no method to force a user to accept recovery information.

- Use the Administration Client to access statistics and configure monitoring of important databases, communications pathways, and hardware.

- Be able to identify the use and configuration of active and passive monitoring tools. Remember the relationships between statistics, alarms, monitors, and events.

- Be able to use the Domino Web Administrator to monitor domain servers via a browser session. Remember the requirements for administering the domain with a browser.

- Follow methodical procedures to identify communications problems. Logically isolate whether the problem is in the network or client configuration before taking action.

Section 2: Implementing a Domino R5 Infrastructure: Exam 521

ABOUT EXAM 521

Exam Number	**521**
Minutes Allowed	**60**
Single-Answer Questions	**No**
Multiple Answer with Correct Number Given	**Yes**
Multiple Answer without Correct Number Given	**No**
Choices of A–D	**Yes**
Choices of A–E	**No**
Scenario-Based Questions	**Yes**
Objective Categories	**Yes**

▶ Creating/Registering Certificates (Hierarchical)

▶ Creating/Registering Groups

▶ Creating/Registering Servers

▶ Creating/Registering Users

CHAPTER **6**

Creating/Registering
System Resources

In this chapter, you will explore the creation or registration of a particular set of system resources. These resources include IDs, groups, servers, and users. These are not the only resources you can create in a Lotus Notes/Domino environment, but they certainly are the most common that you would work with on a daily basis.

CREATING/REGISTERING CERTIFICATES

Certificates make it possible for you to create users, servers, and other certificates. Certificates are much like a user's ID in that they contain unique keys and names that cannot easily (if at all) be reproduced. In general, there are two categories of certificates: the organization and organizational units; these certificates can be International or North American. The two types of security for IDs: hierarchical and flat. These categories of certificates (International versus NA) and ID types (Hierarchical versus Flat) are explained in the following sections.

International Versus North American IDs

The decision about whether to use International IDs and certificates should be made very early on in the creation of a Lotus Notes/Domino infrastructure. Changing your mind later can be a taxing ordeal (especially when re-creating a server). Federal laws govern the use of North American IDs—specifically, no North American ID or software should leave the United States or Canada. This is because the North American version uses stronger encryption (128 bit) than the International version (48 bit). The U.S. Government does not want strong encryption keys to be distributed outside of North America. Most large companies with business divisions overseas will decide to make the entire structure International. The administration process is much easier with one type of security structure.

Hierarchical Versus Flat IDs

A hierarchical server or user ID can contain the following:

- **Common name.** Server, or first and last name of the user. Can be up to and including 80 characters.

- **Organizational unit (OU).** Usually a department or location name. Can be up to four OUs, each of no more than 32 characters. Organizational units are optional, but can help to further distinguish users and servers.

- **Organization name (O).** A required element of the ID. It can consist of between 3 and 64 characters.

- **Country.** Uses the ISO standard two-letter abbreviation for the country. It is recommended that you use OUs rather than these country codes to specify location. Typically you would have to create many more IDs if you used the country codes, and the two-letter restriction could be a hindrance.

An example of a hierarchical ID follows:

CN=Tim Greeney/OU2=Sales/OU1=Atlanta/0=ChairCreations/ C=US

In this example, the common name is Tim Greeney. The first organizational unit is Atlanta and the second organizational unit is Sales. The Atlanta OU was used to create the Sales OU. The organization is ChairCreations. The country code is US. If you want to sound really impressive, the way the above is written is referred to as the *canonical* format. An abbreviated format would be as follows:

Tim Greeney/Sales/Alanta/ChairCreations/US

Lotus Notes version 3 and older versions used non-hierarchical (often called flat) certificates. A flat ID contains only the name of the person or server. With each new release from Lotus, you lose more functionality with flat IDs. Version 5 will likely be the last release that even allows flat certificates. Hierarchical certificates help determine who has rights to databases and also distinguish individuals from one another in the directory.

Making the Organizational Certifier

When you created the first server in your organization, the certificate for your company was born. It was saved on your server as CERT.ID in the data directory of your server. For such a small (about 3KB) and innocent-looking file, it has amazing significance. This file is used to create all future IDs (servers, people, and OUs). This first certificate is referred to as the organization certifier.

You will also find that the first server setup creates a SERVER.ID and a USER.ID. However, you will not find the USER.ID in the data directory as you will the CERT.ID and the SERVER.ID. The USER.ID is stored in the directory until the client is installed and configured. Storing IDs in the directory is a convenient way to distribute new IDs to a client or server. It does also present a security risk, however. If an individual knows that the ID is stored in the directory, he can simply detach the ID to his machine. If the correct password is used with the ID, that person has then stolen the identity and can send messages or create records under the new identity.

Organizational Units

After the organization certificate is born, it can be used to create new organizational units (OUs). Organizational units further help to secure and identify users and servers attached to your network. An OU can simply be the name of a location or department in which a person or server belongs. Let's take the example of FastCars, Inc. In the directory, we find Michael McCaw/Support/Atlanta/FastCars. The organization in this case is FastCars. The OU, Atlanta, was created from the FastCars CERT.ID. Atlanta, in this case, is actually referred to as OU1. The support OU (OU2) was created from the Atlanta/FastCars OU. The Michael McCaw client ID (user) was created from the Support/Atlanta/FastCars OU. An organization can have up to four levels of OUs. It is recommended not only that you limit the number of OUs that you have but also that you use names that are unlikely to change. Figure 6.1 shows an example of an organization, OUs, and common names.

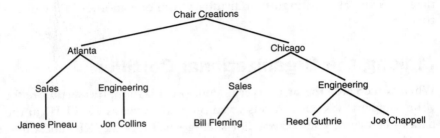

FIGURE 6.1
Organization, organizational units, and common names.

The Cert Log

To re-certify or change IDs of any type, you must have a certification log file (CERT.LOG). You can simply create the certification log file by clicking on File, Database, New. You then must name the file CERT.LOG. Be sure to use the Certification Log Template. The file must be placed in the root of the server's data directory. If you are using your own machine, select the server you will be using to register IDs. Then, click OK.

Creating OUs

To create a new OU, you can click the Registration button on the Configuration tab in the Administration panel. You must have at least Editor access and be a member of the Net Modifier role. An example of the Configuration panel is shown in Figure 6.2. For more information on roles in the Directory, please see Chapter 11, "Setting Up/Configuring Domino Infrastructure Security."

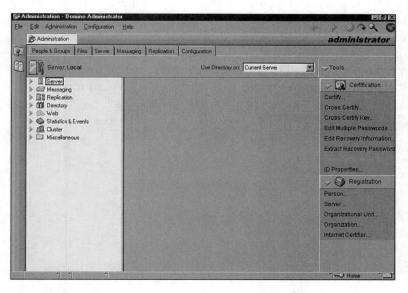

FIGURE 6.2
Administration panel—Configuration tab.

Organizational Unit is the third option at the lower right of the panel. Just like creating a new user or a server, you must first determine which certifier ID file you will use. Then, you will need to supply the correct password for that certificate. After you supply these items, you will then be presented with a dialog box requesting the name of the registration server and you also have the opportunity to change certifiers. (See Figure 6.3 for an example.)

As previously implied, you can use the original organizational certifier or an organizational unit certifier to create an OU. The first item to select is the registration server. This server can be any server within the domain. If you are using your own machine, Local will simply add the certificate record to your own personal address book, so you must select a server in your domain instead. The Set ID button lets you name the file before it is created. This is very helpful later when you want to use the certifier to create servers and people. Then specify the name of the new OU. You should also specify a password for your new certifier. Notice that you can determine how strong the password will be. This is based on its length and how unique the word or phrase is. If the word is found in the spell checker dictionary included with Lotus Notes, it is considered to be a weak password. You must also determine whether the OU will be a North American security type or an International security type. For explanation of these security types, please refer to the earlier section "International Versus North American IDs" in this chapter.

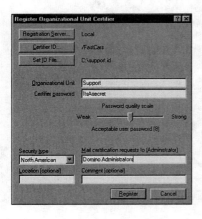

FIGURE 6.3
Register Organizational Unit Certifier dialog box.

After you click Register, an ID is created with the name you specified and a record is created in the directory in the Miscellaneous, Certificates view. You are not prompted for how long you want the new OU to exist. This is because all cerificates (organizational or organizational units) are usable for 100 years. Be sure to mark your calendar to re-register these when they expire!

CREATING GROUPS

Groups can be used to distribute mail or grant access to files. Groups are created by opening the directory and selecting Create Group. Five different types of groups are defined in the following list:

- **Multi-Purpose.** Used to send email and grant access to databases, servers, and so on.

- **Access Control List Only.** You cannot use this group to distribute email. It is used only to grant access to databases and servers.

- **Mail Only.** This group is strictly for sending messages to many people at once.

- **Servers Only.** Members of this group are servers, not people. The Servers Only group can be useful for establishing mail routing and replication with many servers at once.

- **Deny Access Only.** This group type is used to populate a list of terminated employees. This group name must be added to the Deny Access field of the server.

The default for a new group is Multi-Purpose. Changing the group from Multi-Purpose can make your server run more efficiently because the server has separate indexes for mail, servers, and access. Deny Access groups cannot be seen in the general Group view. To see these groups, you must select the Servers, Deny Access Groups view.

Groups often are created because a new application is deployed and you want to use groups rather than individual names in the Access Control List (ACL). This is especially convenient when new people are hired. You can simply add them to the group rather than going to each database. For example, suppose you are deploying a new action items database. You may need individuals who will read, create, or edit the documents within the file. You might create a group called MarketingActionsReaders and place all members in the Marketing department within this group. Individuals who also create new documents could be placed in the MarketingActionsAuthors group. Those who need higher access might also be placed in the MarketingActionsEditors group. If a person is in all three groups, the highest access overrides the other two. You could even make one more group called MarketingActionsAdministration so that the department managers can alter the groups. This group name would need to be added to the Administration field of the group records. If there are individual names in an Access Control List, the groups are ignored. See Table 6.1 for an explanation of different scenarios in the ACL.

TABLE 6.1

DIFFERENT SCENARIOS FOR GROUPS IN THE ACL

Individual's Name	Editor Group	Author Group	"Winner"
X	X	X	Individual
	X	X	Editor
		X	Author
			Default

CREATING/REGISTERING SERVERS

The three categories of servers in an organization are mail server, application server, and hub server. By determining what kinds of databases will reside on a server, you can better configure the system for the tasks needed for the type of data on that server. A mail server will provide mail files to the users. An application server will house any database applications (such as discussions, libraries, and sales reporting) that have been created. The hub server is used as a central point to distribute all mail and/or replications.

The first server in an organization creates an organization (CERT.ID) and directory (NAMES.NSF). Any additional server is created from the Administration panel (Configuration tab) using Registration, Server. To create new servers, you must have at least Editor access and be a member of the Server Creator role in the directory's Access Control List. First you will be prompted for the password of the last certifier you used. If this certificate is the one you will be using to register the new server, simply enter in the password. Otherwise, press Esc on your keyboard and select a different certifier. This may or may not be the very first certificate that you created. You must supply the password for the certificate you have chosen. The next dialog box you see will allow you to select the registration server, certifier, security type, and expiration date (see Figure 6.4).

If you are using your personal machine, it is important that you change from Local to some server in the domain. Assuming you are replicating all your servers, it does not really matter which server you use. Most administrators will use a mail hub if one is available. Notice that the server will not expire for 100 years. You should change this date if you know that the server is a transitional server (such as a test server). For an explanation of North American and International IDs, please refer to the earlier section "International Versus North American IDs" in this chapter.

As shown in Figure 6.5, the second dialog box you see will prompt you to name the server and specify a password.

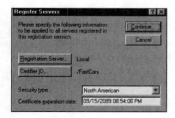

FIGURE 6.4
First dialog box for server creation.

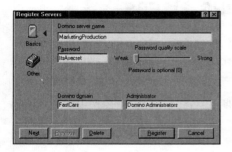

FIGURE 6.5
Second dialog box for server registration.

It is a good idea to leave the password at its weakest setting so that no password is needed to restart your server. However, you must type in a password initially so that the ID is securely stored in the directory. You can then later remove the password after the ID is removed from the server record during installation. Installation of a server is addressed in Chapter 7, "Installation."

You may optionally select the Other tab in this second dialog box. As shown in Figure 6.6, you can specify a title, enter a network name, and select where you want to store the new ID.

Network name does have some significance as it relates to mail routing. This name will populate in the Network section of the server record. If servers belong to the same network name, they will appear for the user in the Open Database dialog box. For more information on Named Networks, please see Chapter 10, "Setting Up/Configuring Distribution and Monitoring."

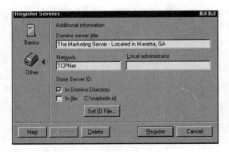

FIGURE 6.6
The Other tab in the server registration dialog box.

CREATING/REGISTERING USERS

Creating people is a daily process of most Lotus Notes/Domino administrators. Fully understanding how to register users can save you a lot of headaches in the long run.

First, let's examine what is in a Lotus Notes ID. The following are stored in an ID file:

◆ **The user's common name.** The user may also have one alternate name. A certifier ID may contain multiple alternate names.

◆ **The license for the individual.**

◆ **The public and private keys for an individual.** These keys are used for authentication and mail encryption.

◆ **Certificates from the certifier ID.**

◆ **Optional encryption keys.** This would be used if a designer uses encryption for specific fields on a database.

◆ **Optional Internet certificates.** This certificate is used to secure Internet connections with SSL.

◆ **Recovery information.** This can be used to obtain a password if it is forgotten by the user.

To create new users, simply click the People, Register option in the People & Groups tab (see Figure 6.7). You must have at least Editor rights to the directory and be a member of the User Creator role.

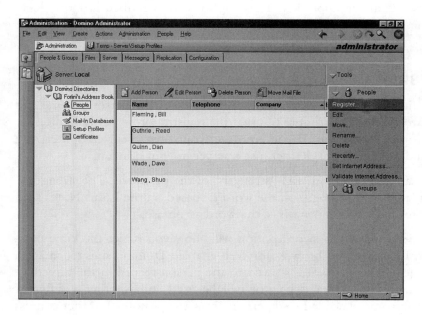

FIGURE 6.7
Registering users.

The first item you are presented with is the password for the last certificate you used. If you will be using the same certificate, you can simply enter in the password. If you want to use a different certifier, you can select Cancel and select a different certifier. Unless your company is very small, you will likely use an OU to register new users. For an explanation of OU certifiers, please refer to the "Creating/Registering Certificates" section earlier in this chapter.

The dialog box you are presented with is broken up into five tabs:

- The Basics tab
- The Mail tab
- The ID Info tab
- The Groups tab
- The Other tab

Some of these options will not appear unless you click the Advanced check box at the upper left. These options are described in more detail in the sections that follow.

Basics

The first tab you see is primarily used to enter the person's name and password. Notice in Figure 6.8 that the registration server is a button at the top of the screen. If you are using your own client computer, you should not use Local. Rather, use a server in your domain.

You can also determine the "strength" of the password. The strength is calculated by how common the word is (based on the Lotus Notes spell checker file) and the length of the word or phrase.

The Set Internet Password option will allow you to set the same password for use with a browser for Web-enabled Domino sites (such as an intranet). This password is saved to the person record in the directory. You can choose what separator will be used and whether a different domain name is needed to determine how the person's Internet address will be configured.

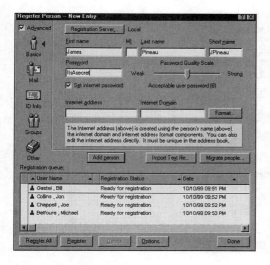

FIGURE 6.8
The Basics tab of people registration.

Mail

The Mail tab can be used to specify the person's server and options for the mail file (see Figure 6.9). The first button, Mail Server, allows you to select which server the user will use to receive mail. This server should be as geographically close to the user as possible. Selecting Local while using your personal client will cause the file to be created on your machine

The Mail File Template option allows you to select the template that will correspond to the client you are installing. For example, if you are currently using R5, but you know the new installation of the user will be R4.6, you should use the R4.6 template. Otherwise, the user will get many script errors.

You have the option to select Lotus Notes, Other Internet, POP, or IMAP for the user's mail. Lotus Notes is the default and requires the Lotus Notes client to read and send messages. The other three options allow you to send and receive mail with an Internet browser. You will obviously lose some functionality (such as Calendaring and Scheduling and To Do's) by using a browser.

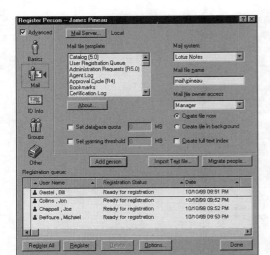

FIGURE 6.9
The Mail tab of people registration.

The Mail File Name box will automatically use the first letter of the first name and seven characters of the last name. If you know that there is another user with the same mail file name on the same server, you can change the name before you register the user. If you forget, or you are not certain, you will be prompted when you register the user.

The default access right to the mail file is manager. This means that the user can change the rights to the mail file and even delete the file. You can change this so that the user has a lower access level (such as designer). You should be aware that designer access would not allow the user to grant access to his or her mail or calendar. For more information about access levels, please see Chapter 11, "Setting Up/Configuring Domino Infrastructure Security."

You can choose to create the database immediately or create the file in the background. This second option will use AdminP to create the file later. There is also an option to immediately create a full text search index for searching within the mail file.

The Set Database Quota option gives you the ability to limit how large the mail file will get. It is a good idea for a company to have a policy on mail file sizes and general usage for mail. The unit of measurement is megabytes. If you are using quotas, it is a good idea to set a warning threshold that will be lower than the quota. This allows you (as the administrator) and the user to know that the quota could soon be reached. Warning notices are written to the LOG.NSF file.

ID Info

The ID Info tab allows you to view and make changes to the certifier type. You can use a different certifier or change the current ID to International or North American. You can also determine how long the ID will exist before expiring, and you can set the location of the ID after it is created.

The default expiration date is two years from the time you register the user. Saving the ID to the address book is convenient when you install the client, but it also poses a security risk because someone could detach the ID and use it on her own machine (if she knows the password). For more information on storing IDs, please see Chapter 7, "Installation."

Groups

You can determine what groups a user will belong to with the Groups tab. Groups can be used to distribute mail and grant access to databases. As seen in Figure 6.10, adding a user to a group is quite simple.

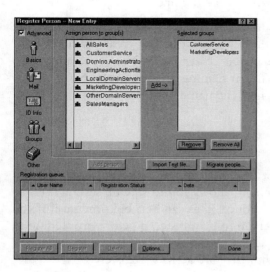

FIGURE 6.10
The Groups tab of people registration.

Other

The Other tab gives you the option to use a setup profile, make comments, or specify an alternate language. These features can make installation easier and make it easier for the user community to identify a person.

You can select the setup profile that you will be using. Setup profiles can save you a tremendous amount of time with installation of clients. You can specify which files to replicate, what connection records to create, what proxy to use, and much more. Please see Chapter 7 for more information about setup profiles and installation.

The unique organization unit can be used to further identify a user. If you had two people with the same name in the same location or department, you could add this to the name so that it would be distinguishable. This does not actually create an OU, but will appear in the person's fully distinguished name. For more information on OUs, please see the "Creating/Registering Certificates" section of this chapter.

Local Administrator allows you to select a name so that mail can be sent when an ID is going to expire. This makes it possible for you to delegate some users to a regional administrator.

The comment line is for information only. You may want to add a comment for the port number of the PC or the like.

If you are a Windows NT administrator and have the rights (and the Domino NT sync service is running), you can also create Windows NT accounts at the same time that you create Lotus Notes accounts. You may very likely be using a different naming scheme in the NT environment so you may optionally enter the name in at this screen.

Three Buttons

Three buttons toward the bottom of the dialog box aid you in registration. The first button, Add Person, allows you to save up several users so that you can register them all at once. This can be a big time saver if you don't want to wait for each person to be registered before proceeding to the next one. Users who are added to the registration queue are placed in the USERREG.NSF file until they are actually registered.

The second button, Import Text File, can be used to create many users at once. You can work within a spreadsheet to enter many names into a structured file. Then you can save the file and register all the users at the same time. This would be particularly useful if you have an installation team working on certain groups of users per day. Use great care with this feature because you could potentially cause a huge mess if even one field of a column is entered incorrectly.

The final button, Migrate People, can be used to migrate from other systems, such as Microsoft Exchange, cc: Mail, and others.

> **NOTE** The migration tools are not part of a standard install. You must request them during a custom install.

More Efficient Registration

You can register users faster by using the Preferences dialog box (see Figure 6.11). This allows you to preset many of the registration prompts.

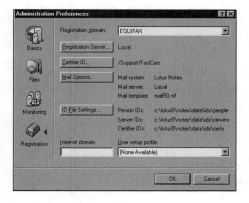

FIGURE 6.11
Set up preferences for user registration.

You can predetermine the domain in which you will often be registering users. This is set at the top of the dialog box. If you find that you are often setting the registration server to MailHub1/ChairCreations, you can set the server so it will automatically populate when you register new users. You can set the most often used certifier with the Certifier ID button. If you would like to preset the mail system, server, and template, you can do this with the Mail Options button. You can optionally select where to save person, server, and certifier IDs on your hard drive or network drive. You can also type in a commonly used Internet domain name if you want. Finally, you can set a commonly used profile record in the User Setup Profile field. Selecting any or all of these options can save you a lot of time when you register users.

Duplicate Names in the Directory

The error message User Name Not Unique means that more than one entry for a person exists in the directory. This can occur because two administrators used two different directories to register a person. When the directories replicate, both entries end up in the directory and mail can no longer be delivered to the user. You can correct this simply by removing the extra person document.

Re-Certifying an ID

Because IDs expire, they must be re-certified from time to time. You must have at least Editor access and be a member of the User Modifier role in the directory to perform this function. You also must be able to edit the Certifcation Log file. A person can be re-certified three different ways:

- **Use the Person View of the directory.** You can use the Re-certify Person Action from the Actions menu.

- **Use Mail to Send the ID.** The user must go to Certificates tab of the User ID dialog box. He must click the Request Certificate button and then type in the administrator's name. After the administrator certifies the ID, it is then sent back to the user, who then merges the new copy using the Action menu.

♦ **You Can Take the Certifier to the User's Machine.** You must first switch to your ID so that you can make the needed update to the directory.

When you re-certify the user, the ID is good for another two years.

ID Recovery

The password recovery feature (similar to the Escrow Agent in R4) can be used to restore an ID in the event that the password is forgotten or the ID is somehow damaged or deleted. To use this feature, you must have set up a mail-in so that you can capture the IDs as they are created. For more information about recovering an ID, please see Chapter 2, "Monitoring, Maintaining, and Troubleshooting Domino Directories, Users, and Groups."

Alternate Name Certifier

You can add an alternate name certifier to an ID so that a person can use a different name in a different country. There can be only one additional name certifier added to an individual. A certifier can contain as many alternate names as there are languages available. When an alternate name is added to the user's ID, the person document will also be updated automatically. As entries are added to ACLs, either can be used. Additionally, users can type either name when addressing mail.

Renaming Users

You can rename a person using the directory. When you rename the user, the server task (AdminP) makes the changes to all entries in the directory, Access Control Lists, and documents that contain the name. This process will not change the Calendar Profile or the Calendar Entries for the person.

Moving a Mail File

You can simply move a person from one server to another quite easily within the directory. From the People view of the directory, you can click the button Move Mail File at the top of the view. The prompt box will request the name of the new server. AdminP will then make a replica copy of the file onto the new destination server.

WHAT IS IMPORTANT TO KNOW

The list below outlines what you need to know to be sure you are prepared for the exam. Make sure you know the following information:

- The difference between an organization (O) and an organizational unit (OU).
- The difference between a hierarchical and a flat ID.
- How to create the Certification Log file.
- Where the organization certifier comes from.
- How to create organizational units (OUs).
- How to create groups.
- How a user is granted access rights with groups.
- The four different types of groups.
- The necessary rights to create certifiers, servers, and people documents.
- How to register servers.
- The structure of an ID file.
- How to register new users.
- The difference between a registration server and a home server.
- The process of re-certifying an ID.
- The default expiration time of certifier, server, or user ID.
- How to speed up the user registration process.
- How to use the Alternate Name feature.
- How to move mail files from one server to another.

▶ Installing Clients of Different License Types

▶ Installing Servers of Different License Types

CHAPTER *7*

Installation

Installing servers and workstations is a common task for support personnel and administrators. The server installation is, of course, much more complex than that of the typical workstation. For that reason, server installation is covered first.

INSTALLING SERVERS

This section is devoted to an explanation of installing and configuring servers. The first part of this section explores the installation of the software. The second part of the section covers the setup of a first server. The third part embarks on configuring additional servers.

Installing Software

Before you install software on a machine, you should be certain that you meet the minimum requirements for the software and traffic that the server will be hosting. You can install Lotus Notes software from a CD-ROM or a network drive. If you use the CD, the install wizard will appear (shown in Figure 7.1) and you can select the button for the server you are installing.

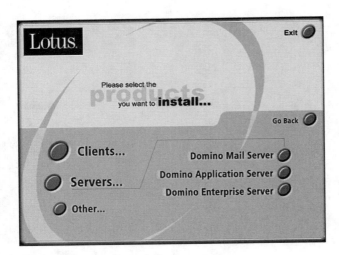

FIGURE 7.1
The install wizard.

Notice that within the install wizard, there are options for the type of server you will be installing:

- Domino Mail Server

- Domino Application Server

- Domino Enterprise Server

Selecting the type of server you are installing will offer more services (such as transaction logging). Each of these server types is explained in more detail in Chapter 8, "Setting Up Infrastructure, Servers, and Workstations."

If you are installing from a network drive, you will want to find the servers directory and then find the appropriate directory for the operating system you are installing (W32Alpha or W32Intel for Windows NT). After you run the setup.exe file, you will see the same install wizard that you would see if you were using the CD.

You will see a welcome screen and then the license agreement for the software. After selecting Yes, you will be prompted for your name and the company name. Because you are installing a server, you may want to simply put the company name in both places. There is a check box at the bottom of this screen that will allow you to install the server as a partitioned server. Partitioned servers allow you to have multiple server installations on one machine.

The next screen you will see allows you to change the default directories where the files will be installed. The defaults are Lotus\Domino for the executable files and Lotus\Domino\Data for the working directory. The data directory will actually appear as the "root" of the server to the end user. In past releases, the defaults were Notes and Notes\Data, respectively.

You are then given the option to choose what type of server you will be installing. These options are the same as the install wizard explained previously. Chapter 8 defines the server types in more detail.

Select the custom button to pick and choose the options you want to install. These options are defined as follows:

- **Common Data.** This option is for files that are shared by both the Notes client and the Domino server.

- **Data Files.** These files are essential for the client to function.

- **DECS.** DECS is used to pull data from external sources so that the information can be used in a Lotus Notes database.

- **Domino Data Files.** These files reside in the root of the Domino server and are a necessary component of a server.

- **Domino Server Planner.** This helps you determine the response time you should expect with the configuration you are using. You will be better able to gauge when it is time for more hardware.

- **Domino Server Program Files.** These files are necessary for your server to function.

- **Domino Web Services.** You may want to omit these files if the server will not be using HTTP and hosting Internet/intranet sites.

- **Help.** If this is a hub or server that does not have mail users, you may decide to omit this file.

- **Notes Program Files.** These files are needed to use the client on the same machine.

After you have installed the selected options, you will then proceed to the registration screen. If you register with Lotus, you can be informed of updates and changes to products. You can then exit the installation program.

You should then launch the server for the first time. When you launch the software, it will automatically recognize (because the NOTES.INI is mostly empty) that you have never used the server before and prompt you to set up the server. An example of this screen is shown in Figure 7.2.

You can then select whether this is your first server or an additional server to the domain. These options are quite significant and are explained in two sections that follow, "Setting Up a First Server," and "Setting Up Additional Servers."

If you select the advanced setup, a third setup screen will appear as shown in Figure 7.3.

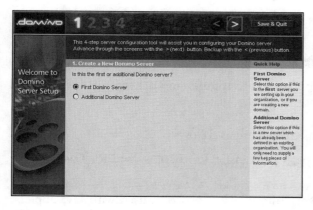

FIGURE 7.2
An example of the first server setup screen.

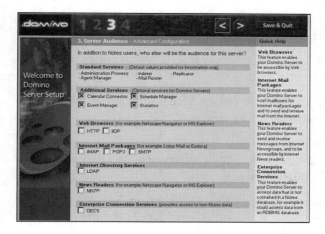

FIGURE 7.3
Third setup screen.

At this screen, you can see that several server tasks will run by design and several others can be added. The tasks that will be automatically added are as follows:

- **Administration Process.** This is used to change names, add files, and trigger many other processes that are automated for the administrator.

- **Indexer.** This task will update views and full-text search indexes.

- **Replicator.** This task carries out all replication events.

- **Agent Manager.** The agent manager task will periodically check to see if there are agents to run and then run these agents as needed.

- **Mail Router.** This is used to transfer and deliver mail for the users of the system.

The tasks that you can change are as follows:

- **HTTP.** The Hypertext Transfer Protocol is used for hosting Web sites.

- **IIOP.** The Internet Inter-ORB Protocol is used with Java applets.

- **IMAP.** The Internet Mail Access Protocol can be used to retrieve mail.

- **POP3.** POP3 is used to deliver mail using the Post Office Protocol 3 with a Web browser.

- **SMTP.** Internet mail is transferred and delivered using the Simple Mail Transfer Protocol task.

- **LDAP.** The Lightweight Directory Access Protocol is used to collect address information from various Web sites and other companies.

- **NNTP.** The Network News Transfer Protocol can be used to collect messages from news groups.

- **DECS. The Domino Enterprise Connection Service** is used to extract or change data from other non-Notes databases such as Oracle or Sybase.

Page four of the setup is shown in Figure 7.4.

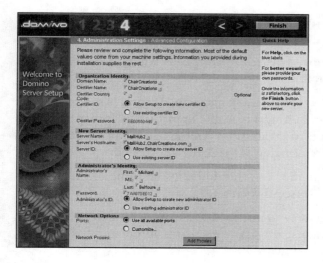

FIGURE 7.4
Page four of the setup menu.

On page four of the setup menu, you will establish the names of the following items. Think ahead as you create these names. They can potentially be used and seen by everyone within and outside your company:

- **Domain name.** The domain name is used to address mail—as an example: DavidVotta@ChairCreations.

- **Certifier name.** This appears at the end of all IDs that are created in your organization—for instance: Shuo Wang/ChairCreations. For information about IDs, please see Chapter 6, "Creating/Registering System Resources."

- **Country code.** Each country has a two-letter abbreviation that can be used to identify the location of servers and clients. You may prefer to use an OU. See Chapter 6 for more details.

- **Certifier ID.** You may already have a certifier ID created and you are setting up a server in a different domain. If not, you should leave this option set to create the ID during the current setup.

- **Certifier password.** You may want to change this to something you can easily remember. If you do not, be sure to write down the password.

- **Server name.** Every server in your domain must have a unique name, and it should not contain spaces or unusual characters.

- **Server host name.** This is how the server will be identified on the Internet if applicable.

- **Server ID.** If you have already made an ID for this server, you can use it rather than making a new one immediately. It may have been necessary for you to create OUs with a "throw away" server, and you therefore are using an ID you already created.

- **Administrator name.** You should fill in the name of the administrator that will oversee this server.

- **Password.** You may want to use a password that is easier to remember. If you use the password that is automatically generated, be sure to write it down.

- **Administrator ID.** You may have already created an administrator's ID. If you have, select the Use Existing Administrator's ID option.

- **Ports.** If you are connecting via a LAN, you likely do not want to change the port settings because Notes will automatically configure them.

- **Network proxies.** If you must use a proxy, enter the address by clicking the Add Proxies button.

- **Serial port.** If you will be connecting your server with a modem, you can set up the appropriate com port.

- **Modem.** If available, you should select the modem you are using from the list. If not, you can use Auto Configure.

You are presented with the final screen and have one final button to further configure the server. The Set Access Control List feature will save you a great deal of time by adding a name or group to all of the files that Lotus puts on your server by default. After you are finished setting the Access Control List, you can select Exit Configuration. You will then be ready to launch your server for the first time.

Setting Up a First Server

The first server in an organization is rather unique. It automatically creates two elements that may never be created again:

- The directory
- The organizational certifier

Because the first server potentially dictates how your entire Lotus Notes/Domino infrastructure will ultimately look, it is a good idea to handle the process with care and forethought. You may want to consider policies about naming (for certifiers, servers, people, and so on), mail, new applications, connecting to other companies, and more. The earlier you set up such policies, the easier it is to maintain the environment in the future. If people have established habits of large mail files, poor naming conventions, and illogical connection settings, they are difficult to change and correct.

The Domino Directory

The directory is the heart of a Domino infrastructure. The directory is used to determine how to route mail, who can access a server, when to replicate, certificates for authentication, distribution lists, and much more. The directory is called Names.nsf and is found in the data directory (c:\lotus\domino\data). The following document types can be found in the Domino directory:

- **Group.** Distribution of people or servers for access control lists and mail distribution.
- **Person.** An individual's name, home server, mail file, and other required and optional information.
- **Certificate.** Holds data for each certifier in the organization.
- **Configuration.** Can be used to change parameters of servers.
- **Connection.** Used to determine when to connect to servers for replication and mail routing.
- **Domain.** Used to set up an SMTP Internet mail server, fax gateways, foreign domains, and more.

- **External Domain Network Information.** Used to connect users from their home server to a server outside of their domain.

- **File Identification.** Used with MIME messages to associate extensions with programs.

- **Holiday.** Allows you to enter the holidays that will be recognized in your company for each country.

- **Mail-In Database.** Some applications will require mail delivery. Very similar to a person record except it is for a database.

- **Program.** Used to trigger executable files to launch at specified times. This can be great for backup routines or virus protection programs.

- **Server.** Configuration settings for a server such as ports, Agent Manager, HTTP, access rights, and much more.

- **Setup Profiles.** Used to aid in the registration and setup of users.

The Organizational Certifier

The organizational certifier is the final element that appears at the end of all IDs in a hierarchical ID structure. After this ID is created, it is used to create all IDs in the future. For more information about creating and registering IDs, please see Chapter 5, "Monitoring, Maintaining, and Troubleshooting Domino Systems."

Setting Up Additional Servers

Setting up additional servers is quite different from creating a first server. To set up an additional server, you must first have an ID registered with a certifier that can authenticate with another server in your domain. You will need the server ID either stored in the directory or placed on a floppy disk. You also must connect in some manner to another Domino server in the domain. At the first setup screen, you will want to select Additional Domino Server.

Functions at Server Startup

When you launch the server after you have completed setup, you will see many functions run for the first time. A sample is shown in Figure 7.5.

Each of these functions are defined here:

- ◆ **Creating Administration Request Database.** The Administration Request database is used to change names, add databases, change ACLs, and so on.

- ◆ **Database Replicator Started.** The replicator task makes replication of databases possible.

- ◆ **Creating New Mail Box File.** The mailbox (mail.box) is used to store mail while mail router is determining the destination.

- ◆ **Index Process Started.** The Index process will update views and full text search indexes.

- ◆ **Agent Manager Started.** Agents will run tasks periodically on a server.

- ◆ **Calendar Connector Started.** The Calendar Connector is used when a user is checking for free time on calendars that are on connecting servers.

FIGURE 7.5
A sample of the server startup screen.

- **Java Virtual Machine Initialized.** A Java Virtual Machine is an adding program that helps read compiled Java bytecode as data and then executes the resulting program that is gleaned from the bytecode.

- **Creating Statistics and Event Database.** You can collect information about disk space and usage with the Events task. After you have Statistics and Events fully configured, you can be notified before serious problems with your servers occur.

- **Schedule Manager Started.** The Schedule Manager gathers information about calendars in the BusyTime.nsf database.

- **Stats Agent Started.** This allows for the Show Statistics command. The Show Statistics command will give you information about the server since its last restart.

- **Maps Extractor Started.** With this task loaded, you can graphically see router and replication schemes within the Administration Client.

- **Database Server Started.** This means that the server can now accept requests from clients for File, Database, Open.

Server Tasks

Table 7.1 lists common server tasks and, if applicable, the Notes.ini equivalent.

TABLE 7.1

SERVER TASKS AND NOTES.INI EQUIVALENTS

Command Line Examples	Description	Notes.ini Equivalent
Show Users	Lists all users currently attached to the server.	None
Show Tasks	Lists all tasks currently running on the server.	None

Command Line Examples	*Description*	*Notes.ini Equivalent*
L Compact Mail\ Smith	Reduces the amount of space the file is using and makes the file more efficient. There are also several switches.	None
L Design	Conforms a database to all design elements that are in the template associated with the file.	ServerTaskAT1= Design
L Updall Names	Reindexes views and Full Text Search Indexes.	ServerTasksAt2= Updall
Rep MailHub1/ATL/ ChairCreations	Replicates all databases in common with the MailHub1 server.	ServerTasks= ...replica,...
Ro MailHub1/ATL/ ChairCreations	Routes all pending mail to the MailHub1 server.	ServerTasks= ...router,...
L Amgr	Used to process scheduled agents in databases.	ServerTasks= ...Amgr,...
T AdminP Process All	Used to make name changes, create replicas, change ACLs, and much more.	ServerTasks= ...AdminP,...

The NOTES.INI File Defined

The NOTES.INI file is a crucial file that contains many settings for a server. The file can be changed with a text editor but any changes will require the server to be restarted. There are many elements of the NOTES.INI file; understanding them can help you in many ways with administering the server. Following is a sample of a NOTES.INI file, and an explanation of many of the lines follows the sample.

```
[Notes]
Directory=C:\Lotus\Domino\Data
KitType=2
SetupDB=Setup.nsf
UserName=ChairCreations
CompanyName=ChairCreations
NotesProgram=C:\Lotus\Domino
```

```
InstallType=3
WinNTIconPath=C:\Lotus\Domino\Data\W32
Timezone=5
DST=1
$$HasLANPort=1
WWWDSP_SYNC_BROWSERCACHE=0
WWWDSP_PREFETCH_OBJECT=0
EnablePlugins=1
Preferences=2147486833
AltNameLanguage=en
ContentLanguage=en-US
WeekStart=1
ViewWeekStart=2
NavWeekStart=2
XLATE_CSID=52
SPELL_LANG=1033
Region=en-US
Passthru_LogLevel=0
Console_LogLevel=2
VIEWIMP1=Lotus 1-2-Worksheet,0,_IWKSV,,
➥.WKS,.WK1,.WR1,.WRK,.WK3,.WK4,,4,
VIEWIMP3=Structured Text,0,_ISTR,,.LTR,.CGN,.STR,,1,
VIEWIMP4=Tabular Text,0,_ITAB,,.PRN,.RPT,.TXT,.TAB,,1,
VIEWEXP1=Lotus 1-2-3 Worksheet,0,_XWKS,,.WKS,.WK1,.WR1,.WRK,,4,
VIEWEXP3=Structured Text,0,_XSTR,,.LTR,.CGN,.STR,,1,
VIEWEXP4=Tabular Text,1,_XTAB,,.LTR,.RPT,.CGN,.TAB,,1,
EDITIMP1=ASCII Text,0,_ITEXT,,.TXT,.PRN,.C,.H,.RIP,,1,
EDITIMP2=MicrosoftWord RTF,0,_IRTF,,.DOC,.RTF,,2,
EDITIMP3=Lotus 1-2-3 Worksheet,0,_IWKSE,,
➥.WKS,.WK1,.WR1,.WRK,.WK3,.WK4,,4,
EDITIMP4=Lotus PIC,0,_IPIC,,.PIC,,8,
EDITIMP5=CGM Image,0,_IFL,,.GMF,.CGM,,8,
EDITIMP6=TIFF 5.0 Image,0,_ITIFF,,.TIF,,18,
EDITIMP7=BMP Image,0,_IBMP,,.BMP,,18,
EDITIMP8=Ami Pro,0,_IW4W,W4W33F/V0,.SAM,,2,
EDITIMP9=HTML File,0,_IHTML,,.HTM,.HTML,,1,
EDITIMP17=WordPerfect 5.x,0,_IW4W,W4W07F/V1,.DOC,.WPD,,2,
EDITIMP21=WordPro 96/97,0,_IW4W,W4W12F/V0,.LWP,,2,
EDITIMP22=PCX Image,0,_IPCX,,.PCX,,18,
EDITIMP28=Binary with Text,0,_ISTRNGS,,.*,,1,
EDITIMP29=WordPerfect 6.0/6.1,0,_IW4W,W4W48F/V0,.WPD,.WPT,.DOC,,2,
EDITIMP30=Excel spreadsheet,0,_IW4W,W4W21F/V4C,.XLS,,4,
EDITIMP31=Word for Windows,0,_IW4W,W4W49F/V0,.DOC,,2,
EDITIMP32=GIF Image,0,_IGIF,,.GIF,,18,
EDITIMP33=JPEG Image,0,_IJPEG,,.JPG,,18,
EDITEXP1=ASCII Text,2,_XTEXT,,.TXT,.PRN,.C,.H,.RIP,,1,
EDITEXP2=MicrosoftWord RTF,2,_XRTF,,.DOC,.RTF,,4,
EDITEXP3=CGM Image,2,_XCGM,,.CGM,.GMF,,8,
EDITEXP4=TIFF 5.0 Image,2,_XTIFF,,.TIF,,18,
EDITEXP5=Ami Pro,2,_XW4W,W4W33T/V0,.SAM,,2,
EDITEXP14=WordPerfect 5.1,2,_XW4W,W4W07T/V1,.DOC,,2,
EDITEXP21=WordPerfect 6.0,2,_XW4W,W4W48T/V0,.DOC,,2,
EDITEXP22=WordPerfect 6.1,2,_XW4W,W4W48T/V1,.WPD,.WPT,.DOC,,2,
EDITEXP23=Word for Windows 6.0,2,_XW4W,W4W49T/V0,.DOC,,2,
```

```
DDETimeout=10
NAMEDSTYLE0=030042617369630000000000000000000000000000000000000000000
➥00000000000000000000001010100000A000000000000000100A0050A0000006400A00
➥50A000000000000000000000000000000000000000000000000000000000000000000
➥000000000000000000000000000009404000000000000
NAMEDSTYLE0_FACE=Default Sans Serif
NAMEDSTYLE1=030042756C6C6574000000000000000000000000000000000000000000
➥00000000000000000000001010100000A0000000000000000008070A0000006400080
➥70A000000000000000000000000000000000000000000000000000000000000000000
➥000000000000000000000000000049404000000000000
NAMEDSTYLE1_FACE=Default Sans Serif
NAMEDSTYLE2=0300486561646C696E6500000000000000000000000000000000000000
➥00000000000000000000001010101 0B0C000000000000000100A0050A0000006400A00
➥50A000000000000000000000000000000000000000000000000000000000000000000
➥000000000000000000000000000009404000000000000
NAMEDSTYLE2_FACE=Default Sans Serif
DefaultMailTemplate=mail50.ntf
ServerTasks=Router,Replica,Update,Amgr,AdminP,CalConn,Event,Sched,
➥Stats,maps
ServerTasksAt1=Catalog,Design
ServerTasksAt2=UpdAll,Object Collect mailobj.nsf
ServerTasksAt3=Object Info -Full
ServerTasksAt5=Statlog
TCPIP=TCP, 0, 15, 0
LAN0=NETBIOS, 0, 15, 0
SPX=NWSPX, 0, 15, 0
LAN1=NETBIOS, 1, 15, 0
LAN2=NETBIOS, 2, 15, 0
LAN3=NETBIOS, 3, 15, 0
LAN4=NETBIOS, 4, 15, 0
LAN5=NETBIOS, 5, 15, 0
LAN6=NETBIOS, 6, 15, 0
LAN7=NETBIOS, 7, 15, 0
LAN8=NETBIOS, 8, 15, 0
COM1=XPC,1,15,0,
COM2=XPC,2,15,0,
COM3=XPC,3,15,0,
COM4=XPC,4,15,0,
COM5=XPC,5,15,0,
Ports=TCPIP,LAN0
DisabledPorts=SPX,LAN1,LAN2,LAN3,LAN4,LAN5,LAN6,LAN7,LAN8,COM2,COM3,
➥COM1,COM4,COM5
LOG_REPLICATION=1
LOG_SESSIONS=1
KeyFilename=C:\Lotus\Domino\Data\server.id
CertificateExpChecked=server.id 10/20/99
CertifierIDFile=C:\Lotus\Domino\Data\cert.id
MailServer=CN=MailHub10/O=ChairCreations
ServerKeyFileName=server.id
Domain=ChairCreations
Admin=CN=Randy Davison/O=ChairCreations
TemplateSetup=55
Setup=59
```

```
ServerSetup=50
DESKWINDOWSIZE=-4 -4 1032 776
MAXIMIZED=1
CleanSetup=1
PhoneLog=2
Log=log.nsf, 1, 0, 7, 40000
TRANSLOG_AutoFixup=1
TRANSLOG_UseAll=0
TRANSLOG_Style=0
TRANSLOG_Performance=2
TRANSLOG_Status=0
MTEnabled=0
SCHEDULE_VERSION=3
```

The second line tells Notes where the working data directory can be found. KitType establishes whether the machine is set up as a client or a server. KitType=1 is a workstation and KitType=2 is a server. The setup=setup.nsf line launches the setup database. Each of the graphical screens that you use to set up a server is actually a document within the setup.nsf database. The username and companyname are simply cosmetic to assign a name and company to the software. The NotesProgram line directs the software to find the executable files. The InstallType line is used to identify whether the server is an enterprise, application, or mail server.

Many of the lines from the InstallType to the DefaultMailTemplate are settings for a Lotus Notes client. There are lines for the path of SmartIcons, Time Zone, Daylight Savings Time, Browser cache, Preferred language, Calendar settings, spell checking, and Passthru connections. There are also many lines associating extensions with the Windows programs they use.

The ServerTasks= line tells Domino what tasks to start when the server is started. Each of these is significant:

- **Router.** Router delivers electronic mail to users.

- **Replica.** The Replica tasks awaits for instructions from a console command or a connection record to replicate with other servers.

- **Update.** This task is used to refresh views and full text search indexes.

- **Amgr.** The Agent Manager task runs agents that are scheduled within a database.

- **AdminP.** The Administration Process is used to change names, add databases, change ACLs, and much more. These changes can be rather involved and time consuming without the help of AdminP.

◆ **CalConn.** The Calendar Connector task will connect servers when a user wants to check a calendar on another server.

◆ **Event.** The Event task sends mail when it reaches triggers that you set to monitor (such as low disk space).

◆ **Sched.** When a user checks other calendars, the Schedule task uses the BUSYTIME.NSF file to deliver the availability of others.

◆ **Stats.** The Stats task waits for the Show Stats command to be requested at the server. It will then display statistics of the server.

◆ **Maps.** The Maps task allows you to view router and replication topologies graphically with the Administration panel.

Server tasks can be set to run with program documents in the directory or with NOTES.INI parameters. Notice in the example that there are four lines that automatically launch server tasks at the military time specified:

◆ **ServerTasksAt1=Catalog, Design.** The Catalog task will make any changes to the catalog database. The catalog.nsf file is essentially just a listing of all databases on the server. The Design task will conform all databases to the template specified in the Properties box.

◆ **ServerTasksAt2=UpdAll, Object Collect mailobj.nsf.** Updall will update all views and full text search indexes at 2 a.m. Object Collect mailobj.nsf is used with shared mail to remove links and message bodies from deleted mail.

◆ **ServerTasksAt3=Object Info - Full.** This line verifies the total number of messages and sizes in the shared mail database.

◆ **ServerTasksAt5=StatLog.** This line updates the statistics database at 5 a.m.

Although you see many lines for port configurations, it is much better to make changes to these settings in the File, Tools, User Preferences, Ports dialog box. The KeyFileName tells Domino what ID was last used. This setting is actually for the client, and the ServerKeyFileName is for the server. CertificateExpChecked records the last time the ID was checked for expiration. CertifierIDFile is simply the last certifier that was used. The MailServer setting specifies the home server for the client. The Domain setting is used when sending mail so the client knows what domain the user is in. The Admin line establishes who the local administrator of the server is. The remainder of the lines are primarily for the client to recall where the window settings were last.

The Server Record

There are many fields to a server record that further configure and enhance the many tasks that run on a server. You can view or change a server record in the Domino directory from the Server, Servers view. The sections of the server document are broken up as follows:

- **Basics.** This area lists the name of the server, name of the local administrator, Domino release number, and many other informational settings.

- **Security.** You can set a vast array of different settings for the users on the server. For more information, see Chapter 11, "Setting Up/Configuring Domino Infrastructure Security."

- **Ports.** This area used with the Ports settings dialog box is used to configure network ports. See Chapter 8, "Setting Up Infrastructure, Servers, and Workstations" for a more in-depth look at this section.

- **Server Tasks.** In this section you can change configurations for Administration Processing, Agent Manager, Domain Indexer, Directory Cataloger, Internet Cluster Manager, and Web Retriever.

- **Internet Protocols.** You can change settings for HTTP, Domino Web Engine, IIOP, LDAP, and NNTP in this section.

- **MTAs.** If the server is servicing Internet Mail, cc:Mail, or X.400, you can further configure the tasks in this section.

- **Miscellaneous.** This area is only for information purposes and allows you to add location and contact information.

- **Transaction Logging.** This will allow you to further configure transaction logging. Transaction logging is useful when restarting a server.

- **Administrators.** You can set the owner and administrator fields in this area.

Figure 7.6 shows an example of a server record.

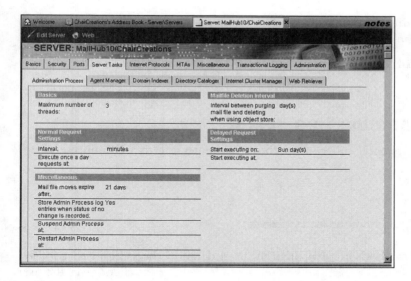

FIGURE 7.6
A sample of a server record viewed at the Server Tasks section.

INSTALLING CLIENTS

A typical company will install a hundred times the number of clients compared to servers. So, you will likely become an expert in no time. It is not advisable to install the client software on the server if it can be avoided. A Lotus Notes client cannot be set up to authenticate with a server unless an ID exists for the new user. Registration of IDs is covered in more detail in Chapter 6, "Creating/Registering System Resources." When an ID exists for the user, you can either obtain the ID from the directory or carry the ID to the machine on a floppy disk (or access it via a networked drive).

Installing the Software

You can install Lotus Notes from CD-ROM or a network drive. You will want to find the appropriate drive and install program for the machine to which you are installing. You can install one of the four options listed below:

- **Lotus Notes.** This option allows use of all databases and mail.

- **Domino Designer.** This selection gives you the needed tools to develop Lotus Notes databases.

- **Administrator.** To perform administrative tasks, you must install the Administration client.

- **All Clients.** This option installs all the preceding clients.

Connecting to a server

There are three different methods of connecting to a Domino server:

- LAN

- Modem

- RAS (Remote Access Server)

These methods are explained in more detail in the sections that follow. The first screen that you will see when launching the client gives the user an explanation of what is needed to connect to a Domino server. The next screen allows you to determine whether you will be connecting to a server or using the client independently. There are some rare cases that may require you to set up the client as a standalone and then create location and connection records after setup is complete. However, if at all possible you should reach a Domino server and connect at the time of setup. After you select I Want to Connect to a Domino Server, you will see the screen shown in Figure 7.7.

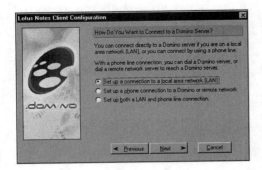

FIGURE 7.7
Selections for connecting to a Domino server.

You can then decide whether you want to connect via a LAN or modem, or you want no connection. Options for establishing a connection to a server are explained in the sections that follow.

LAN Connection

Connecting via a LAN requires the client to connect to the company network with a network card. As long as you can connect to network printers and other servers, there is a good chance that you can connect to a Domino server. You can simply enter in the fully distinguished name of the user and the name of the Domino server. If you are using DNS (Directory Names Service) to resolve TCP/IP addressing, the client will find the server and connect.

Modem Connection

To connect via modem, you will need the phone number of either the home (primary) server for the user or a Passthru server. You will also enter in the name of the user and select a driver for the modem.

RAS (Remote Access Server) Connection

You can use Global Dialer or other Remote Access Server services to connect to your server. Either will allow you to connect to a server and obtain an IP address. This sort of connection will essentially act as if you are attached to your network (only slower). You must have the ID and password for the Global Dialer account.

Further Settings

You will see a series of screens as you continue your setup of the client. You can optionally set up an Internet address, newsgroups, and LDAP, POP3, and ISP connections. Of course, you cannot set up any of these options if you don't have servers running these tasks.

The final steps involved in the setup include copying the ID to the client (if needed), establishing a bookmark for the mail file and the directory, creating a personal address book with location and connection records, and removing the ID from the person document (if applicable).

Creating Additional Connections

It may be necessary to set up more connections to servers after the client installs. This will give the user more flexibility if he will be traveling with a laptop. This process can mean changing settings for ports, location records, and/or connection records.

Changing Port Settings

Ports can be changed and configured within the Ports dialog box. If you want to add a modem, for instance, you would go to the File, Preferences, User Preferences, Ports. To add a port, you can click on New. However, it is best to use the ports that are ready and waiting for use. Simply find the port that corresponds to the COM port you are using and click COMX Options. If at all possible, select the port that matches the name of the modem. If that is not available, you can use the Auto Configure option. You can also change any settings you find necessary for speed, volume, time out, and more. Finally, click on OK and then select the Port Enabled check box. You can then click OK to exit the User Preferences dialog box.

Location Record

After the modem is configured, you then will want to change the location record. There are two connection records available for modems: Home and Travel. If you want, you can add a new one as shown in Figure 7.8.

You can easily switch to a connection record by clicking on the second to the last rectangle at the bottom right of the Lotus Notes client. You can also edit the current record by clicking on the same button and then selecting Edit Current. The following sections are contained in the Location Record:

- **Basics.** This contains information about the type of connection (such as LAN, Notes Direct Dial, or Internet), the name of the location record, proxy information, and Internet mail addressing.

- **Servers.** This area contains the fully qualified names of the servers that are used for mail, Passthru, searching, and LDAP.

- **Ports.** This section contains the available network and modem ports.

- **Mail.** This area contains the name and location of the user's mail file and settings for features to be used when sending and addressing mail.

- **Internet Browser.** This allows you to choose the browser you prefer.

- **Replication.** This section holds settings for enabling replication on a schedule.

- **Phone Settings.** This lets you configure settings for using your phone line and credit card if needed.

- **Advanced.** This area holds settings for the time zone, the user ID that should be used, configuring the Web retriever, Java security, TCPIP optional servers, and MIME conversion.

To finish setting up a modem, you must ensure that the modem is enabled in the Ports section. You may also want to disable ports that will not be used while dialing. You should also consider changing the settings for the directory that you will be using and settings for how mail will be configured to retrieve names.

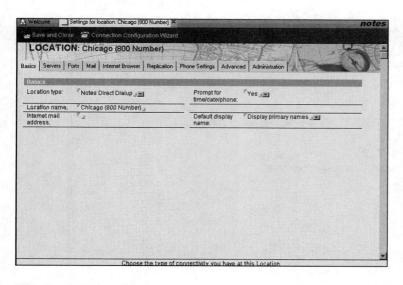

FIGURE 7.8

An example of a connection record.

Connection Record

A connection record can be used to establish a connection to a server, provide an avenue to pass through a server, or set up newsgroups. To create a connection record, you simply open the personal address book for the user. You can then switch to the advanced section by clicking the page with the "mechanical gear" at the bottom of the navigator. The connections view is the second choice. You make new connections by clicking on the Add Connection button. You should then select whether the connection will be via direct dial, Passthru, network dial (RAS), hunt group, or LAN. Last, fill in the protocols or phone numbers needed. An example is shown in Figure 7.9.

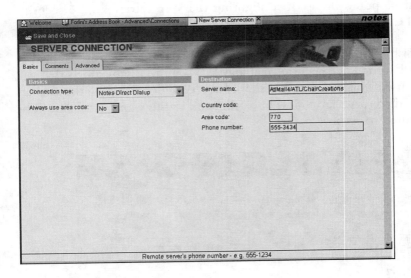

FIGURE 7.9
An example of a connection record.

WHAT IS IMPORTANT TO KNOW

The following bullets will help you check yourself to see whether you are prepared for the exam:

- Generally understand how to install server software and the different options available while installing.

- Have a general understanding of the directory structure after the software is installed.

- Know the difference between a first server and additional servers.

- Be very familiar with the Domino directory.

- Understand how the original certifier is created and what it is used for.

- Have a firm understanding of how to create and install additional servers.

- Understand the tasks that start when the server is launched.

- Have a working knowledge of executing server tasks.

- Have a general understanding of the Notes.ini file, particularly lines that are specific to the server.

- Understand what tasks run at night and early in the morning as specified in the Notes.ini file.

- Be familiar with the server record.

- Understand how to install clients.

- Know how to connect clients to a server using a LAN connection or a modem connection.

- Understand how to add ports and configure them for use on the client.

- Be familiar with location and connection records.

CHAPTER 8

Setting Up Infrastructure, Servers, and Workstations

In this chapter, we will further explore setting up servers and workstations. The concepts presented throughout the chapter are based on the assumption that you have servers and workstations installed and now you want to enhance and configure the systems further.

SETTING UP INFRASTRUCTURE DOMAINS

In Chapter 7, "Installation," you learned that a *domain* is defined as multiple servers using a single directory. You also discovered that the first server in an organization creates a *directory* and all other servers are added to same directory in most cases. There are instances that dictate the need for multiple domains in a company. These include the following:

- **Testing environments.** In this case, you need more than one domain to test applications separately from your production environment.

- **Public Internet sites.** To ensure that you are secure from unwanted mail and attacks, you can place Internet servers in a separate domain.

- **External communication server.** You can securely connect to other companies that have Lotus Notes.

To create an additional domain, you can either install another "first server" or create a new directory. Especially if you intend to create another organization certifier, creating another "first server" is a much easier method than creating a new directory. When you launch a new installation of Domino on a computer and select First Server rather than Additional Server, you are prompted to fill in the name of the server, domain, organization, and administrator. After you finish setting up the server, you will have a new domain, organization, and server. Following are a few caveats that you should be aware of with a new domain and new organization certifier:

◆ Making a new certifier means that your users and servers will not authenticate with each other until you cross-certify. For information about cross certification and authentication, see Chapter 11, "Setting Up/Configuring Domino Infrastructure Security."

◆ A separate Domino directory will not contain any of the server records, person records, groups, and so on. This can cause denial of access to databases that are put on the new server even if the database was originally on a server in the same domain.

If you prefer, you can create another domain by creating a new names.nsf database file. This is done by clicking on File, Database, New. The New Database dialog box appears as shown in Figure 8.1.

You will want to name the file something other than Names.nsf when you create the domain. You can change the name to Names.nsf when you place it on a server. Because the NAMES.NSF file is constantly in use on both a workstation and server, you would have to close either the workstation or server to put a new file of the same name in place.

As you can see in Figure 8.2, the first item that comes up with the new file is a profile record. You can simply fill in the name of the new domain and set the options for a Directory Catalog (if one exists), group sorting, Internet password strength, and alternate language support. After the new file exists, you can simply copy person, server, or group records to the new directory file from your current domain. You then must change the domain field for all server, person, mail-in database, connection, and domain documents in the documents that have been pasted. You then can take the file to the server that will be in the new domain. While the server is not running, you can use the operating system to copy over the current NAMES.NSF file with the new file you have created. You should also delete the MAIL.BOX (make sure there is no mail in the file), CATALOG.NSF, and LOG.NSF files. Finally, change the domain line of the NOTES.INI file and you can restart a server in a new domain.

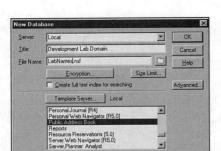

FIGURE 8.1
Creating a new Domino directory.

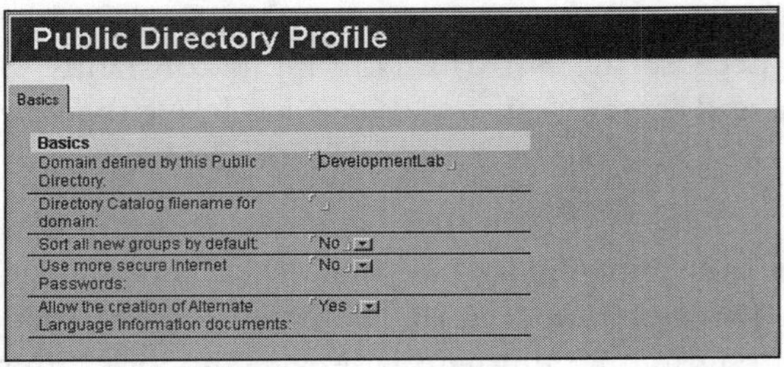

FIGURE 8.2
The Directory Profile record.

SETTING UP INFRASTRUCTURE DOMINO NAMED NETWORKS

Named networks are established when you set up a first server or register additional servers. Even if you don't give the named network a name, you will discover that the registration process will give it the name *Network1*. *Named networks* are defined as two or more servers that share the same protocol and network.

In other words, a server should not be within the same named network if the server uses SPX and all other servers use TCP/IP. The server should be a part of the same named network only if it is constantly connected (rather than connected via modem) to another server in the same domain. There are two reasons for this. Mail will automatically attempt delivery if the servers are within the same named network. This can present a problem if the server does not share a common protocol or must use a modem to connect. The second reason for separate named networks is that when users try to access servers, they use File, Database, Open to see what servers are available. If the user attempts to use a server that is actually only modem connected, he will most likely not reach it. It is actually possible to set up "Cause Calling." The response time, however, will be inferior to what the user should be accustomed to.

SETTING UP INFRASTRUCTURE PROTOCOLS/PORTS

Lotus Notes and Domino offer the flexibility to have many protocols running on servers and workstations. Most companies have found it best to run TCP/IP for all systems in the company. In some cases, the network decision-makers will not even allow another protocol to run in the company. There are some cases, however, that warrant other protocols such as NetBIOS, SPX, Apple Talk, or Vines. Adding a protocol to servers involves changing the network settings for the operating system, changing the Port options in the client software, and editing the settings in the server record.

Ports cannot be changed unless you first down the server. So, you should quit the server task and then launch the client software at the server. To change the port within the client software, you should click on File, Preferences, User Preferences, Ports. There is a good chance that the port name already exists. Look through the list of ports and find the one you are setting up. If it does not exist, you can click New. Simply give the port a name and select the appropriate driver. Be sure to select Port Enabled in either case, and then click OK. The following protocols can be used with Lotus Notes and Domino:

- ◆ **TCP/IP.** By far, this is the most popular protocol, at least partially due to the increasing focus on the Internet.

- ◆ **NetBIOS over IP.** A Domino or Notes system can use NetBios over IP rather than TCP over IP.

- ◆ **IPX/SPX.** This is often used with Novell and small networks.

- **NetBIOS over IPX.** You can optionally use NetBIOS over IPX rather than TCP over IP.

- **NetBEUI/NetBIOS.** This does not work with routed networks and is best in a small environment.

- **Vines.** This protocol is used with Banyan networks, but Banyan also supports TCP/IP.

- **AppleTalk.** This is used with Apple Macintosh networks. Apple will also support TCP/IP, however.

If you have just added a new modem, there is no need to change the server document. Only network ports will need to be enabled on the server document. To change the server document, you should open the Domino directory and locate the corresponding server document in the Servers view. After you are in Edit mode, you can then select the Ports, Notes Network Ports tab (see Figure 8.3). You will then want to enter the name of the port and specify the appropriate network name. Network names are explained in more detail in the Domino Named networks section of this chapter. The net address must be the TCP/IP dot address if you are enabling TCP/IP; it can be the server name for all other protocols. You can then choose to enable the port and save the document.

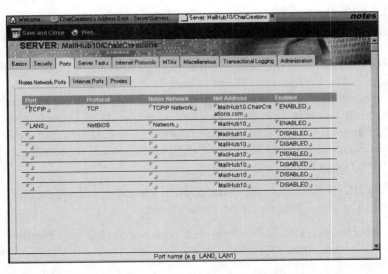

FIGURE 8.3
The network section of the server document.

SETTING UP SERVERS FOR DIFFERENT FUNCTIONS

Servers can be created to host particular functions. The more specialized or well-defined you make your servers, the more efficient you can make the server's function and the happier the end user will be. You can create the following servers to host specialized functions:

- Mail
- Applications
- Passthru
- Hub
- External communication

Each of these servers is explained in detail in the next five sections.

Mail Server

When a server is hosting only mail files, you can remove many tasks that will allow the server to function better. You should have no need for HTTP (although you may want to keep it running if you are using POP3 mail) or replication (although you may want to keep it to replicate the directory). You will need CalConn (the calendar connector), Sched (the free time search feature), and of course Router (for mail routing). The Sched and CalConn tasks work together to alert you to the availability of fellow workers in the same domain.

Applications Server

An applications server will not need any calendar functions or, perhaps, mail routing. Unless you have added a room reservation database to your application server (they really should be placed on your mail server), you will not need CalConn or Sched. You also will not need HTTP if you are not hosting Web sites. You will not need to load Router if you are not using any mail-in database files on the server.

You should have a good understanding of the Agent Manager section of the server record because applications typically have a lot of agents. As shown in Figure 8.4, the Agent Manager section is found in the Server Tasks, Agent Manager tab. Notice that you can change the number of agents and the length of execution, and you can change these parameters between day and night.

Passthru Server

A Passthru server is a central call-in server for remotely connected users (see Figure 8.5). The advantage is that a mobile user can call one server and access many. The primary concern for the server setup involves the access rights section of the server record. It is recommended that you use a common mail server to provide a Passthru connection. This means fewer connection records and better performance on those clients that will be using the same server as their mail server does. It also means that you would not need to purchase another server just for providing connection to other servers.

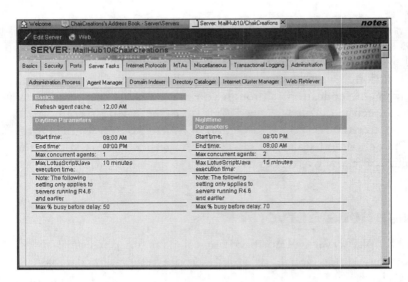

FIGURE 8.4
The Agent Manager tab.

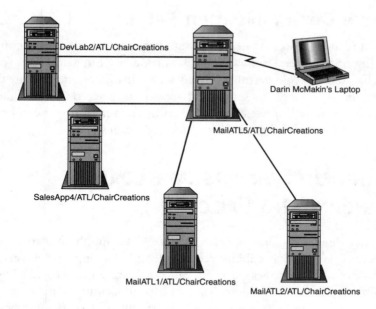

FIGURE 8.5
A Passthru server configuration.

Hub Server

A hub server can be used either to deliver mail or as replication for all other servers in the company. You may have a need for multiple hubs if you have a large organization. In a hub and spoke topology, *spokes* allow users to connect for mail and applications, and the *hub* delivers mail or database changes to other servers. Because communicating with other servers can be taxing, it is best to offload this traffic to the hub; this allows the users to get a better response from the mail and application servers. Hub servers typically do not have any users attached to them. You might consider limiting server access only to other servers and the administrators. For more information about security, see Chapter 11, "Setting Up/Configuring Domino Infrastructure Security."

External Communication Server

For added security, you may decide to set up a server dedicated to communicating with other Domino servers outside of your company. You will not likely need a powerful server to serve this function. The greatest advantage to having this server is that you can place only those files that will replicate with other companies on the server, and you can better control the access rights to the outside companies.

SETTING UP SERVERS FOR LOAD BALANCING AND FAILOVER

Servers that deliver crucial applications should be highly available. To maintain this level of accessibility requires load balancing or failover to another server. Two or more servers can be clustered to provide high availability to the users. *Clustering* involves replicating databases to another server in the same network. On clustered servers, replication is essentially immediate between the two servers. Configuring normal replication is covered in more detail in Chapter 3, "Monitoring, Maintaining, and Troubleshooting Domino Messaging and Replication." If a server becomes unavailable, the records are still intact and the user is just redirected to the same files on the other server.

To create clustered servers, simply open the Administration Client and select the Configuration tab. The view labeled Cluster will allow you to remove and add servers to clusters. When you add the server to a new cluster, you must give the cluster a name. As you add additional servers, you can simply select the name of the cluster to which to add the servers.

SETTING UP SERVERS FOR WEB/INTERNET CONNECTIVITY

There are a few considerations with servers that host Internet or Web sites. Using Domino to host Web sites is becoming more popular every day; you must have a good understanding of the options you have as an administrator of the server. You may need to work with the developer who will create the site to discuss what tasks may be needed and what may need to be done to secure the site. There are two tabs on the server record that are used for the HTTP settings: HTTP and Domino Web Engine. These are found by opening the Server record for the corresponding server and selecting Internet Protocols.

Notice that there are many fields in the HTTP tab of the server record. Figure 8.6 shows all but the last two. These are broken into the following categories:

- **Basics.** In this section you can determine the host names and set the parameters for active threads. Notice the field for browsing databases. Most companies will set this to No so that a person cannot find data without being taken to the file (or page in this case). Also notice that the Home URL field in the Mapping section (if used) will supersede the default home page.

- **Mapping.** You can alter the mapping section if you desire a more structured directory setup. Notice that you can also set the desired starting database with the Home URL field.

- **DSAPI.** You can specify the filter file names for a DSAPI (Domino Server Application Programming Interface).

- **Enable Logging To.** In this section, you can set the desired database to capture log information.

- **Log File Settings.** You can set the amount of logging and frequency in this section.

- **Log File Names.** With these settings you can specify different directories and filenames for logging different data.

- **Exclude From Logging.** You can optionally set what items are not important to log.

- **Time Outs.** These settings can keep the client from waiting for long periods of time to execute input and output data.

- **Web Agents.** You can set the agents to run serially or asynchronously, and you specify the maximum wait in seconds before a timeout error.

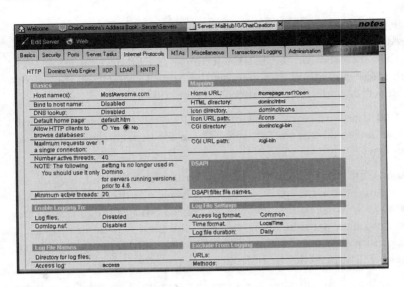

FIGURE 8.6
The HTTP tab of the server record.

You can further configure a Web server with the Domino Web Engine tab of the Server document (see Figure 8.7). An explanation of the fields follows.

- **HTTP Sessions.** You can establish whether you want to require a username and password, how long an idle Web client can remain on the server, and how many users the server will allow.

- **Java Servlets.** *Servlets* are Java programs that run because a Web client has requested them. You can determine where the Servlets will live on the server, and set parameters for how long they will run and how many can run at once.

- **Generating References to this Server.** In this section you can configure settings for IIS, the Host name, the port to use, and the protocol you want to use.

- **Memory Caches.** You can establish when to discard the most recent commands, design, and user information.

- **Post Data.** With these settings you can set the maximum amount of data that a user can place on the site and determine the compression ratio for that data.

- **Conversion/Display.** You can determine whether you want to use GIF or JPEG file formats and set options for how the images will appear. To enable Interlaced Rendering means that you want to draw an image line by line rather than displaying the image after it has been completely received.

- **Disk Cache for Images and Files.** Here you can specify where you want to store the server's most currently used images and files.

- **Character Set Mapping.** This section determines how characters will appear on a Web page. Changes are generally made only if the Web page has used non-Western languages.

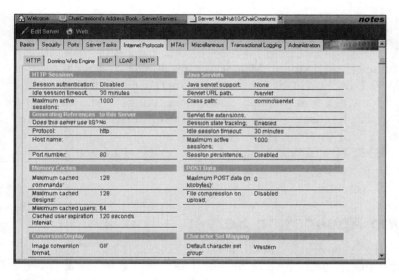

FIGURE 8.7
The Domino Web Engine tab of the server record.

SETTING UP SERVERS OF DIFFERENT TYPES

There are three types of servers that you can set up during the install process. No matter what option you select, all servers will have the Administration Process (AdminP), Agent Manager (Amgr), Indexer (Update), Mail Router (Router), and Replicator (Replica) running.

These install types include the following:

- Domino Mail Server
- Domino Application Server
- Domino Enterprise Server

When you select from the server options during the install process, a line is written to the almost empty NOTES.INI file. For instance, the line InstallType=3 means that you have selected the Mail Server install type. These install types are described in more detail in the three sections that follow.

Domino Mail Server

When you select the Domino Mail Server install type at setup, the server is configured to host Domino and Internet mail, Calendaring and Scheduling (which can include room scheduling) and, potentially, Domino discussion databases. Servers that host primarily mail files need CalConn, Sched, Router, Agent Manager (Amgr), and possibly HTTP and POP3. HTTP and POP3 might be desired if you are going to allow Internet connections to read mail.

Domino Application Server

This selection sets InstallType=5 in the NOTES.INI file. The assumption is that the application server will host all of the same features as the mail server, plus many customized Domino databases. Application servers may not need the Calendar tasks (CalConn and Sched), HTTP, or POP3. You must pay close attention to the Agent Manager section of the server record because an application server typically has many agents running throughout the day and night. If you want to use the applications with a Web browser, you could optionally use HTTP as well.

Domino Enterprise Server

This option sets the NOTES.INI line InstallType to equal 4. Enterprise servers are assumed to run all of the same tasks as the Domino mail server and the Domino application server, plus Domino and Internet clusters and, potentially, partitioned servers. You might consider eliminating any tasks that are not needed on your enterprise server. As you remove tasks, you improve performance.

RUNNING PROGRAMS AUTOMATICALLY

You can run batch and executable files automatically with program documents. You can create program documents by opening the Domino directory and selecting the Programs view. When you click the Add Program button, you can configure the program that will run (see Figure 8.8) and the times you desire to run them. The times are specified in the Schedule tab. These documents can be especially handy with backup programs or tasks that run late at night and normally would be triggered manually.

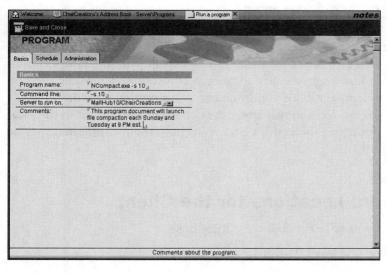

FIGURE 8.8
A program document.

SETTING UP WORKSTATIONS FOR DIFFERENT CLIENTS

There are three major Workstation Install types, and each is significantly different from the other:

- **Lotus Notes.** The client can send and receive mail and open and use databases. The InstallType is set to 0 in the NOTES.INI with this option selected.

- **Domino Developer.** The Domino Developer allows designers to create and change Domino databases. This option sets InstallType=1 in the NOTES.INI file.

- **Domino Administration.** The Domino Administrator is needed to configure and change servers. The NOTES.INI has the InstallType=2 when this feature is added at installation.

SETTING UP WORKSTATIONS FOR DIFFERENT LOCATIONS

A workstation has seven location documents by default. You can add more if needed. The sections that follow explain the standard locations and explain how to create new locations. You should determine early on in your implementation if you intend to replicate the Domino directory to laptops. This decision will affect the configuration you set in the locations, and bringing the laptops back in to have them configured may be a costly endeavor.

Standard Locations for the Client

By default you have the following locations:

- Home (Network Dialup)
- Home (Notes Direct Dialup)
- Internet

- Island (Disconnected)
- Office (Network)
- Travel (Network Dialup)
- Travel (Notes Direct Dialup)

Home (Network Dialup)

This location allows you to use Microsoft's Dialup Networking to access a network. When you request a server (this could be just as simple as trying to open a database on a server), the Dialup Networking software will launch automatically. You should still make a replica copy of the user's mail file and possibly the Domino directory so that the user can work mostly offline.

Home (Notes Direct Dialup)

The Notes Direct Dialup location will dial directly into a Domino server. A connection record is needed so that the phone number is available to the client. Ideally, this server will also provide Passthru connectivity to all other servers the user would need. If you are providing Passthru connectivity, you would also need a Passthru connection record, and you would want to add the Passthru server name to the location record in the Passthru server field.

Internet

The Internet location would allow a user to use Domino servers via the Internet. As long as the user has some method to reach the Internet and establish TCP/IP connectivity, he can reach the Domino servers that are needed. This kind of connection would mean your company has no security concerns about accessing data over the Internet.

Island (Disconnected)

This location is typically used in an airplane or some place where connectivity is not possible. The advantage to using this location is that the client will not attempt to access a server. All settings force the client to search locally for documents and databases.

Office (Network)

The Office location is intended for use with a constant connection to servers. All files are assumed to be readily available through the network. Typically, the only file used locally is the Personal Address Book.

Travel (Network Dialup)

Much like the Home (Network Dialup) location, this location relies on a RAS solution with Microsoft's Dialup Networking. The only significant difference is that you must specify the area code from which you are dialing.

Travel (Notes Direct Dialup)

This location is essentially the same as the Home (Notes Direct Dialup) location, except that you may need to put in additional numbers to ready an "outside line." You may also be using a toll-free number. If that is the case, you should specify that the connection record containing the toll-free number be used only when traveling. You can use the PassThru connection record for both locations.

Adding New Location Records

Many administrators believe that adding more location records will make life easier for the user. You can add one for each location to which they travel, for example. If you are using a service such as Global Dialer, you might consider making a different location record for each city to which the user travels. However, a large number of location records can contribute to user confusion and can be quite difficult to support if there is a problem.

To add location records, simply open the Personal Address Book. Then, click on the icon that looks like a paper and mechanical gear. In the Locations view, click the Add Location button. As you can see in Figure 8.9, you have several tabs that can be used to configure the location record. You will want to select whether the connection is constant (LAN) or via modem (Notes Dialup or Network Dialup), and specify the location of the mail file and directory as well as the phone number, if needed.

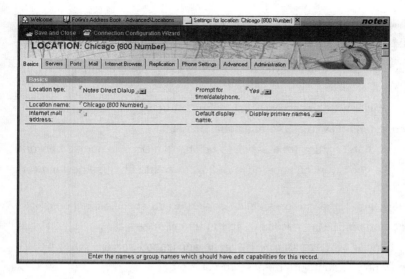

FIGURE 8.9
A location record.

Directory Catalog

If you decide that you want to replicate the directory to mobile users, you should consider using a Directory Catalog. A Directory Catalog can significantly reduce the size of the directory by making a new database using the DirCat5.ntf template. You also must run the DirCat task on the server. This task will keep the file up to date and keep the file a reasonable size for replication.

WHAT IS IMPORTANT TO KNOW

The following bullets will help you determine whether you are prepared for the exam:

- Be familiar with how to establish an infrastructure domain.
- Understand how to create additional domains.
- Know what it means for a server to belong to a Domino named network.
- Have a good working knowledge of how to create and use new network ports.
- Know what it means to establish servers to do specific functions.
- Understand what is necessary to run a mail server.
- Be familiar with agents running on an application server.
- Know how to configure a Passthru server.
- Have a working knowledge of a hub server.
- Understand how to create clustered servers.
- Be very familiar with how to establish and configure servers to host Web sites.
- Be able to change a server record to redirect a URL.
- Have a working knowledge of the difference between mail, application, and enterprise Domino servers.
- Have an understanding of how to create and configure program documents.
- Be familiar with the different client types (Notes, Domino Developer, and Domino Administrator).
- Have a good working knowledge of the different standard location documents for clients.
- Understand how to create new location records.

▶ Setting Up/Configuring Directories (Domino, Catalog, Assistance)

▶ Setting Up/Configuring Calendaring and Scheduling

▶ Setting Up/Configuring ID Backup and Recovery

▶ Setting Up/Configuring License Tracking (Certlog)

▶ Setting Up/Configuring Transaction Logging

C H A P T E R 9

Setting Up/Configuring Database Resources

This chapter covers database resources on the Domino server and how they are configured.

SETTING UP/CONFIGURING DIRECTORIES (DOMINO, CATALOG, ASSISTANCE)

The first three resources that we want to examine are the Domino Directory, Calendaring, and Transaction logging. The Domino Directory is the name and address book for the entire Domino domain. The Calendar database is used by Domino users to define shared schedule information. Transaction logging is used to ensure data integrity and provide administrators with the ability to recover lost or corrupted data.

The Domino Directory

Prior to Domino Release 5, the Domino Directory was commonly referred to as the name and address book. The default file name, NAMES.NSF, remains the same, but can be changed if desired. The Directory contains information, such as server configuration parameters, connection documents, user information, and group information. User information is stored in the Domino Directory in person documents when IDs are created. Server documents are also created when a new server is registered. The Directory is created when the first server in the domain is built. When a new server is added in the domain, the Directory is replicated from the first server to the new server and a server document is added for the new machine.

The Directory Catalog

The Directory catalog is used to gather data from Directories in the local domain. This data is compiled into one database for quick access and contains user and group information. If multiple Directories exist, a Directory catalog can be used to combine the data from all copies of the Directory into a single copy for quick access. A mobile directory can be deployed for laptop users to look up users while they are traveling. The Directory catalog uses the DIRCAT5.NTF as the source template. After the catalog is created using the template, a configuration document will need to be created. To create a new configuration document, select

Create from the menu and then select Configuration. A configuration screen will appear with two tabs: Basic and Advanced. Figure 9.1 displays the Configuration screen.

The fields on the Basics tab include the following:

- **Directories to Include.** Used to define the file names of the directories to consolidate.

- **Additional Fields to Include.** The following fields are default fields:

  FullName. Name of person, name of Mail-in database, or group name

  Listname. Group name

  Type. Person, mail-in database, or group

  FirstName. Person

  MiddleInitial. Person

  LastName. Person

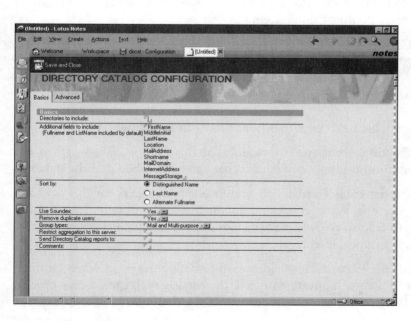

FIGURE 9.1

Use the Configuration screen of the Create option to create a new configuration document.

Location. Person

MailAddress. Person

Shortname. Person

MailDomain. Person, mail-in database, or group

- **Sort By.** This field has three options:

   Distinguished Name

   Last Name

   Alternate FullName

- **Use Soundex.** Default for this field is Yes. Soundex is a tool used to attempt phonetic searching for user names. This search will increase the size of the Directory catalog by four bytes for each catalog entry.

- **Remove Duplicate Users.** Duplicate entries are deleted as they are found. The entry kept in the catalog is the first entry found based on the values entered in the Directories to Include field. If No is selected, user interaction will be required to select the user required from the list of duplicate names.

- **Group Types.** Valid selections are All or Mail and Multipurpose. All should only be selected if Notes API programs are used to resolve members of groups that appear in ACL lists. The default is Mail and Multipurpose.

The definable fields on the Advanced tab are as follows:

- **Packing Density.** The default for this field is 255, which is the maximum number of entries that can be combined in the database

- **Incremental Fields.** The default selection of Yes for this field will store changes in combined documents as duplicate entries. Setting this field to No will make changes in the original fields and not create a duplicate entry.

- **Merge Factor.** This field is used to define the point when Domino will merge duplicate entries in the catalog with the original entries. The default setting is 5 percent of the total entries in the database.

After the fields have been populated, click the Save and Close button on the top of the form to continue.

After the catalog document has been created, the Dircat task must be started. At the server console, type `Load Dircat` to start the process. The Dircat task will combine all defined data in the configuration document and deposit it into the Directory catalog. The most efficient use of the Directory catalog is to create one database and then replicate it to all servers in the domain. Keep the Directory catalog up to date by running the Dircat task regularly.

Problems may occur with the Directory catalog from time to time. Typical errors include the following:

- **Searches on a Directory Catalog Aren't Working.** Proper setup in a Domino domain with the Directory catalog installed requires that each server in the domain contain a replica of the catalog. The Domino Directory must also be set up so that the Public Directory Profile lists the file name for the Directory catalog. Make sure that all replicas of the catalog database have the same file name.

- **Incomplete Entries in the Directory Catalog.** Check the Directory catalog regularly to verify that entries are correct. If names are missing from the catalog perform the following steps:

  1. Open the catalog and select the configuration document. After the document is selected, choose File from the Domino menu and choose Document Properties.

  2. A box appears that has six tabs. Select the second tab (the T-Square). In the left box (a listing of the fields) select the Directories field. Check the directories in the box listed on the right (the field's contents) and make sure that the Dircat task can access these directories.

  3. Next select the Since field on the left and check the right box to verify the last date and time that Dircat ran on the server.

  4. If these items are accurate, open the NOTES.INI file and add the line `Log_Dircat=1` to enable the Dircat task to add log entries in the Log.nsf file. Restart the Domino server and check the log file for errors to troubleshoot the problem.

Directory Assistance

Directory assistance is useful for companies that have more than one Directory or have implemented LDAP directories. The Directory assistance database matches the Domino Directory with a defined hierarchical name. Using this format for searching simplifies the search due to the fact that Domino searches hierarchical names first by design. The Directory assistance database is created using the DA50.NTF database template. Directory assistance is used for secondary directories to do the following:

- Set up security for Web authentication for users accessing the Web server.

- Provide clients with LDAP Directory search capability.

- Provide convenient mail addressing for Notes users to registered Directory users.

Directory assistance is used with LDAP directories to do the following:

- Set up security for Web authentication for users accessing the Web server.

- Confirm registered group membership in an LDAP directory.

- Direct LDAP users connecting to Domino LDAP services to the defined LDAP directories.

- Provide mail addresses for users in the LDAP directories to Notes users.

SETTING UP/CONFIGURING CALENDARING AND SCHEDULING

Domino uses the calendar and scheduling utility to provide users with the ability to set up meetings. Company holidays can be defined for employees to access and users can import the holidays into their personal calendars. Schedule Manager, defined by the task Sched, is a tool provided with Domino along with Calendar Connector, defined by the Calconn task. At the time of the server build, Sched and Calconn are automatically added to the NOTES.INI file. The BUSYTIME.NSF database is created when the server first starts for servers that are not in a cluster. The file name in a clustered server environment is CLUBUSY.NSF. Users who have completed a Calendar Profile have an entry created in the BUSYTIME.NSF (or CLUBUSY.NSF if the users home mail server is found to reside within a cluster) database to facilitate meeting scheduling. Users manage their own personal calendars and create personal calendar profiles. In the profiles, users designate other users who can access their free time information and determine when they are available for meetings. When a user is invited to meetings, Domino verifies that the user is available by accessing his schedule to determine whether he is free. If the user is available, the information is updated in the database and the user's time is scheduled.

Domino scheduling should be set up based on the location of users in the Domino domain.

Scheduling within a single Domino domain is configured automatically. Should the administrator want to make available rooms and other resources for scheduling within the domain, she would simply need to create a Resource Reservations database and subsequently define the various resources. To allow for scheduling between users in adjacent Domino domains, however, the administrator will need to create an adjacent domain document.

1. Click the Configuration tab in the Domino administrator. From the left view pane, select the Messaging view, then select the Domains view. In the main view window, a list of available domains will be displayed. Select the adjacent domain and click the Edit Domain tab.

2. Select the Calendar Information tab. This tab has one field to complete: Calendar Server Name. This field is used to define the name of the adjacent domain server that processes requests for the selected domain.

Non-adjacent domains cannot access schedules between them directly. A Calendar server in an intermediate domain will provide access for both domains to inquire about free time information. The Domino Directory will require non-adjacent domain documents for the domains to communicate. To set up the nonadjacent domain scheduling, perform the following steps:

1. Click the Configuration tab in the Domino Administrator. From the left view pane, select the Messaging view, then select the Domains view. In the main view window, a list of available domains will be displayed. Select the non-adjacent domain and click the Edit Domain button.

2. Select the Calendar Information tab. This tab has one field to complete: Route Requests Through Calendar Server. This field is used to define the name of the adjacent domain server that processing requests for the selected domains. The server defined in this field will process requests from the source domain to the targeted domain.

Domino also supports users of Lotus Organizer and IBM OfficeVision. Supporting these two types of users requires the creation of a Foreign Domain Document. After the document is defined, perform the following steps:

1. Click the Configuration tab in the Domino administrator. From the left view pane, select the Messaging view, then select the Domains view. In the main view window, a list of available domains will be displayed. Select the non-adjacent domain and click the Edit Domain button.

2. Select the Calendar Information tab. This tab has two fields to complete:

   ◆ **Calendar Server Name.** Server name running OfficeVision or Lotus Organizer.

   ◆ **Calendar System.** Used to select either OfficeVision or Organizer 2.x.

3. Domino users using OfficeVision or Organizer require an entry in their person document that defines the CalendarDomain field with the foreign domain.

SETTING UP/CONFIGURING ID BACKUP AND RECOVERY

From time to time, users will lose their IDs or forget their passwords. Administrators can prepare for this situation by keeping copies of the user IDs in a mail-in database. To set up recovery, perform the following steps:

1. Create a database for users to access via email (either a mail or mail-in database).

2. Set the Default ACL access to No Access and set Reader access for administrators.

3. Open the Domino Administrator and select the Configuration tab. From the field on the right, select the Certification tab. A menu of items will be displayed. Select Edit Recovery Information.

4. A dialog box will appear. Select the certifier ID and enter the password.

5. The Edit Master Recovery Authority List dialog box will appear (see Figure 9.2).

6. The number of authorities must be defined in this box. The suggested number is three, with one being the default.

7. The center of the dialog box will display the current recovery authorities. To add additional users, click the Add button. The Domino Directory will display a list of users. Select the users to be added to the list and click OK to continue.

8. The Address button is used to identify the recipient address that will be used to store the encrypted ID files.

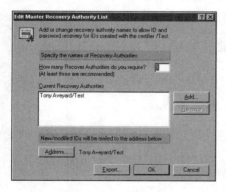

FIGURE 9.2

The Master Authority List is used to define users authorized to recover passwords.

If recovery information is defined in the certifier ID before users are created, the user IDs are automatically set up with recovery information. If this was set up after an ID was created, the information must be updated in the ID and then it will be sent into the database.

Perform these steps to update existing user IDs with recovery information:

1. Open the Domino Administrator and select the Configuration tab. From the field on the right, select the Certification tab. A menu of items will be displayed. Select Edit Recovery Information.

2. A dialog box will appear. Select the certifier ID and enter the password.

3. The Edit Master Recovery Authority List dialog box (refer to Figure 9.2) will appear.

4. Click the Export button. After entering the certifier ID's password, a new dialog box will appear. This information will be used to update user's recovery information. The following fields need to be completed:

   - **To.** This field is used to select users and groups that need to be backed up.

   - **CC.** Users and groups to whom to send a copy of the recovery message.

   - **Subject.** This field is used for a message to the users and groups receiving the update. The default message is "New ID file recovery information is attached. Please add it to your ID file by using the Actions menu's Accept Recovery Information option."

   - **Memo.** Used to include information for users. This text will appear in the body field of the message.

After the user message is received, the user must complete the following actions:

1. Open the message and open the Action menu. Select Accept Recovery Information and enter the password.

2. The following fields must be completed:

- **To.** This field is used to identify the mail address or mail-in database that has been set up to store the backup user ID. Domino will automatically enter the name of the database.

- **CC.** Users and groups that should receive a copy of the message.

- **Subject.** This field will be used for Administrator information. If the field is left blank, a default message will be entered.

- **Memo.** Used to include information for users. This text will appear in the body field of the message.

SETTING UP/CONFIGURING LICENSE TRACKING (CERTLOG)

After the first Domino server in a domain is created, the first database that should be created is the Certification Log. The database must have a file name of CERTLOG.NSF. The domain only requires one certification log. After a log is deleted, the information stored in the previous log cannot be recreated. New users and servers that are added to the domain are added to the log. A document is created for each item that includes the following:

- Name and license type of users

- Date of certification and expiration

- Name, license type, and ID of the certifier ID used to create or re-certify the ID

To create the Certification Log, execute the following steps:

1. Choose File from the menu and select Database, New. The New Database dialog box will appear (see Figure 9.3).

   The following fields required to create a new Certification log:

   - **Server.** Select the Domino server to store the log file.

   - **Title.** The title of the database should be Certification Log.

   - **Template Server.** Select a server in the domain that contains the CERTLOG.NTF file template.

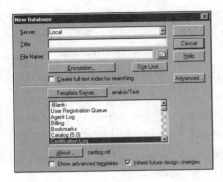

FIGURE 9.3
Use the New Database dialog box to create and configure databases on the server.

2. Select OK to create the database. After the database is created, set the ACL for administrators to at least Editor.

> **NOTE**
>
> Remember that if the certification log is created from an administrator's workstation instead of at the server, the administrator's name must be properly defined in the server document as a user who has the ability to create new databases or the database creation will be unsuccessful.

SETTING UP/CONFIGURING TRANSACTION LOGGING

When a system failure occurs, the most efficient way to recover is to stop and restart the server. When the Domino server task is restarting, Domino initiates database recovery to fix databases that were open at the time of the server crash. Transaction logs are used by Domino to update transactions that were in process or open at the time of the crash. By default, transaction logging is disabled.

To set up transaction logging, the following steps must be completed. Keep in mind that all databases to be logged must be placed in the Domino data directory. The databases may be located in the root of the data directory, or a subdirectory.

1. Open the Administrator client and select the Configuration tab.

2. Select the server from the Use Directory on Selection box above the main view pane window.

3. Select the Configuration tab under the servers view. The main view pane window will display the list of servers. Select the view defined as Current Server Document. This will open the server document for the previously selected server. Now select the tab titled Transactional Logging to define the task. The available fields on this tab are as follows:

   - **Transactional Logging.** The default setting is Disabled.

   - **Log Path.** Defines the location of the log on the server. Lotus recommends that the log be stored on a separate, mirrored device with hardware redundancy enabled. The recommended size for log space is 1GB.

   - **Use All Available Space on Log Device.** If a separate device is being used to store the log, select Yes to this field. If Yes is selected, the field Maximum Log Space does not require attention. If No is selected, however, the size defined in the Maximum Log Space field is used.

   - **Maximum Log Space.** This field defines the maximum size of the log file. The maximum size of the file is 4GB, and the recommended minimum size is 192MB.

   - **Automatic Fixup of Corrupt Databases.** The default for this field is Enabled. If transaction logging is unable to fix a corrupted database then Domino will launch the Fixup task to correct the errors. After this happens, a new DBIID is assigned to the database and the server generates a message that a new database backup is required. If this field is set to Disabled, then the administrator is notified to execute the Fixup task with the option of –J to repair corrupted databases.

   - **Runtime/Restart Performance.** This field is used to determine how server performance will be affected during the times when recovery checkpoints are recorded in the log file. The options for this field are as follows:

     - *Standard.* This is the default. This option assigns checkpoint to occur on a regular basis.

- *Favor Runtime.* Selecting this option will instruct the server to record fewer checkpoints and will maximize system performance.

- *Favor Restart Recovery Time.* Checkpoints are recorded regularly and will allow the time required for server restart to be minimized.

- *Logging Style.* The default for this field is Circular. This option will allow the log files to be reused and will overwrite old transactions. The problem with this option is that limitations are set in that only the transactions stored in the log can be restored. If the option selected is Archive, then log files are not overwritten, but the log file names are incremented.

4. When all options have been selected, click Save and Close to continue.

Editing documents on the Domino server is a typical example of a transaction. Domino supports a process called transaction logging. Transaction logging is a tool that assists administrators in recovering from a system crash. As database changes occur, Domino records them in the transaction log.

The benefits of transaction logging include the following:

- In the event of a system crash, the server will typically restart more quickly because the Fixup task will not have to repair databases that were open at the time of the failure.

- Database updates are delayed until a time when the server load is decreased. Because the transactions are recorded sequentially in log files it is more efficient than random updates in database files.

- Because transaction logging records change, only the log file needs to be backed up, saving the administrator from having to back up the entire system.

- In the event of a media failure, supported third-party backup API programs can force these transaction logs to be replayed against the most recent backup copy of the database. Consequently, none of the data since the time of the last backup is lost as a result of the media failure.

> **N O T E**
>
> Important: Transaction logging will only work on databases that are formatted in release 5 format.

A database instance ID (DBIID) is assigned to each release 5 database on the server that has transaction logging enabled. For each transaction undertaken in the database, the DBIID is added to the record to match the transaction to the correct database. A new DBIID is assigned to a database when system maintenance activity occurs. Compact running on a database with options defined will change the DBIID on a database, and the records in the transaction database will no longer match. New DBIIDs are assigned to databases when any of the following occurs:

- Transaction logging is activated for the first time.
- The compact executes task with any options.
- Database corruption is repaired using Fixup.
- The log path or maximum log size is changed after it is set up and used.
- A database is moved from one server to another—or to a server that does not have logging enabled.

> **N O T E**
>
> Important: When the DBIID for a database is changed, the backup should be generated as quickly as possible. If a media failure were to occur and a backup copy did not exist, the only option would be to revert to the previous copy and data would be lost.

Some problems that may occur with transaction logging are an invalid transaction log path and a damaged or corrupt transaction log. The following sections will explain how to deal with these problems.

There Is an Invalid Transaction Log Path

This error occurs if the server cannot find the path to the transaction log path. When this error appears, perform the following steps:

1. Make sure the path to the log file is in place.

2. Verify that the server has write access to the log path.

3. After the path has been verified as correct, reboot the server.

4. If rebooting the server does not fix the problem, verify that the system does not have hardware problems. If the hardware is operating error free, change the NOTES.INI file setting TRANSLOG_PATH to a different location.

5. Reboot the server. After the server has been rebooted, Domino will create a new log file and assign new DBIIDs to the databases.

6. If the server document is set to run Fixup automatically on corrupted databases, the files will be repaired without further intervention. If it is not set, run Fixup from the server prompt.

7. After the problem is fixed, perform a full backup on the server.

Transaction Log Is Damaged or Corrupt

This error takes place when a read or write fail occurred in the transaction log file. The error that appears on the server console will state that the log is damaged, or that a database may require media recovery or Fixup. To correct this error, perform the following steps:

1. Restart the server and see if the error reoccurs. If the error does not reappear the file is not damaged and no action is required. If the error reoccurs, the log file is damaged.

2. Stop the server and delete the transaction log file and control files.

3. Restart the server and Domino will re-create new log files and control files and will assign new DBIISs to the databases that are in release 5 format.

4. If the server document is set to run Fixup automatically on corrupted databases, the files will be repaired without further intervention. If it is not set, run Fixup from the server prompt.

5. After the problem is fixed, perform a full backup on the server.

WHAT IS IMPORTANT TO KNOW

- The Directory contains information, such as server configuration parameters, connection documents, user information, and group information.

- The Directory catalog is used to gather data from Directories in the local domain. This data is compiled into one database for quick access and contains user and group information.

- The Dircat task will combine all defined data in the configuration document and deposit it into the Directory catalog.

- The Directory assistance database matches the Domino Directory with a defined hierarchical name. Using this format for searching simplifies the search due to the fact that Domino automatically searches hierarchical names first.

- Non-adjacent domains cannot access schedules between them directly. A Calendar server in an intermediate domain will provide access for both domains to inquire about free time information.

- Domino also supports users of Lotus Organizer and IBM OfficeVision. Supporting these two types of users requires creating a Foreign Domain Document.

- The Certification Log contains Name and license type, Date of Certification and expiration, Name, license type, and ID of the certifier ID used to create or re-certify the ID.

- Transaction logging is a tool that assists administrators in recovering from a system crash. As database changes occur, Domino records them in the transaction log.

- A database instance ID (DBIID) is assigned to each Release 5 database on the server that has transaction logging enabled. For each transaction entered into the database, the DBIID is added to the record to match the transaction to the correct database.

- ▶ Setting Up/Configuring Message Distribution Performance Enhancements (Multiple routers, Multiple MAIL.BOX Files)

- ▶ Setting Up/Configuring Message Distribution Tracking

- ▶ Setting Up/Configuring Message Distribution using Force

- ▶ Setting Up/Configuring Message Distribution using Non-Notes/Internet-based Mail

- ▶ Setting Up/Configuring Message Distribution using Notes-Based Mail (Shared, Message-Based)

- ▶ Setting Up/Configuring Message Distribution using Schedules

- ▶ Setting Up/Configuring Messaging Distribution using a Mixed Messaging System

- ▶ Setting Up/Configuring Monitoring Administration Tools (Preferences, Logs, Web-based, Remote)

- ▶ Setting Up/Configuring Monitoring Monitors (ACL, File, STAT, Probes)

- ▶ Setting Up/Configuring Monitoring Statistics (STATS)

- ▶ Setting Up/Configuring Replication Distribution through Force

- ▶ Setting Up/Configuring Replication Distribution through Scheduling

CHAPTER 10

Setting Up/Configuring Distribution and Monitoring

This chapter will discuss the various ways that Domino can be configured to provide the maximum throughput for messaging and replication.

SETTING UP/CONFIGURING MESSAGE DISTRIBUTION PERFORMANCE ENHANCEMENTS (MULTIPLE ROUTERS, MULTIPLE MAIL.BOX FILES)

Using new features implemented in Release 5, Administrators can optimize mail routing on a Domino server. These new features include the use of multiple routers and multiple MAIL.BOX databases.

When a Domino server is processing excessive mail traffic, the server may try to deposit mail in the MAIL.BOX file while the router task is processing mail in the database. Domino is designed so that when processing is occurring in the MAIL.BOX database, the database is locked for exclusive use by that particular task. Based on the hardware configuration of the server, this can cause a bottleneck in processing the mail for delivery.

Domino addresses this problem by providing the ability to run multiple router tasks as well as multiple MAIL.BOX databases on the same server. Using this methodology, when one MAIL.BOX database is locked for use, the Domino server will mark the database as "in use" and will look for additional MAIL.BOX server tasks to use. There is no limit on the number of MAIL.BOX databases that can be used on a server; however, each additional file sequentially decreases the benefit in performance increase.

Multiple MAIL.BOX files are defined using the administrator client. Open the server configuration document and click on the Messaging tab. Select the Configurations item to display the available configurations. If a configuration does not exist, select Add Configuration to create one. The first tab displayed is the Basics tab. Before defining the number of MAIL.BOX files for the server, the group or server name must be defined on the Basics tab. The option is available to select a specific server or group, or to alternately select a global default setting. Figure 10.1 shows the Basics tab and the options for defining the server.

After the new configuration has been created, select the Router/SMTP tab and enter the number of mailboxes to run on the server. Press the Escape key and select Yes to save the new configuration. Figure 10.2 shows the Router/SMTP tab with three MAIL.BOX files selected.

The server task must be stopped and restarted to initialize the new configuration. Figure 10.3 shows the server task running and the new MAIL.BOX files being created as MAIL1.BOX, MAIL2.BOX, and MAIL3.BOX.

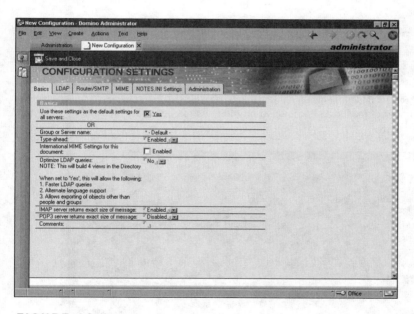

FIGURE 10.1
Complete the fields in the Basics tab to define parameters used in SMTP routing.

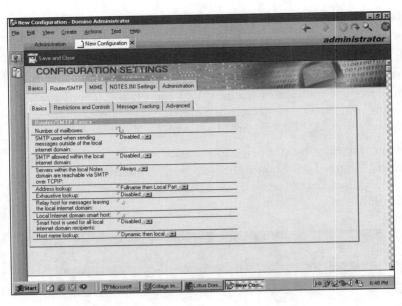

FIGURE 10.2
The number of mailboxes to be used on the server is set using the Router/SMTP tab.

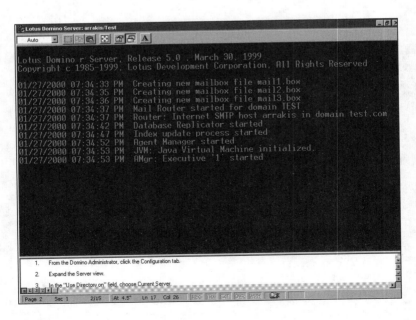

FIGURE 10.3
The new mailboxes defined in the SMTP tab will be created when the server is
restarted.

SETTING UP/CONFIGURING MESSAGE DISTRIBUTION TRACKING

Occasionally an administrator will need to verify that messaging is operating properly. Domino uses message tracking to verify that a message makes it to the intended user. Mail usage reports are instrumental for providing an administrator with data regarding mail delivery problems as well as information that can be used for determining if the server is running optimally. Mail probes are used when an administrator requires specific information regarding mail routes.

The database MTSTORE.NSF, or Mail Tracking Store database, is used to record message-tracking data. MTC, the mail tracking program, uses the directory MTDATA in the Notes data directory to store the MTSTORE.NSF database. The MTSTORE.NSF database is created when the mail tracking program is started, either in the NOTES.INI file or by loading the program manually by using the Load MTC command at the server prompt. Message tracking will display one of the following results:

- **Delivered.** The delivery to the mailbox on the server was successful.

- **Delivery Failed.** The delivery to the mailbox was unsuccessful. The person may not exist on the server or a hardware configuration error, such as insufficient disk space, may be occurring.

- **In Queue.** The server has queued the message to the router and the router is processing the message.

- **Transferred.** The message was successfully sent from the originating server to the destination server.

- **Transfer Failed.** The message was unable to be transferred to the next destination server by the router.

- **Group Expanded.** Delivery to a group was successful and the designated group was appended by the addressee names.

- **Unknown.** Status of message delivery is unknown.

From time to time it may be necessary to create reports that examine trends in message delivery. The Mail Tracking Store database will allow an administrator to access data generated over time and analyze it for problem tracking. These reports provide data such as message size or a ranking of usage by users. In addition, a report can be generated that would allow an administrator to determine whether a company's policy for proper mail usage is being abused. The Mail Tracking Store database is used to create mail usage reports, and the Reports database is used to store the generated reports.

Setting Up Message Tracking

To set up message tracking, perform the following steps:

1. Open the Administrator client and select the Configuration tab.

2. Select the server from the Use Directory on Selection box above the main view pane window.

3. Select the Configuration tab under the servers view. The main view pane window will display the list of servers. Select the view *- [All Servers] and double-click on it to open it.

4. Select the Basics tab and make sure that the selection Use These Settings as the Default Settings for All Servers has been selected in the box marked Yes. If the Default Setting box is not checked, the specific group or server must be selected in the Group or Server Name field. After these steps are completed, click on the Save and Close field at the top of the document.

5. Select Configurations and select *- [All Servers] and open it.

6. Open the Router/SMTP tab. Select the Message Tracking tab. The fields on this tab will need to be defined to enable message tracking. Click on the Edit Server Configuration field to change the fields on this tab. The fields are defined as follows:

   ◆ **Message Tracking.** The default setting for this field is Disabled. Select Enabled to use the Mail Tracking Store database to enable logging for activity related to message routing.

   ◆ **Don't Track Message For.** The default for this field is Empty. If there are users or groups whose business requirements dictate that their messages are not tracked, enter them here. If this field is left blank, all users and groups will be tracked.

- **Log Message Subjects.** The default for this field is No. Change this field to Yes to generate message logging in the Mail Tracking Store database.

- **Don't Log Subjects For.** The default for this field is No. Entering names of users of groups in this field will disable the logging of the subject line in the messages.

- **Message Tracking Collection Interval.** The default for this field is 15 minutes. This field is used to tell the Domino server the frequency in minutes for logging messages in the Mail Tracking Store database. Keep in mind that the more times that the server logs messages, the greater the load will be on the server.

- **Allowed to Track Messages.** The default for this field is blank. This field is used to determine servers or users who have permission to track messages on the server. If this field remains blank, only the group LocalDomainServers will be able to track messages.

- **Allowed to Track Subjects.** This field is blank by default. If the field is left blank, the LocalDomainServers group will be able to track messages by the subject field in the message. Use this field to enter names of servers or users who can track messages by the subject field.

After mail tracking is enabled on the server, the results are stored in MTSTORE.NSF. To generate reports using this data, perform the following steps:

1. Open the Reports database and click on the Run Report button above the main view window. After the button is selected, a dialog box will appear. The fields that need to be completed are as follows:

   - **Report Type.** This field is used to define the type of report to run. The valid choices are as follows:

     Top 25 users by count
     Top 25 users by size
     Top 25 senders by count
     Top 25 senders by size
     Top 25 receivers by count

Top 25 receivers by size
Top 25 most popular "next hops"
Top 25 most popular "previous hops"
Top 25 largest messages
Message volume summary
Message status summary

- **Created By.** User who is generating report, typically the administrator.

- **Created At.** Date and time report is created.

- **Created on Server.** Server where report is created.

- **Description.** Comment field to describe report.

- **Time Range.** Amount of time to base report on. The possible selections for this field are as follows:

Today
Yesterday
Over the last week
Over the last two weeks
Over the last month
All available information

- **Execution Interval.** This field is used to establish the frequency of the report. The available options are as follows:

Once
Daily
Weekly
Monthly

- **Earliest Message Found.** Set the beginning date to search for messages.

- **Latest Message Found.** Set the ending date to search for messages.

- **Report Should Be.** Three options are available to set the disposition of the report: Saved, Mailed, and Saved & mailed.

Special options are selectable at the bottom of the form. The fields for the special options section are as follows:

- **Sender's Name.** The name can be set for an exact match or a search that can contain the name of a user.

- **Recipient's Name.** The name can be set for an exact match or a search that contains the name of a user.

- **Delivery Status.** Parameters for delivery statuses are defined as *"is"* or *"is not"* "delivered," "not delivered," or "being processed."

- **Message Size.** Defined as *"is greater than"* or *"is less than,"* followed by an empty field to define a size to search by.

2. After all the parameters are set for the search, click OK to being the operation.

SETTING UP/CONFIGURING MESSAGE DISTRIBUTION USING FORCE

Situations will occur when mail is not routing, or there may be an instance when a message needs to be routed immediately and the threshold has not been met to initiate mail delivery. When either of these situations occurs, the administrator has the ability to force mail to route by either entering commands at the server prompt or using the Domino administrator client. The syntax to route mail at the server prompt is *Route servername.* The hierarchical name should be used when forcing mail to route. If the name of the server is more than one word in length, the server name must be enclosed in quotes.

In order to force mail routing using the Domino Administrator client, perform the following steps:

1. Start the Administrator and select the Server tab, and then select the Status tab.

2. Select the Server button on the right. A menu will be displayed with valid server tasks. Select Route Mail.

3. A new dialog box will appear. Select the name of the destination server to force mail routing by using the drop-down menu or by

typing in the complete hierarchical name. After the selection has been made, click the Route button to continue and force the mail to be sent.

SETTING UP/CONFIGURING MESSAGE DISTRIBUTION USING NON-NOTES/ INTERNET-BASED MAIL

Prior to the release of Domino R5, administrators would have to install an additional product to enable the server to send mail outside of the local notes domain to the Internet. SMTP mail routing is now accessible directly in the server configuration. Using SMTP, users can send and receive mail directly from the Internet. SMTP can be set up on one or all servers in the domain.

Domino is flexible in that it has the capability to communicate with non-Notes mail systems. Using message transfer agents, or MTAs, Domino can exchange mail with x.400 and cc: Mail systems via SMTP. In addition, Domino includes tools that will allow you to migrate users from the following systems to Domino mail:

- cc: Mail

- Microsoft Exchange

- Windows NT

- LDIF-formatted files

- Netscape Mail Server

- Groupwise4

- Groupwise5

Domino also supports the IMAP protocol. IMAP running on a Domino server permits clients running the IMAP protocol to access the server in a more advanced fashion than a simple POP3 connection. Users running the IMAP protocol can access messages on a Domino server running the IMAP protocol and store them on their local machine. IMAP clients can also make offline copies of messages and then later synchronize them with the online copy of their mail database that is resident on the server.

In order to access a Domino server, an IMAP client must authenticate with the server. Methods used between the IMAP client and server include name and password authentication, SSL authentication, and SSL encryption. After an IMAP client has successfully accessed the server, an IMAP client can access only its own mailbox. When an IMAP client is accessing the Domino server, the Domino folders display as IMAP mailboxes.

The IMAP service is started by either adding IMAP to the servertasks= line in the server's NOTES.INI file, or by manually loading the task at the server console. In addition to loading the IMAP service, at least one server must be running the SMTP server task and the SMTP listener must be enabled.

SETTING UP/CONFIGURING MESSAGE DISTRIBUTION USING NOTES-BASED MAIL (SHARED, MESSAGE-BASED)

Shared mail is a feature that is specific to Domino. A special database is used on the Domino server that is designed to save space on the server by using a single copy of a message stored for multiple users. A single message is kept in the database when multiple recipients are defined and a message header is then stored in each user's mailbox. The users are unaware that a single copy of the message exists only in the database, and there is no degradation in performance. Users can make changes to the message without causing edits to appear to other recipients. A Domino server task Object Collect runs daily to perform maintenance on the database.

In order for a router on a Release 5 Domino server to access a user's mail database file, the router examines the users person document in the Directory to determine the way that Internet mail will be processed.

If the message is in Notes format and the person document is set for Prefers Notes Rich Text, then the router will process the message as normal. If the person document is set for Prefers MIME, then the router will convert the document to MIME format before the delivery is made. If the person document is set for No Preference, then no conversion takes place and the message is delivered because Domino reads the message and automatically converts the message to MIME for Internet clients using the IMAP and POP server tasks.

If the message is in MIME format when the message is received and the person document is set for Prefer Rich Notes Text, then the router performs the conversion to Notes format and delivers the message. If the person document is set for Prefer MIME or No Preference, no conversion is required and the message is delivered as normal. Encrypted messages in S/MIME format are converted to attachments and a new Notes format message is sent to the user with the attachment explaining that the message is encrypted and cannot be converted to Notes format.

SETTING UP/CONFIGURING MESSAGE DISTRIBUTION USING SCHEDULES

Domino uses connection documents to define the parameters used to route mail between servers in different Domino Named Networks in the most efficient manner. To set up a connection document, perform the following steps:

1. Open the Domino Directory and select the Connections view. If there are existing connection documents, they will be displayed in the main view window. Select the Add Connection button to create a new connection document.

2. The Replication/Routing tab is used to define parameters for the mail router task. The page contains the following fields regarding mail routing:

    ♦ **Routing Task.** Establishes the type of mail that will be routed on the server. These selections include Mail Routing, X.400 Mail Routing, SMTP Mail Routing, cc:Mail, and None.

    ♦ **Route at Once If.** Defines the number of messages to queue before transferring mail. The default is 5 messages.

    ♦ **Routing Cost.** Used to determine the most effective route to use to route mail from the server. The default is 1.

♦ **Router Type.** This field defines the type of mail routing to occur on the server. The available options are Push Wait, Pull Push, Pull Only, Push Only. The default is Push Only.

3. To save the new connection document, click on the Save and Close button.

SETTING UP/CONFIGURING MESSAGING DISTRIBUTION USING A MIXED MESSAGING SYSTEM

Domino Release 4 does not support SMTP routing or MIME messaging without installing an MTA. Domino Release 5 provides built-in support for MIME and SMTP.

When a Domino Release 4 server receives a message from a Release 5 server and the name and address book does not contain a person document for the recipient, the Release 5 server will handle the message in one of two ways:

♦ The message is converted from MIME to Notes format and then transferred to the user's mailbox. Although the size of the message is compressed in this manner, there may be some loss of message integrity.

♦ The message is converted to Notes format from MIME format, and an attachment is added to the message as a file attachment. This conversion will secure message integrity, but will require increased disk space.

In a domain containing Release 4 and 5 servers, MIME messages may require special attention. MIME and native Notes format messages must be processed before being sent to the Internet.

SMTP mail processing in a Release 4 mail environment is facilitated with the SMTP MTA. Incoming messages that are in the MIME format are processed as usual to the Notes router. Outgoing messages are changed to MIME format and then sent out the SMTP MTA.

In a mixed Release 4 and Release 5 environment, a Notes-formatted message is processed as usual. If a MIME-formatted message is queued for delivery, the person document must be checked to determine if the receiving mailbox is set to receive MIME messages.

If the person document is set for Notes Only or Prefers Notes Rich Text, the message is converted to Notes format and transferred as normal. If the person document is set for Internet Only or Prefers Mime, then the message is converted to MIME format and then delivered to the user's mail file. If the person document is set for Notes and Internet or No Preferences, the message is converted to Notes format and an attachment is added containing the original message in MIME format. If a router cannot locate a person document for a user the default conversion is to MIME format.

SETTING UP/CONFIGURING MONITORING ADMINISTRATION TOOLS (PREFERENCES, LOGS, WEB-BASED, REMOTE)

Domino provides various tools and utilities that will assist and administrator in monitoring messages and its related tasks. This portion of the chapter will discuss setting up the tools.

Mail probes are used to provide data on mail routes. Using a mail probe an administrator can test mail routes and gather statistics on routes.

Before a mail probe can be created, the ISpy task must be started. At the server prompt, enter this command: **load runjava ISpy**. The command is case sensitive. The ISpy task can also be loaded in the NOTES.INI file.

You can monitor your mail network by configuring probes to test and gather statistics on mail routes. To set up a mail probe, perform the following steps:

1. Using the Domino Administrator, select the Configuration tab.

2. Select Statistics and Events view in the navigator pane. The view will expand into three nested views: Domino Server, Mail, and TCP Server. Select the Mail view. In the main view pane, the view

will change and the option to create a New Mail Probe will display at the top of the main view window. Click on the New Mail Probe field to continue.

3. Three new tabs will be displayed: Basics, Probe, and Other. The Basics tab is displayed by default. The following two fields need to be completed:

   ◆ **Probing Servers (Source).** This field is used to define the originating server that will start the probe. Select the server from the box displayed by the selection arrow, or type the name of the server in the box.

   ◆ **Target Mail Address (Destination).** The purpose of this field is to define the user's mail route that is being checked. Select the user from the box displayed by the selection arrow, or type the name of the user in the box. More than one user or a Domino defined group is not a valid entry for this field.

   Do not check the box All Domino Servers in the Domain Will Probe Themselves, or only local mailboxes will be checked.

4. Select the Probe tab and complete the following fields:

   ◆ **Send Interval.** This field is used to determine the frequency that probes will be transmitted.

   ◆ **Time Out Threshold.** This field is used to determine the amount of time the originating server will wait for a response from the destination server before logging a failure state.

5. Select the Other tab and complete the following fields:

   ◆ **Event.** This field is used to select the severity of the event to be reported if the probe fails. The possible selections are: Normal, Warning (low), Warning (high), Failure, and Fatal.

   ◆ **Enablement.** Check this box to disable the probe. The probe can be re-enabled by deselecting the box.

6. After the tabs have been completed, select OK to save the probe data. Notice that the new probe is now displayed in the main view window.

SETTING UP/CONFIGURING MONITORING MONITORS (ACL, FILE, STAT, PROBES)

Domino uses monitors to track server performance. The monitors are created in the Statistics and Events database. The file name of the database is EVENTS4.NSF. The monitors that can be created are the ACL change monitor, Statistics monitor, Replication monitor, and File monitor.

ACL Change Monitor

This monitor is used to report changes in database ACLs, either by replication or a change generated by a program modification. To set up an ACL change monitor, perform the following steps:

1. Select the Configuration tab in the Administrator tab. Expand the Statistics and Events tab and select Monitor. Select ACL Change and in the main view window click the New ACL Change Monitor button.

2. The ACL change monitor has two pages to be defined. The first tab is the Basics page. Complete the following fields:

    ♦ **File name.** The name of the database to be monitored.

    ♦ **Server(s).** Select either All in the Domain or Only the Following and enter a server name to be monitored. Servers can also selected by using the Servers button.

3. The second tab displays the Other page. The fields on this page to be completed are as follows:

    ♦ **Generate a security event of severity.** The following options are available: Fatal, Failure, Warning (high), Warning (low), and Normal.

4. To disable this monitor, select the Disable This Monitor box.

5. To enable this monitor, select the OK button.

Statistics Monitor

This monitor is used to check the status on a specific statistic task running on the server. The Collect task is used in conjunction with the monitor to report when an alarm threshold has been reached. To set up the Statistics Monitor, perform the following tasks:

1. Select the Configuration tab in the Administrator client. Expand the Statistics and Events tab and select Monitor. Select Statistic and in the main view window, click the New Statistic Monitor button.

2. The Statistics monitor has three pages to be defined. The first tab is the Basics tab. Complete the following fields:

   ◆ **Server(s) to Monitor.** Select either All in the Domain or Only the Following and enter a server name to be monitored. Servers can also selected by using the Servers button.

   ◆ **Statistic to Monitor.** This field is used to select the statistic to monitor. As you select a field, the description will change and more selections may appear so that the statistics parameters can be more qualified.

3. The Threshold tab has three fields that are defined by selecting a radio button. These radio buttons will generate threshold events based on the following three conditions:

   ◆ The statistic is LESS THAN the threshold value.

   ◆ The statistic is GREATER THAN the threshold value.

   ◆ The statistic is a MULTIPLE of the threshold value.

   Below the radio buttons is a box used to define the threshold. A suggested default is listed in the box.

4. The third displays the Other page. The fields on this page to be completed are as follows:

   ◆ **Generate a Security Event of Severity.** The following options are available: Fatal, Failure, Warning (high), Warning (low), and Normal.

5. To disable this monitor, select the Disable This Monitor box.

   These settings are used in order to allow a statistical alarm to be promoted to a statistical event. In effect, this enables administrators to assign a higher priority to resource measurements when they breach a certain threshold.

6. To enable this monitor, select the OK button.

Replication Monitor

This task is used to report problems related to replication. To set up the Replication Monitor, perform the following tasks:

1. Select the Configuration tab in the Administrator tab. Expand the Statistics and Events tab and select Monitor. Select Replication and in the main view window, click the New Replication Monitor button.

2. The Replication Monitor has two pages to be defined. The first tab is the Basics tab. Complete the following fields:

    ◆ **File Name.** Enter the name of the replicating database.

    ◆ **Server(s) to Monitor.** Select either All in the Domain or Only the Following and enter a server name to be monitored. Servers can also selected by using the Servers button.

    ◆ **Servers(s) with Which the Database Must Replicate.** The possible selections for this field are All in the Domain or Only the Following. If Only the Following is selected, the name of the server must be entered.

    ◆ **Replication Timeout.** This field will establish the amount of time the server will wait for a timeout to occur.

3. The third displays the Other tab. The fields on this page to be completed are as follows:

    ◆ **Generate a Security Event of Severity.** The following options are available: Fatal, Failure, Warning (high), Warning (low), and Normal.

4. To disable this monitor, select the Disable This Monitor box. This monitor is enabled by default.

File Monitor

The File Monitor is used to establish database integrity and usage history. To set up the File Monitor task, perform the following tasks:

1. Select the Configuration tab in the Administrator tab. Expand the Statistics and Events tab and select Monitor. Select File and in the main view window, click the New File Monitor button.

2. The File Monitor has three pages to be defined. The first tab is the Basics tab. Complete the following fields:

    ◆ **File to Monitor.** This field is used to select the file to monitor.

    ◆ **Server(s).** Select either All in the Domain or Only the Following and enter a server name to be monitored. Servers can also selected by using the Servers button.

    ◆ **Monitor Unused Space.** Select this field to monitor unused space in the file.

    ◆ **Monitor for User Inactivity.** Select this field to monitor the file and determine its usage on the server(s).

3. The second tab is the Unused Space page. The fields on this page are as follows:

    ◆ **Trigger the Event When the Unused Space Exceeds.** This field is defined by setting a percentage for database size to monitor.

    ◆ **Automatically Compact the Database When the Above Condition Is Met.** Selecting this box will cause the database to compact when the selected size in the unused space field is met.

4. The third tab is the User Inactivity page. The fields on this page are Time Periods to Monitor and Minimum Session. The time periods to monitor are definable by daily, weekly, and monthly.

5. The fourth tab is the Other page. The fields on this page to be completed are as follows:

    ◆ **Generate a Security Event of Severity.** The following options are available: Fatal, Failure, Warning (high), Warning (low), and Normal.

6. To disable this monitor, select the Disable This Monitor box.

7. Select the OK button at the top of the page to enable the File Monitor.

SETTING UP/CONFIGURING MONITORING STATISTICS (STATS)

Domino statistics provide the administrator with a report on the status and integrity of the server. Statistics on the server are available at the server console by typing the command **Show Stats**. The Collect task pulls data from the server and deposits the information in the Statistics database (STATREP.NSF). To view statistics reports on the server, perform the following steps:

1. Open the Administrator client, elect the Server tab, and select Analysis.

2. Select the Statistics Report view.

   The Statistics Report view expands to display the following views:

   - Statistics Reports
   - Calendaring Scheduling
   - Clusters
   - Communications
   - Mail & Database
   - Network
   - System
   - Web Server & RetrieverAlarms
   - Events
   - Spreadsheet Export
   - Graphs
   - System Loads

♦ System Resources

♦ System Statistics

♦ Server Access

♦ Single Copy Object Store Statistics

SETTING UP/CONFIGURING REPLICATION DISTRIBUTION THROUGH FORCE

Domino servers in a domain are set up to replicate databases based on a predetermined schedule. A Domino administrator typically creates connection documents that will replicate databases during times of decreased server activity, such as after hours or on the weekend. Situations may dictate that a database, such as a discussion database, replicates hourly to maintain message thread continuity in the domain. Replication errors may occur on the server that will require the administrator to troubleshoot the error by forcing the database to replicate outside of the scheduled connection times. Replication is forced on a Domino server by executing one of the following commands at the server console prompt:

♦ **Replicate.** Use this command to send and receive updates from a specified server. The format is `replicate servername filename`.

♦ **Pull.** Pull is used to retrieve changes only from a specific server. The format is `pull servername filename`.

♦ **Push.** Use push to force changes to a specific server. Changes are only sent, not received. The format for the push command is `push servername filename`.

In addition to forcing replication from the server prompt, it is also possible to replicate databases from the workspace and select the type of replication that will be used. Perform the following steps from the workspace:

1. Open the database to be replicated.

2. After the database is open, select File, Replication, and Replicate.

3. A dialog box appears that offers two options: Replicate via Background Replicator and Replicate with Options. Select Replicate with Options and click OK to continue.

4. Select the server to replicate with or type in the server name.

5. The options available are Send Documents to Server or Receive Documents from Server. When receiving documents from the server, two optional parameters are available: Receive Full Documents, or Receive Summary and 40KB of Rich Text. Set the options for the file and click OK to start the replication.

SETTING UP/CONFIGURING REPLICATION DISTRIBUTION THROUGH SCHEDULING

Domino, as in previous version of Notes, uses scheduling for database replication. The hardware configuration of the server, as well as the setup of the network infrastructure, plays a key point in successful replication. An administrator should keep in mind that network traffic and user activity will have an effect on how efficiently a database replicates. The default scheduled replication time is from 8:00 a.m. to 10:00 p.m. with a repeat time of 360 minutes. Time Zones should be considered when setting up replication schedules. To define replication schedules, perform the following steps:

1. Open the Domino Directory and select the Connections view. If there are existing connection documents, they will be displayed in the main view window. Select the Add Connection button to create a new connection document.

2. The Replication/Routing tab is used to define times and dates as well as files and directories to be replicated. This page contains the following fields:

    ◆ **Replication Task.** This field is used to enable or disable the replication task.

    ◆ **Replicate Databases Of.** This field sets the priority of the databases to be replicated. The options are Low, Medium, or High.

- **Replication Type.** Select the type of replication to be executed on the server. The options available are Pull Pull, Pull Push, Pull Only, and Push Only.

- **File/Directories to Replicate.** Specify a specific file, files, or directory to replicate.

- **Replication Time Limit.** Defined time limit to replicate files.

3. Click on the Save and Close button to save the new document.

NOTE

Remember that the viable topologies in a Notes Network are Line – 2 to 4 servers, Ring – 4 to 6 servers, Hub and Spoke – 6 or more servers.

WHAT IS IMPORTANT TO KNOW

- Domino can utilize multiple routers and mailboxes to optimize system performance.

- The database MTSTORE.NSF, or Mail Tracking Store database, is used to record message-tracking data.

- IMAP running on a Domino server permits clients running the IMAP protocol to access the server in a more advanced fashion than a simple POP3 connection.

- The Mail Tracking Store database will allow an administrator to access data generated over time and analyze it for problem tracking.

- MIME and native Notes format messages must be processed before being sent to the Internet.

- Using a mail probe, an administrator can test mail routes and gather statistics on routes.

- Time Zones should be considered when setting up replication schedules.

- A Domino server task, Object Collect, runs daily to perform maintenance on the shared mail database.

- After mail tracking is enabled on the server, the results are stored in MTSTORE.NSF.

CHAPTER 11

Setting Up/Configuring Domino Infrastructure Security

SETTING UP AUTHENTICATION

Authentication is the process of verifying a server or user ID with a server's ID. You may recall from Chapters 7, "Installination," and 8, "Setting up Infrastructure, Servers, and Workstations," that IDs are created from certifiers. When these IDs are created, there is a public and private key pair kept in each ID. These keys are used to encrypt and decrypt data to ensure the ID is official. In the following example, Jill Hobby/ATL/ChairCreations is a user and Mail27/ATL/ChairCreations is a mail server:

1. Jill Hobby attempts to use Mail27.

2. Mail27 sends a random number to Jill Hobby.

3. Jill Hobby's workstation encrypts the number and sends it back to Mail27.

4. Mail27 uses Jill's public key to decrypt the response. If the number is the same as the random number picked in step 2, Jill is verified.

5. The process is then reversed: Jill's workstation generates a random number and the server must encrypt the information and the client must decrypt and verify.

SETTING UP/CONFIGURING AGENT ACCESS

Agents can automate tasks such as updating documents, routing mail, changing data in fields, and much more. You should use great care in granting rights to creating and executing agents. They can be quite helpful or quite damaging. They also can cause an undue burden on the server if you have too many people with the rights to run agents. Agent access involves two elements:

- The Access Control List
- The Server Document

The Access Control List

You can limit who can create and use agents with the Access Control List (ACL). As you can see in Figure 11.1, there are two different options within the Access Control List that limit agent privileges:

◆ **Create Personal Agents.** You can limit who has the rights to create personal agents. Personal agents can only change records that a user has rights to.

◆ **Create LotusScript/Java Agent.** LotusScript and Java are very powerful languages. Generally, you would give rights only to a seasoned developer for LotusScript and Java.

Of course, you cannot run agents that change records unless you can see the records and you have rights to change them. There are other limitations that can be put in place to prevent clients from seeing or changing documents:

◆ **Using No Access in the ACL.** This would prevent the client from access to the overall database.

◆ **Using Reader Access in the ACL.** This would allow the client to see the records, but an agent could not change any records.

◆ **Using a Reader Name field in the database.** If a user is not listed in a Reader Name field, the documents will not appear.

◆ **Using Author Access in the ACL and an Author Name field on the documents.**

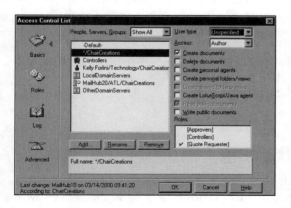

FIGURE 11.1
An Access Control List dialog box.

The Server Document

You can also limit who can run agents on the server with the Agent Restrictions section of the Server document. You can find the Agent Restrictions section by opening the server and clicking on the Security tab. The bottom left section of the tab contains the Agent Restrictions section.

Each of the fields for the Agent Restrictions section are explained in the following list:

- **Run Personal Agents.** This field limits who can run personal agents on the server. If there is no entry in the field, everyone can run Personal Agents.

- **Run Restricted LotusScript/Java Agents.** Users listed (usually within a group) in this field can use LotusScript and Java Agents to make changes within databases. To run agents that call operating system commands and C programs, the user must be a member of Run Unrestricted LotusScript and Java agents. No entry in this field means that no one is allowed to run agents of this type.

- **Run Unrestricted LotusScript/Java Agents.** Users (usually within a group) can run all LotusScipt and Java Agents. If this field is blank, no one can use LotusScript or Java agents.

- **Run Restricted Java/JavaScript.** If you run Domino IIOP, users in this field can use a limited set of Java or JavaScript with a browser. An empty field means that no one can run Java or JavaScript with a browser.

- **Run Unrestricted Java/JavaScript.** This allows a user to use Java and JavaScript with a browser as long as Domino IIOP is running. If there is no entry in this field, a user will not be able to use unrestricted Java or JavaScript.

Setting Up/Configuring Database Access

You should use care when sharing drives and directories through the operating system. If users can map a drive to a Domino server with Windows Explorer, the user could potentially have full access to a file. He might even be able to delete the file or entire directories. If you need to share the directories for a backup program, be sure to share only the directory for the server that will be performing the backup.

The Access Control List is the most commonly used method to limit who can use a database and what can be done within the database by a user. The Access Control List is composed of seven different access rights. It is important to specify whether the entry in the Access Control List is a server or person. If you specify that the entry is a server, you also will prevent the database from being opened manually with Server's ID. The Default entry of a database is the access assigned if a user does not appear explicitly, by wildcard (such as */ATL/ChairCreations), or in a group. The seven access rights are described as follows:

- **No Access.** Members of this selection are denied access to the database (assuming the Read Public Documents and Write Public Documents check boxes are not used).

- **Depositor.** Persons or groups with Depositor access can only create records. They cannot see even the records they create.

- **Reader.** Persons or groups with this privilege can read but not alter documents. Each person or group would also need to be a member of a Reader Names field if one exists.

- **Author.** This security option gives persons or groups the ability to create and change only documents that they created. Each document must have an Author Names field or the user will have the ability to only read documents.

- **Editor.** Persons with this right are able to read and change all documents in the database.

- **Designer.** Individuals or groups with this security option can change all records in the database and create or change design elements such as Forms, Views, agents, and so on.

- **Manager.** Persons or groups with this privilege can do all that a Designer can, plus make changes to the Access Control List or delete the database from a server.

As you can see in Figure 11.2, there are check boxes that assist you further with determining what functions to give users. The following options can be set for each person or group listed in the ACL:

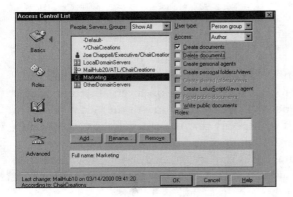

FIGURE 11.2
A sample of an Access Control List.

- **Create Documents.** With the Author Access selected, you can toggle the ability to create new documents. With all other access rights, this option is grayed out.

- **Delete Documents.** This option can be used with the Author and higher rights. The user can still use her keyboard to mark the document for deletion but after responding Yes to delete the records, Lotus Notes will reply You not authorized to delete documents in this database.

- **Create Personal Agents.** This gives a user the ability to create agents that can change many documents at a time rather than individually.

- **Create Personal Folders/Views.** This determines where a view is stored. If the check box is selected, private views are stored on the server. If it is not selected, private views are stored in the DESKTOP5.DSK file.

- **Create Shared Folders/Views.** Typically this option is selected for users with Editor access. New views can be made available to other users of the database. To make changes to views, the user would also need to have the Domino Designer client.

- **Create LotusScript/Java Agent.** When this check box is selected, the user or group can create agents that use LotusScript or Java code. To run the agents on the server, the server record must also grant additional rights.

- **Read Public Documents.** This option allows users to see only records intended for everyone using the database. The Calendar of a mail file is a common example of using this option. Users can read another person's calendar but not the mail of the other person.

- **Write Public Documents.** This option allows a person or group to create entries in a database for public viewing.

If you have a very sensitive database that should not be seen by most people in the organization, consider making the database hidden when using File, Database, Open. This is done within the Database Properties menu of the database. If you click on File, Database, Properties, you will see a Design tab (it has a T-square and a Right Triangle). The check box Show in "Open Database" Dialog can enable or disable the appearance of the file. This is not really a security feature because the user can type in the file name and still open the file if the access rights are not set securely. See Figure 11.3 for an example of the Database Properties box.

There are three other sections of the Access Control List:

- Roles
- Log
- Advanced

These areas are defined in the sections that follow.

FIGURE 11.3
An example of the Database Properties box.

Roles

Roles can be used to dynamically change rights for users in a specific database. By specifying the role name in a form, view, or agent, you can then use the role to grant rights to use the elements. Roles will appear to the right of the Access Control List in brackets ([ ]). To create roles, you simply select the Roles tab within the ACL. You can then add the names of the roles you want to use. To use a role in a form, you can open the Properties menu for the form and select which role can create or read records with the form. An example is shown in Figure 11.4.

You also must add the user or groups to the corresponding role you will be using to grant access. This is done very easily in the ACL. You simply select the name or group you want to add to the role and then click on the role name at the bottom-right corner. You should be certain to include server names or groups so that the documents will replicate. This is necessary only in cases where the role has been used with the Form Read Access option, not the Form Create Access option.

Log

The log simply lets you know when the Access Control List has been changed and by whom. This can be particularly handy when you are trying to diagnose a problem because you have a brief history of recent changes.

FIGURE 11.4
An example of using roles for a form.

Advanced

The Advanced tab has powerful and important options. Notice a sample in Figure 11.5.

These options are explained in the following list:

- **Administration Server.** For AdminP to carry out changes to the Access Control List, an Administration Server must be selected in this option. The server that is selected will have a key placed next to it when viewed in the Access Control List. If the database replicates to many others, be sure to select only one server as the Administration Server. Notice that you can also determine whether AdminP will alter the Reader and Author fields of the database. For more information on AdminP, please see Chapter 13, "Domino Infrastructure."

- **Enforce a Consistent Access Control List Across All Replicas of This Database.** This option enables the Access Control List locally (it acts the same as opening the database from a connected client). Without this option, accessing a database locally yields Manager access. This option should be used on a limited basis because replication can be disabled if the Access Control List is changed on another server. Many administrators prefer to change an ACL for the servers they are responsible for. When this feature is engaged, whether you work on a server copy or a local copy of a database, you will enjoy exactly the same level of access to the database.

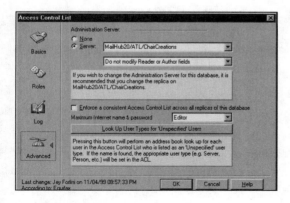

FIGURE 11.5

A sample of the Advanced tab of the Access Control List.

- **Maximum Internet Name and Password.** Regardless of how a user is listed in the ACL, he will get only as high as this setting. Limiting the maximum rights provides added security to Web-based applications.

- **Look Up User Type for "Unspecified" Users.** This button will allow to you use the Domino Directory to determine whether the entry in the ACL is a server or a person.

SETTING UP/CONFIGURING FORMS AND VIEWS ACCESS

You can limit who can use forms and views with the Properties dialog box. You can see a sample of view security in Figure 11.6. Form security restricts the use of a form to create new documents. If you have an application that is generally read by most people in the company and only a few individuals create the documents, this is a handy feature. View security restricts who can use a view. However, there is a loophole with view security. If a person has Designer access to a database, she can create an equivalent view.

FIGURE 11.6
A sample of view security.

SETTING UP/CONFIGURING DOCUMENT ACCESS

With Author Names and Reader Names fields, you can limit who can edit and read documents. Each document should have an Author Names field if you are going to be using the Author Access right. The Author Names field typically captures the name of the creator of the document so that the same person can later edit the document. Without an Author Names field, selecting Author Access will not allow document creators to change their documents. The Reader Names field allows only specific users or groups to read a document. In addition to user names and groups, roles or the asterisk (*) wildcard can also be used to allow access with the Reader Names or Author Names fields. It is important to include server names (or use LocalDomainServers) in the Reader Names field so that replication can occur. The designer of the database creates Reader and Author Names fields on Forms.

You can also limit modifiable areas of a form (ultimately the document) with sections. Sections are created simply by selecting the area you want to protect and selecting Create, Sections, Controlled Access. You can then determine who will be able to edit the section of the documents. Others will be able to only read the section.

SETTING UP/CONFIGURING FILE SECURITY

File protection documents can be used to secure files on the server's hard drive from Web browser clients. The file protection document can be used to prevent changes to CGI scripts, servlets, and agents. To create file protection documents, open the address book and locate the server document you desire to change. At the top of the screen, you will see a button labeled Web. Upon clicking this button, you can see that File Protection is the third option. The first screen you see is used simply to enter in the path that you will be protecting. This is relative to the data path (Lotus\Domino\Data). The second tab allows you to specify the Access Control for the files. An example is shown in Figure 11.7.

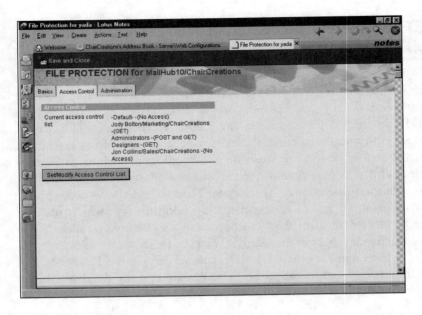

FIGURE 11.7
A sample of File Protection access control.

You have three options for setting access to files:

- Read/Execute access (Get method)
- Write/Read/Execute access (Post and Get method)
- No Access

To retrieve and make changes to file protection documents, you can open the Domino Directory and select Server, Web Configuration view. This view will allow you to see the file protection documents for each directory of each server. To make changes, you need only edit the document.

After you create or make changes to file protection documents, you must restart the HTTP process. You can do this very simply by issuing the Tell HTTP Restart Server command.

SETTING UP/CONFIGURING SERVER ACCESS

Server Access is primarily granted by authentication and server document fields. Authentication is covered in detail in the Authentication section of this chapter. Figure 11.8 shows an example of a server document's security section.

After you open the server document, you can make changes to security by navigating to the Security tab. You will need to be in Edit mode (you can just click on the red pencil). The security section of the server document is broken into the following areas:

- Security Settings
- Web Security Access
- Server Access
- Passthru Server
- Agent Restrictions
- IIOP Restrictions

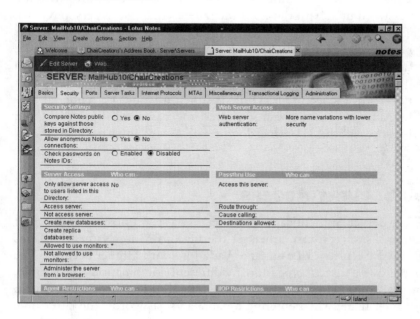

FIGURE 11.8

A sample of a server document's security section.

The first four areas are described in the sections that follow. For information on Agent Restrictions and IIOP Restrictions, please refer to the "Setting Up/Configuring Agent Access" section of this chapter.

Security Settings

Each field in this section is described in the following list:

- **Compare Notes Public Keys Against Those Stored in the Directory.** When a client attempts to use the server, the public key in the ID must match the one stored in the Domino Directory. This option allows for a very secure server. If an ID is lost and you issue a new one, the old ID will have a different public key.

- **Allow Anonymous Notes Connections.** Enabling this option means the server no longer will do authentication and allows any ID to use the server. This may be useful for servers distributing communications with many outside companies that use Lotus Notes.

- **Check Passwords on Notes IDs.** This feature ensures that the password used with the ID is the same as that in the person record. This feature can also be used to force users to change passwords periodically. Not only does this feature ensure that a user enter the same password found in the password digest field of the person document, but it also means that all ID files must share a common password. Hence, if an ID file is stolen it would be rendered useless after the administrator cleared the password digest field and had the rightful ID owner log in with a new notes password.

Web Security Access

The Web Server Authentication field secures a server hosting an Internet or Intranet site. You can either set the field to More Name Variations with Lower Security or Less Name Variations with Higher Security. The former allows a user to type in many different combinations (first name, last name, common name, short name, fully distinguished name, and so on) of their name when entering a name and password. The latter only allows names that appear in the full name field of a person record.

Basic authentication can be used with IIS and an NT account. When a user enters an ID and password, a corresponding NT account will be used to verify the password. Domino does not use the password in the person document in this case.

Server Access

There are many options within the Server Access section. Each of these is described in the following list:

- **Only Allow Server Access to Users Listed in This Directory.** Only if a user has a person record in the Domino Directory is he allowed to use the server. Note that a server would not have a Person record.

- **Access Server.** Only users or groups listed in this field can access the server. It is far more common for administrators to leave this field blank, which allows all users to access the server unless they are denied by the Not Access Server field. An asterisk (*) can also be used as a wildcard (such as */ChairCreations).

- **Not Access Server.** This denies access to any person or groups listed. This is typically the name of a group that lists all terminated employees.

- **Create New Databases.** Only people or groups listed in this field can place new databases on the server. Leaving this field blank means that anyone can add new databases to the server.

- **Create Replica Databases.** This field allows people or groups to replicate copies of databases to a server. If this field is empty, no one can add new replicas.

- **Allowed to Use Monitors.** All persons and groups listed here can set up headlines to search databases for changes. An asterisk (*) is placed in the field by default because an empty field denies everyone.

- **Not Allowed to Use Monitors.** This field denies listed users or groups the ability to search databases for changes using the Headlines feature.

- **Administer the Server from a Browser.** Users or groups added to this field can issue server commands and changes from an Internet browser.

Passthru Use

A Passthru server allows a mobile user to call into one server and access many. An example is shown in Figure 11.9.

Each server that will be accessed will need to be configured to allow for Passthru server access. These fields are defined as follows:

- **Access This Server.** This field will allow the specified users or groups to use the server while passing through another. If the field is empty, no one can access the server indirectly.

- **Route Through.** You can specify who can use a server to route to others. A blank field means that no one can Passthru the server.

- **Cause Calling.** If another server is available only via modem, this field can force the server to call the destination. If there are no entries in this field, the server will not automatically dial another when requested.

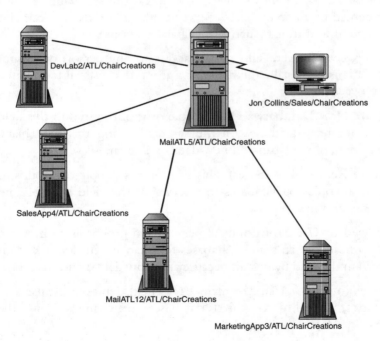

FIGURE 11.9
An example of Passthru Server.

- **Destinations Allowed.** You can selectively determine which servers can be used from a Passthru server. An empty field means that there are no limitations and all servers can be reached through the server.

SETTING UP/CONFIGURING USER ACCESS

In addition to the user access issues addressed in registration, authentication, and database access, there is the issue of user needs with regard to Passthru access. Users can be restricted from using servers, databases, documents, sections, and fields. Access can be granted by using the fully distinguished name of the user, groups, the asterisk wildcard, or roles. Server access is controlled with the Server document for that server. Database access is controlled with the Access Control List and roles for that database. Documents and fields can be restricted with Reader Names. Section security can be added to a form to limit who can change a section. Hide When can be used to limit access to fields. For more detailed information, please see the sections of this chapter that address the respective topics.

SETTING UP/CONFIGURING SECURITY FOR THE DOMINO DIRECTORY

The Domino Directory includes roles that allow you to delegate actions for administration. Each role allows either creation or updating of only certain records in the Domino Directory. These roles are defined in the following list:

- **GroupCreator.** Members of this role can create new groups in the Domino Directory. Typically you would assign this right to those individuals who also create new users.

- **GroupModifier.** This role allows administrators to change groups. You can also delegate this for each individual group. This comes in handy for departments that change access for new hires. To allow changes by a user for a specific group, you can add the name of the individual to the Administrators field of the Administration tab for the group.

- **NetCreator.** The NetCreator role grants the ability to create connection, mail-in database, program, configuration, user profiles, and many other documents. Essentially this role allows you to create every record except persons, groups, and servers.

- **NetModifier.** The NetModifier role allows you to change connection, mail-in database, program, configuration, user profiles, and many other documents. In a nutshell, this role allows you change every record except persons, groups, and servers.

- **ServerCreator.** Members of this role can create new server documents. New servers should be a fairly rare event so most administrators will limit this ability to very few people.

- **ServerModifier.** This role allows users or groups to change server records.

- **UserCreator.** You must be a member of this role to register new users in the Directory.

- **UserModifier.** This role will allow a person or persons to edit all person records. Each user is also allowed to modify fields that contain personal data.

TIP

Although a user may have Author access to a document along with the appropriate modifier role, if a user has only ACL Author access there still may be certain fields that cannot be edited. This is of course the result of the Must Have at Least Editor Access to Modify field property being turned on. For these fields to be modified, one would require at least Editor access in the ACL.

The default access on the Domino Directory is Author, but no check boxes are selected. This means that users can change the records that they own (just their own Person record) but not create or change any others. You will also see that Anonymous is added to the Access Control List too. The entry is set to No Access; in the event that you allow your Directory to be browser enabled, it will be secure and you must authenticate to read the information.

WHAT IS IMPORTANT TO KNOW

The following list will help you determine if you are prepared for the exam:

- Understand how authentication works.
- Have a good working knowledge of how to set security for agents.
- Be very familiar with the Access Control List and how to grant rights for databases.
- Know the seven different levels of securing for the Access Control List.
- Be familiar with roles.
- Understand how to grant rights to forms and views.
- Be familiar with using Author Names and Reader Names fields.
- Have a working knowledge of File Protection Documents.
- Have a good understanding of granting and denying rights to servers.
- Be familiar with granting access with roles to the Domino Directory.

SECTION 3: DEPLOYING DOMINO R5 APPLICATIONS: EXAM 522

About Exam 522

Exam Number	522
Minutes Allowed	60
Single-Answer Questions	No
Multiple Answer with Correct Number Given	Yes
Multiple Answer without Correct Number Given	No
Choices of A–D	Yes
Choices of A–E	No
Scenario-Based Questions	Yes
Objective Categories	Yes

CHAPTER 12

Database Architecture

OBJECTIVES continued

▶ Deploy Applications Based on Design Elements: Shared Versus Non-Shared

▶ Deploy Applications Based on How Attachments Are Handled

▶ Deploy Applications Based on Why Elements Are in the NSF

▶ Deploy Applications Based on Document Characteristics

▶ Deploy Applications Based on Document Characteristics: Archiving

▶ Deploy Applications Based on Document Characteristics: Author Access

▶ Deploy Applications Based on Document Characteristics: Reader Access

▶ Deploy Applications Based on Document Characteristics: View Hierarchies

▶ Deploy HTML-Based Applications

▶ Integrate with Host Data

▶ Design Secure Applications

▶ Secure Applications, User Authentication: Notes ID

▶ Secure Applications, User Authentication: Web

▶ Secure Applications: ACLs for Replication

▶ Secure Applications: Consistent ACLs

▶ Secure Applications: Authors

▶ Secure Applications: Groups

▶ Secure Applications: Read Only views

▶ Secure Applications: Readers Fields

▶ Secure Applications: Roles

▶ Secure Applications: Sections

▶ Secure Applications: Security Versus Deterrence

▶ Secure Applications: Web Users

DEPLOY APPLICATIONS BASED ON BACKWARD COMPATIBILITY

There are many new code functions and script that will not work in previous versions of Lotus Notes. If you will be working in a mixed environment, you should either limit the use of these new code enhancements or be sure to upgrade those clients that will be using the database. If you intend to use R4 clients with R5 servers, you should be certain to name the file extension .NS4 until the clients are upgraded. If you compact files on an R5 server but want to keep files as R4, you can use the Compact –R command. The following table illustrates when files can be used by clients and servers without issues of compatibility:

	R4 Database	*R5 Database*
R4 Server	Yes	No
R4 Client	Yes	Yes (see below)
R5 Server	Yes	Yes
R5 Client	Yes	Yes

An R4 Client using an R5 database on an R5 server will not be able to use R5 functionality.

DEPLOY APPLICATIONS BASED ON CODING

All Lotus Notes applications contain coding. Even a simple view will contain formulas that reference field names so that the columns will show data. The Lotus Domino Designer license and software is required to create applications with code. It is possible to create databases with the Lotus templates or make separate (non-replica) copies of databases that require no changes or additions of code. In such cases, no additional license or software is needed.

To place new applications on a server, either you will need the rights for that server or you will need to send the database to the Domino Administrator. Rights are granted on the server record. For more information on server rights, please see the Server Access section of Chapter 11, "Setting Up/Configuring Domino Infrastructure Security."

Coding a Lotus Notes database consists of the following:

- Formula Language
- JavaScript
- Java
- LotusScript

These different coding languages are explained in the sections that follow. There are other languages (such as C++) that can be used with Lotus Notes, but they are beyond the scope of this book. Code can be placed in many areas of a Lotus Notes applications, such as views, on forms in fields or agents. As you can see in Figure 12.1, there are separate panes for the creating a form, changing code, and creating actions.

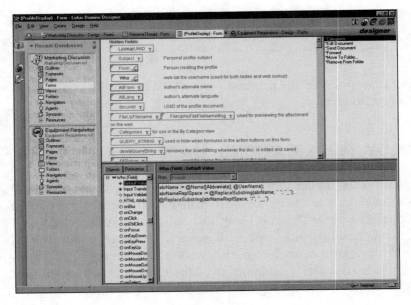

FIGURE 12.1
A sample of the Domino Designer and the coding panes.

Deploy Applications Based on Coding: Formula Language

For many years, formula language was the only code available in Lotus Notes. The following is a sample of code for a column in a view written in Formula Language:

```
REM "Variables to translate";
PrivateTxt := "PRIVATE: ";
ExpiredTxt := "EXPIRED: ";
REM "End variables to translate";
Author := @If(Form = "MainTopic" & Subject = ""; " (" + @Name([CN];
➥From) + ")"; "");
useSubject :=
@If(form = "ResponseToResponse"; ImmediateParentSubject; form =
➥"Response"; OriginalSubject; "");
@If(readers != ""; PrivateTxt; ExpireDate != ""; ExpiredTxt; "") +
➥Subject + @If(useSubject != ""; " (RE: " + useSubject + ")"; Author)
```

A typical formula will contain a function (such as @If), text (enclosed in quotations), and field names. Notes will evaluate formulas from top to bottom and left to right. A few @Commands (equivalent to pull-down menus) and the @PostedCommand are the only exceptions. They evaluate after all other formulas have completed.

Deploy Applications Based on Coding: JavaScript

JavaScript provides more processing at the client (browser) rather than the server. This can reduce server overhead and traffic. JavaScript is useful for evaluating fields, mouse effects, numeric calculations, and simulated dialog boxes. JavaScript cannot be used in Agents. A sample of JavaScript is shown here:

```
function authProf()
{
var pathname = window.location.pathname;
filename = pathname.substring(0,(pathname.lastIndexOf("nsf")+4))
➥key = document.forms[0].AbrFrom.value
var newWindow = window.open(filename + "LookupPersonalProfiles/" +
key +
"?OpenDocument&hw=1","secondary_window","toolbar=no,location=no,
➥scrollbars=yes,directories=no,height=500,width=625")
}
```

Deploy Applications Based on Coding: Java

Java is used with Domino through predefined classes. It is a very powerful programming language that can be used in many areas of an application including agents. You can configure the Internet Protocols, Domino Web Engine section of the server document for Java servlets as follows:

- **Java Servlet Support.** You can select None, Domino Servlet Manager, or Third Party Servlet Manager.

- **Servlet URL Path.** Specify the URL that will call servlets. The default is /servlet.

- **Class Path.** Standard libraries are already included when you install Domino in the domino\servlet directory. You can either change the directory or add additional servlets to the same directory.

- **Servlet File Extensions.** A list of URL file extensions that reference servlets.

- **Session state tracking.** When enabled, the Domino Servlet Manager tracks the HTTP sessions for idle sessions.

- **Idle session timeout.** You can specify what constitutes and idle session. The default is 30 minutes.

- **Maximum active sessions.** You can determine the total number of "users" for your site. As the maximum is reached, the longest idled session will be terminated. The default is 1000.

- **Session persistence.** You can change the default to enable caching of HTTP sessions. The information is saved to a file call SESSDATA.SER.

You can also use File Protection Documents to secure CGI scripts, servlets, and agents. For more information on File Protection Documents, please see the "Setting Up/Configuring File Security" section of Chapter 11.

Java applets can be created or imported in the applets design selection of the database. The applets design area is found by expanding the Resources option in the Design pane. Note that Java cannot be used to make changes in a user's workspace.

Deploy Applications Based on Coding: LotusScript

LotusScript is a very powerful and efficient language available for Lotus Notes applications. LotusScript that references fields or changes data is considered *restricted* LotusScript. *Unrestricted* LotusScript refers to instances when operating system commands or calls to C programs are needed. LotusScript offers fewer limitations than Formula Language. It is possible to do many operations with LotusScript that cannot be done with the Lotus Formula Language. However, for some instances the Formula Language is the only option (such as changing text attributes, changing design elements, and more). A sample of LotusScript for News Letter summaries is shown as follows:

```
Dim s As NotesSession
Dim db As NotesDatabase
Dim view As NotesView
Dim note As NotesDocument
Dim profile As NotesDocument
Dim newnote As NotesDocument
Dim newsletter As NotesNewsLetter
Dim collection As NotesDocumentCollection
Dim pPersonName As Variant
Dim pCategories As Variant
Dim pEvents As Variant
Dim pAuthors As Variant
Dim pStrings As Variant
Dim pMyName As Variant
Dim pThreads As Variant
Dim searchtype As String
Dim query As String
Dim textlist As String
Dim totalquery As String
Dim failed As Integer
```

DEPLOY APPLICATIONS BASED ON DESIGN ELEMENTS

Design elements are the many pieces that make up the whole application. Design elements are, for the most part, kept within the .NSF file. Design elements include actions, agents, buttons, fields, sections, forms, subforms, views, folders, and navigators. Many of these design elements are discussed in the following sections.

Deploy Applications Based on Design Elements: Actions

Actions can appear in the Actions menu or as buttons for forms or views. They can call menus, run agents, or implement formulas. To view and change agents, you can simply select View, Action Pane. You can then add or change actions as you see fit. In many cases, you do not need to create an action from scratch. You can use the many simple actions that are included. You will notice that there are six predefined actions (categorize, edit document, send document, forward, move to folder, and remove from folder) that cannot be modified, although you can decide whether to display the actions. If you want to create an action from scratch, you can use Formula Language, JavaScript, or LotusScript.

Deploy Applications Based on Design Elements: Fields

Fields are the basic element of a database. They can gather information from users, compute automatically or be changed by agents. There are fourteen different types of fields you can have in an application. Each of these are briefly defined here:

- **Text.** The text field type will accept a limited amount of data (65KB) and does not allow links, graphics, or attachments. Text fields can be shown in views unlike rich text fields (discussed later).

- **Date/Time.** This field type can only accept time and dates. When entering a two-digit year less than 49, the full date will appear with 2000 added. All two-digit dates 50 and over will be assumed to be in the century beginning with 1900.

- **Number.** Accepts only numbers, periods, and the negative sign ($-$). Typically you use this type of field because you will be using the number in a formula. You would likely use a text field to capture a ZIP code or Social Security number.

- **Dialog list.** You can give the user a list of choices that can be presented in a dialog box or allow the user to select the choice just by typing the first few characters. You can do this by typing in the choices for the user or by referencing a column in a view for choices.

- **Check box.** This field type can be used to allow the user to select from a set of predefined options. The user can select one option, multiple options, or none, depending on how the field is validated.

- **Radio button.** The radio button field type limits the user to a set of choices that can be changed. The user must select from the alternatives given.

- **List box.** This field type will give the user a list of choices that can be scrolled through. The user must chose from the list given.

- **Combo box.** Similar to a dialog list, you can allow users to select from the choices you display or the user can add a different option. The difference between the two is that the dialog list will present a separate window if requested.

- **Rich text.** The rich text is the only field type that allows the user to do character formatting, use links, embed objects, make attachments, and much more. Rich text fields cannot be displayed in a view.

- **Authors.** For all users with Author access, the authors field type is required for those users to edit documents. The typical formula for the authors field is @Name([CN];@UserName). This will capture the name of the person that creates the document. You should also use the Computed When Composed evaluation option so that the creator's name is only captured when the document is first created.

- **Names.** The names field type is primarily used to list the names of users who have updated a document. It is not used to secure documents like the authors and readers field types do.

- **Readers.** The readers field can be used to restrict users or groups that are allowed to view a document.

- **Password.** The password field type will allow a user to enter data but it will only appear as asterisks (*) on the screen. This option is not used to capture the password for a Lotus Notes ID; the password screen has been created in such a way that it cannot be reproduced.

- **Formula.** Used with Headline Monitoring (a database property) and subscriptions (a server task). The user can specify what documents of interest will trigger a notification.

Fields are calculated from left to right and top to bottom. Therefore, you cannot reference a field that requires input if it is below or to the right because the referenced field will likely not contain data.

Deploy Applications Based on Design Elements: Forms and Subforms

Forms and subforms are structures that hold fields so a user can view and input data. Subforms can make it easier to build and change an application because they can be shared by many forms. If you are requesting similar information on different forms, you can call subforms and decrease your development time. Making updates are much easier too. Simply go to the subform and the change is made to all the forms that call the subform. Subforms must first be created to use them on a form. Once the subform exists, you can use the Create, Insert Subform menu to add it to your forms.

Deploy Applications Based on Design Elements: Graphics

Graphics can be used in many areas of an application. They can make an application more impressive and more user friendly. Graphics can be used with pages, framesets, forms, navigators, and agents.

Images can be loaded after text by changing the properties of the database. As seen in Figure 12.2, you can enable the Display Images After Loading option to allow Notes to display all the text of the document before loading the graphics. Users can also change their location documents so that images are loaded by request. This is done in the Advanced, Basics section of the location document. In the load images field, you can select Always (the default) or On Request.

FIGURE 12.2
A sample of a Database Properties dialog box for image loading.

Deploy Applications Based on Design Elements: OLE

Object Linking and Embedding allow you to share a file within Lotus Notes. When changes are made, the changes will also be made to the linked document. Users will need to have access to the file through a shared drive. To create a linked file, you simply copy the whole or part of the file. You can then use Edit, Paste Special to create the link. If you do not select the link option, the file will be pasted independently from the original (as an embedded object).

The Action properties also include options for OLE files. You can specify whether you want the action included with an OLE and whether you want the OLE to remain open if the action is used. A sample of this dialog box is shown in Figure 12.3

FIGURE 12.3
A sample of the OLE settings for actions.

Deploy Applications Based on Design Elements: Sections

Sections can control access or break up a form for the user. When documents are long and have areas that are easily divided, sections can be handy. You can add a section by highlighting the area you want to make a section and then by choosing Create, Section. You can then decide if you want the section to be Standard (for cosmetics) or Controlled Access (for security). A controlled access section can be used to limit who can make changes to the section. All users can still read the section.

Deploy Applications Based on Design Elements: Shared Versus Non-Shared

Some applications will require views, folders, or actions to be available for only certain users. Elements can only be made private or shared at the time they are created. When you create a view, folder, or agent, you must decide almost immediately whether the element will be shared or private. An agent is private by default. You must select the Shared check box just below the name of the agent if you want all users to have access to it. Views and folders will default to Shared and you must choose to make them Private (or Private on First Use). If the user does not have the ACL privilege, Create Personal Folders/Views, folders and views that are made private are stored locally within the DESKTOP5.DSK file.

Deploy Applications Based on How Attachments Are Handled

File attachments can be added to forms, pages, and documents (rich-text fields only). Attachments in Lotus Notes are not linked to the original (they are embedded objects). This can cause confusion to users as they make changes to a file. If changes are made, the user can re-attach the file with the updated information. You may also consider using OLE to allow editing of the file with a shared drive. For more information on OLE, refer to the earlier section "Deploy Applications Based on Design Elements: OLE."

Deploy Applications Based on Why Elements Are in the NSF

Most design elements are stored within the Notes Storage Facility (NSF). The exceptions generally relate to Web-based applications. Items such as graphics, HTML code, and Java servlets can be kept in separate directories on the Domino server.

DEPLOY APPLICATIONS BASED ON DOCUMENT CHARACTERISTICS

There are many document characteristics to consider as you construct Lotus Notes applications. Some of these include archiving, Author access, Reader access, and View hierarchies. These topics are explained in detail in the following sections.

Deploy Applications Based on Document Characteristics: Archiving

As databases grow in size, the file can become slower and unmanageable. Archiving can automate the task of moving documents that are no longer needed to a separate file. Archiving is typically set up with the Properties dialog box using a time criteria to determine when to remove documents. A sample is shown in Figure 12.4.

FIGURE 12.4
A sample of the archiving section of the Properties dialog box.

You can also archive by using an agent. You can create code that can be set to automatically purge unwanted documents on a daily or weekly basis.

Deploy Applications Based on Document Characteristics: Author Access

To deploy applications with Author access, an Author Names field must be present. If you have not defined a field as Author Names, users with Author access will not be able to edit the documents they have created. The typical formula for an author names field is @Name([CN];@UserName). When a user wants to edit documents that he or she has created, the Author Names field will be compared to the name that created the document against the name in the user's ID. If the names match, the user can make changes to the document. It is also possible to use groups or roles in the field as either a default formula or with an agent.

Deploy Applications Based on Document Characteristics: Reader Access

You can deploy an application with Reader access to documents with three methods. You can select Reader access with the Properties dialog box for the form. You can create a Reader Names field. You can create actions to mark documents private when needed. All these methods create a field that lists only the users or groups that can read the document. You may prefer to use groups, roles, or the asterisk wild card to grant the access rather than add the user's name explicitly.

Deploy Applications Based on Document Characteristics: View Hierarchies

View hierarchies allow a user to quickly see which documents are parent and which are responses. A hierarchical view is created by placing a few columns in the first part of the view that have formulas that are specific to the parent documents. Then, a single column should be added that has a formula for how responses should appear. You should also check the column property Show Responses Only. A sample of a responses only column in a discussion database is shown here:

```
REM "Variables to translate";
PrivateTxt := "PRIVATE: ";
ExpiredTxt := "EXPIRED: ";
AnonTxt := "Anonymous";
REM "End variables to translate";
REM "the following is for alternate name support";
CNFrom := @If(@Contains(form; "Anonymous"); AnonTxt;@Name([CN];
➡From));
CNAltFrom := @Name([CN]; AltFrom);
Alternatename := @If(AltFrom != "" & AltFrom != From; " [" +
➡CNAltFrom + "]"; "");
@If(readers != ""; PrivateTxt; ExpireDate != ""; ExpiredTxt; "") +
@If(Subject != ""; Subject + "  "; "") + "(" + CNFrom +
➡AlternateName + " " + @Text(@Created; "D2S0") + ")"
```

DEPLOY HTML-BASED APPLICATIONS

You can use HTML in forms, views, agents, pages, and framesets. HTML is used to create more impressive applications for the Web. To improve the look of your application, you can assign HTML attributes to fields and other elements in a Lotus Notes database. Often you need only one line of code that will move a field to a better position on Web page. For example, the following line would simply assign dimensions for a body field:

```
"height = \"300\" width = \"625\""
```

INTEGRATE WITH HOST DATA

You can collect information from backend systems with add-on products. You can collect this information as a batch process or you can use live data. ODBC is often required to perform the backend process of accessing enterprise data. OBDC can be used with DECS (Domino Enterprise Connection Services) or other third-party data integration tools (such as Replica Action) to gather data from systems outside the Lotus Notes environment.

DESIGN SECURE APPLICATIONS

You have many different options to securing Lotus Notes databases. The first line of defense is authentication. You can have a user authenticate a server with a Lotus Notes ID or via and ID and password. The second most common security method for applications is the use of Access Control Lists (ACLs). With the ACL, you can determine what users or groups have rights to the database you have constructed. You also have the ability to limit use of documents, sections of documents, agents, views, and more.

Secure Applications, User Authentication: Notes ID

To use Lotus Notes authentication, an ID must be created with the Registration process. The user ID will contain certificates and keys that will be checked as the user attempts to use a server. Because the ID is generated with certificate keys that are in common or because cross certification has been done, the ID can use the server. For more information on authentication with a Lotus Notes ID, please see Chapter 11.

Secure Applications, User Authentication: Web

You can force authentication for the Web with person records. To change the strength of Web authentication, you can simply change the security section of the server document. The field Web Server Authentication can be set to More Name Variations with Lower Security or Fewer Name Variations with More Security. If you intend to have hundreds of users authenticate with a user name and password that are not part of your company, you should strongly consider using a different directory to house the many person records that will be needed. Each person record need only contain a name and an Internet password to allow authentication. An example is shown in Figure 12.5.

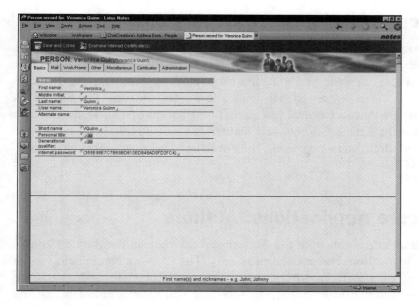

FIGURE 12.5

A sample of a person document with Web authentication.

If you do not want to use authentication, you can use the anonymous entry in the Access Control List. Anonymous access allows access to data on a Web site without being prompted for a user name and password. Anonymous access typically does not get higher than Reader access.

Secure Applications: ACLs for Replication

The Access Control List (ACL) is the most common cause of replication failure. As you specify entries in the ACL, you must be certain to include all users, groups, and servers that will need to access the file. The most common mistake is not including the servers in the ACL so that replication can occur. The server will need to be included either explicitly or within a group (usually the LocalDomainServers group). The server must have high enough rights to carry out changes you make. For example, if you want to make design changes and have a hub server distribute these changes to other servers, the hub must have at least Designer access.

Secure Applications: Consistent ACLs

Consistent Access Control Lists (ACLs) will enforce the ACL on the server as well as locally on a laptop. The Consistent Access Control List feature can be added to a database by selecting File, Database, Access Control. The Advanced tab will allow you to turn on Enforce a Consistent Access Control List Across All Replicas of This Database. The Consistent Access Control List feature can cause replication to fail if a user or administrator turns off the check box and then makes changes to the ACL.

Secure Applications: Authors

To grant edit rights with the Author security right in the Access Control List, an Authors Name field must exist. The Authors Name field can be created on a form anywhere and it typically will contain some variation of the formula @UserName. @UserName will capture the name of the user so that when the document is later accessed to be edited, that same user can change the document.

Secure Applications: Groups

Groups can be used in the Access Control List (ACL) to dynamically change rights for users. Groups can be accessed and created in the Domino Directory in the Groups view. You can also delegate the changing of the members of the group by placing a name in the administration field of the group. When you add or change members of the group, the server's cache must be refreshed before the change will take affect. Additionally, you might need to replicate with a hub server and run updall on the Domino Directory for the host server to recognize the change. If a user is in multiple groups, the highest access privilege will be the rights granted. If the user is listed explicitly, group access will be ignored for that user.

Secure Applications: Read Only Views

Views can be made so that only certain individuals will see the view in the View menu. To make a view available only to certain users, you can use the View Properties dialog box. The tab with the key allows you to specify what users are allowed to use the view. Although this can be used as security for most users, a user that has the Domino Designer client can create views that are the same.

Secure Applications: Readers Fields

You can deploy an application with Reader access to documents with three methods. You can select Reader Access with the Properties Dialog box for the Form. You can create a Reader Names field. You can create actions to mark documents private when needed. All these methods create a field that lists only the users or groups that can read the document. You can also use roles or the asterisk wild card to grant access.

Secure Applications: Roles

If you have a database that will require users to read or update certain views, documents, or parts of documents, Roles is a flexible way to grant access. You can create the role in the Access Control List from the Roles tab. After you have given the role a name (15 characters or fewer), you can then use the role in the corresponding access properties boxes. For instance, a form can be secured with a role by opening the Form Properties dialog box and choosing the tab with the key. The new role will appear among the people, servers, and groups listed. You can then select the role that you desire and save the form.

Secure Applications: Sections

Sections can be used to secure areas of a form or subform. To create the secured section, you can select the area you desire and then select Create, Section, Controlled Access. You can then select the person, group, or role to which you want to grant access. Users can discover who has rights to the section just by clicking the border of the section.

Secure Applications: Security Versus Deterrence

Many design features can hide elements from users but are really not security measures. You can hide a database from the File, Database, Open menu with the Properties dialog box. In the Design tab (a T-Square and a right triangle), you can select Show in Open Database Dialog. But a user can just type in the full name of the database and still open the file if the Access Control List is not set properly. You can hide a view from use if you use the Properties dialog box or use parenthesis. But, if a user has the Domino Designer client, he can create a view with the same structure. You cannot link a database on a Web site, but if a user knows what URL to type, he will get into a file that has a loosely configured Access Control List.

Secure Applications: Web Users

There are many actions you can take to secure Web applications. Using Web authentication will force the user to type in a name and password to gain access. Placing the Anonymous entry in the Access Control List with minimal or no rights will ensure that the application is secure. Disabling Allow HTTP Clients to Browse Databases will discourage users from finding databases on their own without a link. This field can be found on the server document in the Internet Protocols, HTTP section. You can change the strength of Web authentication on the server record in the security section. The field Web Server Authentication can be set to More Name Variations with Lower Security or Fewer Name Variations with More Security. You can use File Protection Documents to secure CGI scripts, servlets, and agents. For more information on File Protection Documents, please see the "Setting Up/Configuring File Security" section of Chapter 11.

WHAT IS IMPORTANT TO KNOW

- Be familiar with deploying applications that exist in multiple versions of Lotus Notes and Domino.
- Understand issues surrounding applications with formula language.
- Have general knowledge about JavaScript.
- Understand how Lotus Notes and Domino can work with Java.
- Have a good working knowledge of the LotusScript code.
- Understand how to create and use Actions in Lotus Notes applications.
- Know how to create and use fields on forms.
- Understand the difference between forms and subforms.
- Know where you can use graphics in a Lotus Notes or Web-based application.
- Understand how to create and use Object Linking and Embedding as part of an application.
- Be familiar with how to create sections with controlled access.
- Have general knowledge of shared and private database elements.
- Understand how users work with attachments in an application.
- Understand how to implement archiving.
- Have a good working knowledge of creating applications that use Author access.
- Know how to create Lotus Notes applications with Reader Names fields.
- Understand how to construct views with hierarchies.
- Know how to create applications that use HTML.
- Be familiar with how to create applications with host data.
- Have a good working knowledge of authentication with Lotus Notes.
- Understand how to provide authentication with a Web client.
- Be familiar with the caveats of replication and Access Control Lists.
- Know how to enforce Access Control List across all replicas.
- Understand caveats with providing access through groups.

- Know how to create views for specific users.
- Have a good working knowledge of how to implement and use roles for an application.
- Understand how to secure sections within a document.
- Be familiar with design methods that are truly deterrence and not security.
- Know how to secure Web-based applications.

CHAPTER 13

Domino Infrastructure

OBJECTIVES continued

▶ Deploy Server-Based Applications: Running Background Agents

▶ Deploy Server-Based Applications: Securing Agents

▶ Distribute Application Design Changes Based on Design

▶ Distribute Application Design Changes Based on Impact on ACL

▶ Distribute Application Design Changes

▶ Distribute Application Design Changes Based on Replication

▶ Secure Domino Applications Based on Notes Authentication

▶ Secure Domino Applications Based on Web Authentication

CAPACITY PLAN BASED ON APPLICATION SIZE

Before deploying an application, you should have a good understanding of the audience for which it is intended and how large you think the file(s) will be. If there will be users who have laptops and the file could potentially become very large quickly, you should consider some options that will reduce the size of the application when it is replicated (either to other servers or laptops):

- **Reader access fields.** A Reader access field allows only users or groups that are listed to view a document. This security feature is explained in more detail in Chapter 11, "Setting Up/Configuring Domino Infrastructure Security."

- **Replication based on age of the document.** In the Replication Settings menu, you can specify a number of days for the age of a document. Only documents that are fewer than the days you specify will replicate.

- **Selective replication formulas.** You can use a formula to decipher what records will replicate to an individual. Selective replication formulas can require a good deal more maintenance and are not a true security measure. If a user removes a selective replication formula, he or she will replicate the entire database. An example of the Replication Settings dialog box is shown in Figure 13.1.

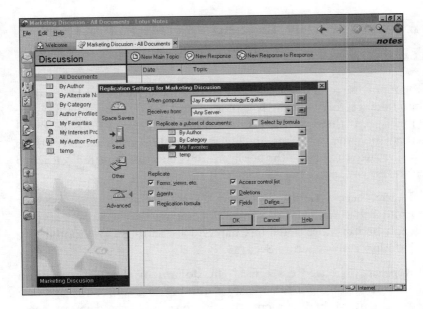

FIGURE 13.1
An example of the Replication Settings dialog box.

CAPACITY PLAN BASED ON INDEXES

Before you deploy an application, you should consider optimizing performance for the database and the server by adjusting the Indexing properties for views. You can change the Indexing properties for each view by selecting the view and choosing Edit, Properties. As shown in Figure 13.2, the tab with the "beanie" (looks like a hat with a propeller) will allow you to adjust the index settings for the view. You have the following options for view indexes:

- **Refresh Index.** You can select how frequently the view will update. You have the following options:
  - *Auto, After First Use.* This option allows you to index the view only after it is used once. Only creating views as they are used conserves disk space and requires less work for the server. This is also the default.

- *Automatic.* Regardless of whether the view is used or not, the index will be created and updated. This option can take up more resources on the server.

- *Manual.* Updates will occur only if the user requests them. The user can request an update if he or she presses F9 or selects View, Refresh.

- *Auto, at Most Every.* You can specify how often (in hours) a view should be updated.

- **Discard Index.** You can determine how often a view index will be deleted before making a new one. Your options are Never, After Each Use, or If Inactive For. The default is Never, but If Inactive For certainly has its advantages. If users are not using a view for perhaps 90 days, why take up server resources and disk space?

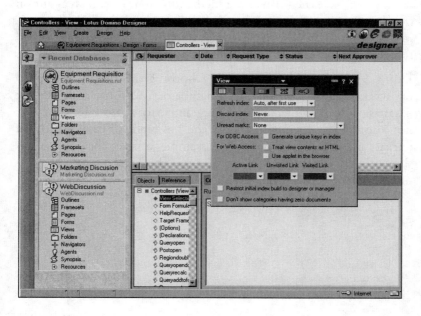

FIGURE 13.2

Index Settings tab of the View Properties dialog box.

CAPACITY PLAN BASED ON PERFORMANCE

You can enhance the performance of a database in many ways. The options that can be changed in the Database Properties dialog box (see Figure 13.3) follow. Please note some of the options are changed in the Basics tab, which is not shown.

- **Display Images After Loading.** This feature will force the text to appear before graphics. This allows the user to focus on the content of the document.

- **Allow Use of Stored Form in This Database.** This option should not be enabled unless the application requires it. If you save each document with the form, it will make the database larger. It will also be more difficult to make changes to the form because the documents have the form embedded and you must run an agent on the documents to remove the field that contains the link. The primary reason to enable this feature is to allow the form to be routed to other databases (such as a mail file).

- **Don't Maintain Unread Marks.** Choosing this option will speed up access and performance of a database. You must compact the database before you will see a change in performance. The user will not know what documents he or she has read, so only use this if unread marks are not needed. A sample of the "beanie" tab is shown in Figure 13.4. You can also use the L Compact –U command to enable this property.

FIGURE 13.3
The Design tab of the Database Properties dialog box.

FIGURE 13.4
The "beanie" tab in the Database Properties dialog box.

- ◆ **Document Table Bitmap Optimization.** Associates tables with the forms used by the documents appearing in the view. This option can significantly improve view performance (especially small views in large databases).

- ◆ **Don't Overwrite Free Space.** As a security measure, all data is overwritten after it is deleted. In the case of a database that is secure or when the data is not sensitive, this feature can be enabled. Enabling the feature will increase the performance of the database.

- ◆ **Maintain LastAccessed Property.** If it is not necessary to capture who last read a document, you can enable this option. Enabling this option will increase database performance.

- ◆ **Don't Allow Headline Monitoring.** Users can be notified of new documents to a database by using the headline monitoring feature. If the application does not warrant headline monitoring, this option can be enabled to increase database performance.

- ◆ **Limit Entries in $UpdatedBy Fields.** Each document in a database will track the last person who edited a document in the $UpdatedBy field. By limiting the number of entries to this field, you can increase the database performance.

- ◆ **Limit Entries in $Revisions Fields.** $Revisions fields are used to track changes to fields in a database. This data can be used to prevent replication conflicts by merging documents that have been updated in different places. Limiting this field to 10 entries can increase performance of the database.

CAPACITY PLAN BASED ON SERVER SIZE

There are tools to determine planning for servers. These tools will help you better understand the performance you should expect with a typical user. These tools are as follows:

- **Domino Server.Load.** Using a script, you can simulate users that will be attached to the server. You can evaluate the performance of the server and better determine the need for CPU, RAM, and disk space.

- **Domino Server.Planner.** Using vendor benchmarking information, you can determine the type of machine you will need for the capacity you have predicted.

- **NotesBench.** NotesBench is available to vendors to test client and servers as they connect to other servers. To acquire the tool and present results, each vendor must be a part of the NotesBench consortium (a non-profit organization that provides performance information for Lotus customers).

CAPACITY PLAN BASED ON SORTING, CATEGORIZING

If you can create views that allow sorting and categorizing, you may be able to eliminate the need for Full-Text Search Indexing. You may not gain much performance with multiple views compared to not using Full-Text Search Indexing, but you will certainly make life easier for the end user. In the case of formulas like @DBColumn, sorting the information may be preferred. To create views that have sorting or categorizing, you need only to change the properties for the column. Notice in Figure 13.5, you must sort to be able to categorize.

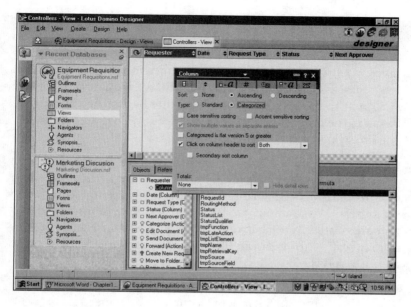

FIGURE 13.5
A sample of the Properties dialog box for a column.

DEPLOY APPLICATIONS BASED ON ACCESS

You have many choices for securing applications that you deploy. You can determine what rights users will have to the database, views, documents, sections, agents, and more. Security to the application is hopefully determined before an application is distributed. After you have established what data is sensitive and how sensitive it is, you can then implement the security that meets the need of the users. The different levels of security and how to implement them are reviewed in Chapter 11.

DEPLOY APPLICATIONS BASED ON CONNECTIVITY

How users connect to the servers can have a significant impact on the design of an application. Especially if you will have any remote users, you must consider the point of view of the end user as you construct an application. You should determine how much (all documents or a subset of documents) will be replicated on servers and workstations. You must also determine how users will act on documents that they receive. For instance, you may need an automated notification to alert a user that there are documents waiting for approval (such as a requisition). If there are doclinks sent to the user, the user must either be attached at the time he or she clicks the link or the database will need to be replicated locally before the link will work.

If the application is large, it may be inefficient for a user or server to receive all the data in the application. Reader Names fields or selective replication formulas may be necessary to reduce the amount of traffic to servers and users. For example, a salesperson may only want new documents that are related to the banking industry. A Reader Names field or a selective replication formula can filter only the accounts for which the salesperson is responsible or documents that relate to banking.

If the user will receive the document by forwarding, the form will either need to be stored with the document or the form will need to be available in the user's mail file. Please see the section in this chapter "Receiving Routed Documents."

DEPLOY APPLICATIONS BASED ON REPLICATION FUNDAMENTALS

There are many factors that can affect replication; understanding these factors can help you build better applications and make it easier to troubleshoot problems with applications. The most common issue with replication is the Access Control List. Please see the later section "Deploy Based on Impact of Replication on ACLs." Two other security features that can affect replication are Reader Names and Author Names fields. Reader Names and Author Names fields limit who has rights to read or change a document, respectively. The replication settings can also affect replication of an application. The replication settings of a database can disable replication of a database altogether, or you can create formulas that limit what a client or server receives.

DEPLOY APPLICATIONS BASED ON ROUTING FUNDAMENTALS

Documents can be sent from one database (including mail files) to another using mail routing. How the document will be sent and received can affect how you design an application. The next two sections outline how you can implement an application that will send or receive routed documents.

Sending Routed Documents

You can send routed documents from a database to another database or to a mail file. You can accomplish this task by using a SendTo field on the form and providing a "send" button or just by using the Actions, Forward menu. In either case, mail routing must be enabled on the server that is sending the mail and there must be a logical path for the router to follow. Servers must either have the same Domino Named Network in common or there must be a connection record that will provide a direction for the routing. If one or the other is not present, the mail will stay in the Mail.Box of the originating server.

If you intend to send documents to another database, some extra steps will be needed. Just like with a mail file, a form must be present to view the documents. Additionally, you will need to create a Mail-In database record. Much like a person record, the record provides the needed direction for the mail router. You must first give the record a name. This name will be used by the agent to send mail and will be used by the router just like a person's name on a person record. You will then specify the server, domain, and path in which the file resides.

Receiving Routed Documents

When needed, you can route documents for applications just like email. You can route documents either to other applications or to mail files for individuals. In either case, for the form to be read the same in the originated application, you must be sure to include the form in the database or use the Store Form in Document option in the form design.

Otherwise, you will get the error Cannot Locate Form: *Form Name*. If available, the default form will be used. In most cases, the data will not correspond to the fields on the default form and the end user will be quite confused.

DEPLOY BASED ON IMPACT OF REPLICATION ON ACLS

The Access Control List (ACL) plays a significant role with Replication. How often and which servers will replicate is very important as you determine how the ACL should be set up. The issue gets more complex when the application is replicated outside of the company. This is because another company will not be using the same Directory and it will therefore not have the same group names and members. This may mean the only option is to include every individual in the ACL that will use the application.

DEPLOY BASED ON IMPACT OF ROUTING ON REMOTES USERS

Remote users can have a myriad of issues that should be resolved before deploying an application. Unfortunately, they are very often forgotten until the phone starts to ring. If an application requires links to be sent via mail, the user must either understand he or she must be connected to servers or have a replica copy of the database. Links can be a very challenging concept for remote users. The user must either understand that he or she needs to remain connected to the server to use a link or he or she must wait until the particular database has replicated before the link will function. If you design the application to use a timed agent, you can delay the mail so that hopefully the user will have replicated before receiving the link in an email message.

> **NOTE**
> Although documents containing links can be accessed from both server and local replica based copies of a database, if the target database of the link cannot be found, Notes will produce a run-time error. Consequently, to avoid these run-time errors when working offline, it is imperative that there be a local copy of the target database.

Users who receive the document must also have the form either included with the Store Form in Document setting or have the form within their mail file. The Store Form in Document setting can be added to a form's property in the first Basics tab. The Form Properties dialog box is shown in Figure 13.6.

FIGURE 13.6
The Form Properties dialog box.

DEPLOY BASED ON LICENSE TYPES

There are license types that have a limited set of databases that can be used. There are no limitations for using databases with the Lotus Notes, Lotus Notes Designer, or Lotus Notes Administrator license types. The Lotus Notes Mail and the Desktop license types are limited to only certain databases. The Lotus Notes Mail license type can use a mail file and the databases created with the basic set of Lotus Notes templates. The Lotus Notes Desktop license type can use all Lotus Notes databases, but cannot use any design or administration features.

DEPLOY BASED ON SERVER'S INVOLVEMENT IN REPLICATION

How often replication occurs between servers can be a concern for an application. If users expect to see data or changes to data in different parts of the world, you may need to construct replication schemes that will accommodate an aggressive replication schedule. In a hub and spoke topology, you will need to consider all the servers involved and where the bulk of changes will occur. For company-wide databases, it is best to make ACL changes only on the hub. If you have servers devoted to hosting applications, you will likely want to replicate much more often than you would a mail server. If the data will also appear with a browser, you should also be sure to replicate with servers that host HTTP (if they are separate machines). To automate replication between servers, you can simply create connection records. The connection records specify the action that will be triggered (replication, mail routing, or both) and what time and frequency are desired. An example of a connection record is shown in Figure 13.7.

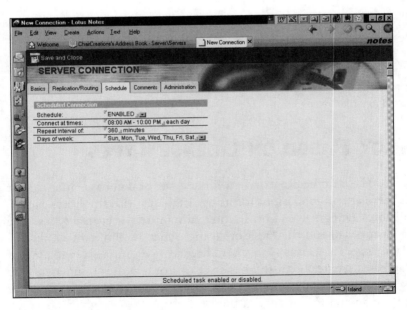

FIGURE 13.7
An example of a connection record.

DEPLOY FOR WEB INTEGRATION

Applications that are built for Web users often use different coding, such as HTML and Java. HTML can be used on fields, forms, pages, and many other areas of a database. Java can be used in agents or incorporated in Java applets to be used in forms and pages. You will also need to be sure the server is running the HTTP protocol and the HTTP server section should be configured for the server. If you intend to use Java applications, you will also need to run and configure the DIIOP task on the server.

You can specify launch properties for a database for both a client and a Web browser. You can allow the Web browser to launch the same options or set one of the following options:

- Open "About Database" Document
- Open Designated Frameset
- Open Designated Page
- Open Designated Navigator in Its Own Window
- Launch First Doclink in the "About Database"
- Launch Designated Doclink
- Launch First Document in View

The launch options can be found in the Properties dialog box for the database. The tab with the rocket ship allows you to configure the settings for a Lotus Notes client or a Web browser.

DEPLOY SERVER-BASED APPLICATIONS

Applications that reside on servers are very common because sharing information is key to almost every application. In some cases, an application may reside on only one server and may not replicate to any other servers or clients. Some applications may be Web enabled and use HTML or Java so that the application will work better with Web browsers. Some applications may use agents and it may be necessary to limit the use of the agent. At times you may also want to change elements in the design of a database. Each of these server-based application issues are discussed in the following sections.

Deploy Server-Based Applications: HTML

Applications that are designed for Web browsers may take advantage of the HTML code. HTML can be used on forms, fields, pages, and many other areas of a database. To use applications with a browser, you must be running the HTTP server protocol. As shown in Figure 13.8, The HTTP protocol can be further configured in the Internet Protocols section of a server document. For more information on the HTTP protocol, please see Chapter 7, "Installation."

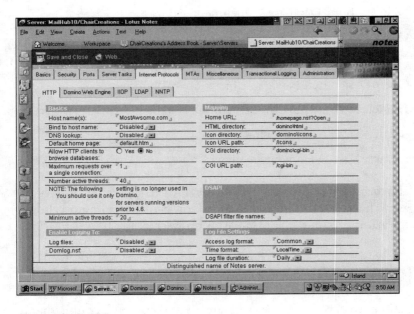

FIGURE 13.8
The HTTP section of a server document.

Deploy Server-Based Applications: Running Background Agents

Applications may require background agents that change documents, mail documents—or links—archive data, and much more. Agents can take up resources, and the more you have running the more performance problems you may encounter. If you can run agents during off-peak hours and limit the number that run at the same time, you can gain some performance back. The Agent Manager (AMGR) task can be further configured on the server record as shown in Figure 13.9.

Notice that you can change the time agents will run, limit the number of concurrent agents and specify a maximum time out. You can also limit who can run agents on the server within the security section of the server document.

It may be desirable to save the agent with the server's ID. This will allow you to send any documents with the server's name instead of a user and it will also prevent problems with access when running the agent even if the developer leaves the company.

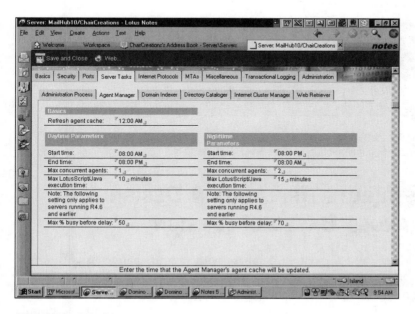

FIGURE 13.9
The Agent Manager section of a server document.

Deploy Server-Based Applications: Securing Agents

Agents should be limited in use because they can be damaging and they take up server resources. The use of agents can be restricted within the configuration of the Security section of the server document. You can restrict Lotus Notes agents as well as Java agents. An example is shown in Figure 13.10.

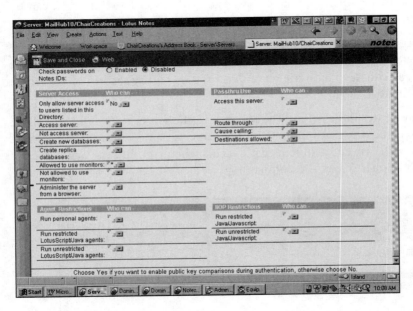

FIGURE 13.10
The Agent Security section of the server document.

DISTRIBUTE APPLICATION DESIGN CHANGES BASED ON DESIGN

The ideal way to update a database with design changes is with a template. If an application has been used for a long time, it is best to test the design changes you will be implementing. You may also want to test the changes with a pilot group to be sure you will not disrupt the population that is using the application. After you have tested the changes you will be making, you can then allow the production database to be updated with a template.

If the application has been developed by an outside firm, it is advisable that you sign the elements of the database. Signing the design elements of a database will prevent problems running agents since an outsider should not be allowed to run agents on a server. It will also eliminate the problem with cross-certification messages that appear as users open the database. The Execution Control List (ECL) on a client should be set to allow only certain privileges to other users in your organization. If the design elements are signed, the users will not encounter an error when they use the file. You can sign a database by launching the Domino Administration software. From the Files tab, you can expand the Database option under the Tools menu. You can then select the file you want to sign and simply click Sign. The file currently in use will sign the elements of the database that you specify. An example of signing a database is shown in Figure 13.11.

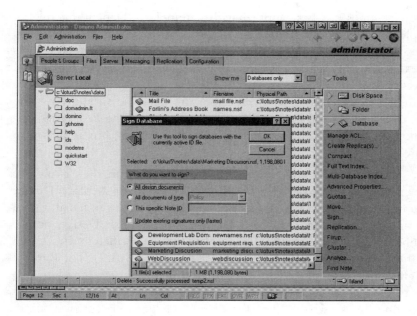

FIGURE 13.11

An example of signing a database.

DISTRIBUTE APPLICATION DESIGN CHANGES BASED ON IMPACT ON ACL

For servers to replicate design changes to other servers, the Access Control List (ACL) must be set appropriately. If you have a hub and spoke topology, it may be adequate to list only the hubs in the ACL. All servers that replicate the changes will need Designer or higher access to the database. When a server replicates with another, it is as if the designer is actually making design changes when the file replicates. If the server has only Editor or lower access to the database, an error will be noted in the log file and the design elements will not be added or changed.

DISTRIBUTE APPLICATION DESIGN CHANGES

Design changes are best applied with a template. Depending on the complexity and number of users an application has, it may be best to also do testing with the changes you intend to apply. A template typically has the extension .NTF and is placed in the data directory of the server. However, you can also simply specify that the database is a template and use the .NSF extension. In either case, the database should have the name of the file in the Design Inheritance option of the Properties dialog box. An example of the Database Property dialog box is shown in Figure 13.12.

After you have made and tested the changes, you can then apply the changes to the database with the Refresh Design or Replace Design options. You can force the design changes by selecting the file and then choosing File, Database, Refresh Design. The Refresh Design option will update the database using the template that is specified in the Design tab of the Properties of the database (refer to Figure 13.9). The Replace Design option will allow you to specify which database template you want to use regardless of what is specified in the properties of the database. You can also simply allow the design changes to occur over night. Each night the server will run the Design server task at 1 a.m. This task will update all databases that have a template associated with them. If the database is on multiple servers, the design changes then need to be replicated and the servers must have enough rights to carry out the changes.

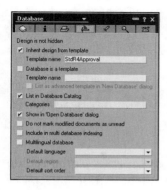

FIGURE 13.12
The Design tab of the Database Properties dialog box.

DISTRIBUTE APPLICATION DESIGN CHANGES BASED ON REPLICATION

After the design changes have been applied to a database, they can be distributed in the company by replication. Replication can either occur when forced with client software or with a server command, such as the following:

```
Rep NotesHub12 Finance\Purchases.nsf
```

The most common method of periodic replication is by scheduling the replication to occur with connection records. A connection record can be created within the Domino Directory. A schedule can be established that will trigger the server to replicate with another at the times and frequency specified. It is also important to have the ACL set correctly so that the design changes can be distributed from one server to another.

SECURE DOMINO APPLICATIONS BASED ON NOTES AUTHENTICATION

Applications that reside on a Domino server and that will be used by Lotus Notes clients will use Notes authentication to access the file. Notes authentication occurs when a user or server presents an ID to the server. It involves verifying the public and private key sets of both the server and client. Notes authentication is covered in more detail in Chapter 11.

SECURE DOMINO APPLICATIONS BASED ON WEB AUTHENTICATION

Users can authenticate with a server via a Web browser. To be certain that authentication is used, the Access Control List must be set low enough to require authentication. Ideally, the Default and Anonymous Access should be set to No Access. This will require the user to verify a name and password before proceeding. The password for the user is kept in the person record for the individual. The user can use his or her short name, full name, or fully distinguished name unless otherwise specified in the server record.

You can also use Secure Sockets Layer (SSL) encryption to secure more sensitive data. SSL encryption uses public and private keys for users and servers to encrypt data during transfer. Data is encrypted with a unique key generated by a client based on an algorithm derived from a public and private key-pair. A new secret key is created for each session.

WHAT IS IMPORTANT TO KNOW

The following list of items will help you better prepare for the exam:

- Understand how to reduce an application that may grow large quickly.
- Be familiar with how to implement replication formulas.
- Understand Reader Names and Author Names fields.
- Know how to improve performance with views and indexing.
- Be familiar with tools that can help you predict performance for servers.
- Know how to plan servers based on the type of applications that will be hosted.
- Understand how to construct views with sorting and categorizing.
- Know how to implement a secured application.
- Be familiar with how to accommodate users that are remotely connected.
- Understand replication fundamentals.
- Know how to automate replication between servers.
- Be familiar with routing documents to and from applications and mail files.
- Understand how the Access Control List can affect replication.
- Know the issues that may impact remote users that receive routed documents.
- Be familiar with the different Lotus Notes client license types and how application deployment may be affected.
- Understand how to deploy applications intended for Web browsers.
- Know the issues involved with server-based applications.
- Be familiar with applications that use HTML and Java code.
- Understand applications that use background agents.
- Know how to limit the use of agents.
- Be familiar with how to distribute application design changes.
- Understand how the Access Control List can affect replication of design changes.
- Know how to distribute application design changes and additions with replication.
- Be familiar with securing an application with Lotus Notes authentication.
- Understand how to secure applications with Web authentication.

INSIDE EXAMS 520, 521, 522

Part II of this book is designed to round out your exam preparation by providing you with chapters that do the following:

- "Insider's Spin." Drawing upon the author's own experiences with no fewer than ten Lotus certification exams, this chapter will provide you with some additional insights into the exam process that may help better prepare you for what lies ahead.

- "Sample Test Questions." These chapters provide practice exams that test you on the actual material covered in Part I.

By the time you reach this point of the book you have no doubt have put in many long hours of study preparing to "write" one or all of the exams leading to Lotus professional certification for Domino R5. Although a sound working knowledge of the product may be enough to ensure you achieve your certification goals, a deeper understanding of the entire exam process is most certainly something from which all CLP candidates can benefit. Drawing upon the author's own experiences with no fewer than ten Lotus certification exams, this chapter will provide you with some additional insights into the exam process that may help better prepare you for what lies ahead.

CHAPTER 14

Insider's Spin

At a Glance: Exam Information

Exam Number:	520
Minutes Allowed:	60
Single-Answer Questions:	No
Multiple Answer with Correct Number Given:	Yes
Multiple Answer Without Correct Number Given:	No
Choices of A–D	Yes
Choices of A–E	No
Scenario-Based Questions:	Yes
Objective Categories:	Yes

Exam 520, "Maintaining Domino R5 Servers and Users" is a computer-administered exam. The exam is designed to measure your ability to monitor, maintain, and troubleshoot the following Domino components: applications, directories, users, groups, messaging, replication, and, finally, systems.

At a Glance: Exam Information

Exam Number:	521
Minutes Allowed:	60
Single-Answer Questions:	No
Multiple Answer with Correct Number Given:	Yes
Multiple Answer Without Correct Number Given:	No
Choices of A–D	Yes
Choices of A–E	No
Scenario-Based Questions:	Yes
Objective Categories:	Yes

Exam 521, "Implementing a Domino R5 Infrastructure" is a computer-administered exam. This exam will measure a candidate's ability to perform the following Domino-oriented tasks: install Domino Server and Workstation software, create and register system resources, set up and configure database resources, set up and configure distribution and monitoring tools, and set up and configure security in a Domino infra-structure.

At a Glance: Exam Information

Exam Number:	522
Minutes Allowed:	60
Single-Answer Questions:	No
Multiple Answer with Correct Number Given:	Yes
Multiple Answer Without Correct Number Given:	No
Choices of A–D	Yes
Choices of A–E	No
Scenario-Based Questions:	Yes
Objective Categories:	Yes

Exam 522, "Deploying Domino R5 Applications" is a computer-administered exam. This exam will assess your ability to deploy Domino R5 Applications as it relates to the following competencies: database architecture and Domino infrastructure.

Each of the three exams consists solely of computer-administered multiple-choice questions. Passing scores will vary over time based on a sampling of the scores taken at a particular point in time, but at press time Exams 520 and 522 required a passing score of 70% and Exam 521 required a passing score of 72%. Although you will encounter 45 questions on Exam 522, only 40 of the 45 questions will be used for the purposes of calculating the final exam score. Unfortunately, you will not know which five questions are being excluded from the final exam score calculation, so it is in your best interest to answer all 45 questions. The remaining exams each contain 40 questions.

Statistics alone indicate that not all individuals who "write" the certification exams will pass. Included among those individuals who fail to achieve a passing grade are administrators who work with the product on a regular basis. Is this then a reflection of their product knowledge? In some cases, perhaps; however, poor exam results can also be attributed to a host of other mitigating factors. Included among this list of factors are the following:

1. Individuals are only familiar with a certain subset of the tasks contained within the Domino environment and are not, perhaps, exposed to the full range of functions that will be tested.

2. The real-world experiences with Domino may not necessarily mirror Lotus' perspective on the product.

3. Individuals are working with a version of the software that offers a range of new functionality that was not available when the exam questions were being developed.

4. Individuals may not be accustomed to the exam format, volume of questions, and time constraints imposed upon them during the exam.

5. Individuals fail to make use of the vast array of resources that are available to better prepare them for the exam.

Although this chapter is principally aimed at assisting those of you who are new to the Lotus examination experience surmount these aforementioned hurdles, veteran test takers may still glean some insightful tips to help them attain higher testing scores. If you have already been exposed to the Lotus testing process, however, and are comfortable with the format and materials that will confront you on the exams, please skip this chapter and move on. Otherwise, continue reading and use the discussion that follows to your advantage.

PREPARING FOR THE EXAM CONTENT: BEING AS PREPARED AS POSSIBLE

To begin, based on this author's experiences with Lotus certification exams it is safe to state that they are a fair test of your knowledge about the product. Rarely, if ever, has this author encountered a Lotus certification exam that posed questions seemingly pulled in from "left field." The same can be said of the exams that are covered in this publication. Provided that you have worked your way through the competency listing which appears in either the R5 Exam Guide or at the beginning of each section of this text, you should not find yourself surprised by any of the topics on the exam.

To be sure, the information provided in the preceding 13 chapters will go a long way toward helping you gain a more complete understanding of how the Domino environment is set up, configured, supported and maintained. Nevertheless, it is still imperative that you reinforce the material covered in this text with actual hands-on experience before dolling out the examination fees. Otherwise, you may simply be wasting your valuable money.

To test the functionality of Domino, you will ideally have access to a series of three networked computers—two of the machines should be loaded with server software and the other should be configured with client software. This configuration will allow you to test many of the features that require more than one Domino server, replication and messaging being two such examples. If for any reason you do not have access to such resources, however, you can certainly configure a single machine with both Domino Server and Workstation software and then, based on the templates that are included in Domino, create a series of database files that are referenced throughout this guide. You will then want to access these local database files and familiarize yourself with the various forms, views, actions, and so on, contained therein. At least this way you will develop a high level of comfort with where you need to be from an interface point of view when changes to the Domino environment need to be made.

PREPARING FOR EXAM CONTENT: THE LOUTS VANTAGE POINT

Certainly many of you will bring to the exam volumes of valuable Domino work-related experience. However, unless you are comfortable with *all* the competencies that will be measured on the exam, do not let the fact that you work with Domino lull you into a false sense of knowledge. Although there can be no denying the fact that your familiarity with the product will be a definite asset at exam time, it must be stated that simply because your job description does not entail working with a subset of features in the product does not mean you have license to ignore them. Lotus' viewpoint is that as a CLP you should be able to walk into any Domino environment and be entirely familiar with the full range of functionality that R5 offers.

In a similar vein, do not let your work-related experience with Domino mask the solution that Lotus is really looking for. For example, your on-the-job experience might lead you to the conclusion that it would be less painful to give birth to a flaming porcupine on the floor of an igloo than it would be to run a Windows NT-based Domino Mail server with the minimum recommended configuration of 96MB of RAM. In spite of the potential merit of your argument, if asked for the minimum RAM configuration required to run a Domino Mail server on Windows NT, the correct answer from Lotus' perspective would in fact be 96MB.

THE TIMEFRAME OF THE EXAM

All three of the exams that are required for your CLP designation have "gone gold." Unlike record sales, this does not mean that there have been one million sales of the exam. Rather, the term *gold* is an indication that the exam has emerged from an evolutionary process to become what the vendor considers to be a fair skills assessment tool. For many vendors, the process involves the following twists and turns:

1. The product undergoes a series of beta releases.

2. Beta testers put each release of the product through rigorous testing to assess its functionality and to offer feedback concerning possible enhancements.

3. The product is "shipped" in its final beta format.

4. In addition to working closely with the vendors, exam writers assess the feedback offered by beta testers to establish objectives for the exam and attach importance to the roles of the various elements within the product—this is why some exams may seem to contain a disproportionate number of questions on one specific facet of a product.

5. The product is released in its gold format.

6. Beta exams are made available for a short period of time and based upon a survey of preliminary exam results, the final battery of questions are then selected.

7. The exam is released in its gold format.

From your vantage point, the preceding process carries with it both good and bad news. Among the positive benefits of sitting the gold exams is the fact that they are shorter in terms of both the number of questions and duration. In their beta format, exams generally contain at least twice the number of questions and require twice as much time to "write." Although some of the questions on these exams would prove to be far less difficult to answer than those on a gold version, it is also not surprising to find an equal number of questions which are at the other end of the difficulty spectrum as well. Consequently, beta exams give Lotus the opportunity to weed out a certain number of these types of questions before pressing ahead with the final battery of questions. In the end, this should mean that the exams will not prove to be overly difficult, but do not assume that they will be overly simplistic either.

The downside of this process, however, is that the questions may not accurately reflect the release of the software that you have employed for your preparation. With each subsequent release of Domino, new functionality is added to the product, as are new "features" or "bugs," and patches to address existing "bugs." Although the enhancements may have introduced new components to the interface, the latter items may have forced you to seek short-term workaround solutions to get the product to perform the way in which it was designed. The biggest concern here is obviously becoming confused by some of the questions that address facets of the product you know do not function as designed or which you commonly configure through an enhanced interface component other than that which is described in an exam question. Although rare, if confronted with this problem remember to consider what Lotus really wants to hear.

FAMILIARIZE YOURSELF WITH ALL AVAILABLE RESOURCES

Too often when preparing for an exam, individuals do not make use of all the preparation materials that are available to them. You have certainly made a good choice in picking up a copy of this book, but there are also a host of other resources that you can use to help prepare yourself.

Practice tests, such as the set included in this book, offer you an excellent opportunity to not only gauge what areas require more study, but they also provide you with an opportunity to familiarize yourself with the exam format. If you want to obtain additional batteries of sample exam questions, log on to www.selftestsoftware.com. For $70 (U.S.) you can order additional exam questions that you can perform in a simulated test environment.

You may also want to consult the Lotus Notes Knowledge Database to pull up some of the technotes concerning the "under the hood" descriptions of how various facets of the product work. The online version of this database can be found at www.lotus.com/support. Similarly, www.notes.net is the defining source for Domino and contains a series of online articles about all components of the software. In fact, these articles are actually written by the folks who write the source code for Domino!

Another site that is particularly useful is www.lotus.com/rw/devchat.nsf. This online forum offers you the opportunity to post a variety of different questions about the product. Use this site as your online tutor for those areas of Domino that you still may find a little unclear.

BOOKING AND SITTING THE EXAM

When you are finally feeling brave enough to take the plunge, you will need to schedule the exam date and time. There are a couple of ways that you can go about booking your exam. The first option is to call 1-800-GOLOTUS. Make sure that before you dial the number, however, you have your Social Security Number or Social Insurance Number (in the case of our Canadian readers) handy along with a major credit card. The exams are roughly $90.00 (U.S.) or $140.00 (CDN) each.

You can also schedule your exams online. Just go to www.lotus.com/ certification and select the link labeled exam registration. If this is the first time that you have used the online scheduling site, you will be forced to register your personal information. After you do manage to log in, however, you will be able to select the exam number, the date and time and the location where you want to be tested. After again, you will need a major credit card, but because this is a secure Web site, you should have few reservations about offering your credit card number over the wire. As a final note, if you do decide to make use of this method, please make sure that your connection to the Internet is using at the very least a 56K modem. As this site will require the downloading and usage of a reasonably large java applet, slow connections speeds may make registration physically impossible.

A day or so before the exam, call the testing center to confirm your exam time and exam number. On exam day, it is a good idea to arrive at the testing center at least 15 minutes prior to the exam start time. At "check in," be prepared to offer two pieces of identification, one of which must be picture ID. As you cannot bring any coats, bags, and so on, into the examination room, it is also a good idea to leave any bulky personal items at home or at the office.

At the appropriate time, you will be escorted into the testing room and seated at a computer. You will then be asked to enter your name and identification number (your SIN, Social Security, or Sylvan Prometric Testing number) for the test to begin. After you click the start test button the 60-minute clock begins to tick. You can monitor the time remaining on the exam by referencing the clock in the upper-right corner of the examination window.

Given the fact that you are likely to be a little nervous at the start of the exam, this author has always found it valuable to look through the first five questions on the exam to help calm the nerves. Nothing can bring on an anxiety attack like looking at the first question only to discover that you don't know the solution. As long as you are not totally unprepared for the exam, there will no doubt be at least a few questions in your initial survey that you know the solutions to. By getting these questions answered correctly you will find your confidence grow and you will then at least be able to return to the others with a clearer head.

Through a series of buttons at the bottom of the computer window, the exam interface provides you the opportunity to undertake the following actions:

1. Move forward to subsequent questions.

2. Go back to previous questions.

3. Flag questions that you want to return to at a later point in the exam.

4. Preview all questions that you have flagged in #3.

5. End the exam.

Getting Inside the Questions

For those questions that you have flagged for later review, make certain that you have selected at least one of the possible solutions provided before moving on. Given the fact that blank questions are graded as incorrect, if you run out of time on the exam, at least you have a 25% chance of getting those questions answered correctly.

Four potential solutions will be provided for each question and these solutions will be presented to you in an A, B, C, and D radio button-based format. Without getting into the specific details associated with the questions on each of the exams, you will find that they are likely to fall into one of the following generic formats:

1. If an administrator needed to perform/undertake a specific task in Domino, in what location within the interface would an administrator need to be, or why would it be done, and/or what would be entered?

2. Using Lotus-based terminology, identify the solution that best describes a particular component/task in the product.

3. What are the limits (numeric in most cases) associated with the various configuration options?

4. What could be said about the functionality of –*put component here*– in the Domino environment?

5. Administrator A did the following; what is the outcome, or it is not working—what did he do wrong?

When you are confident that all the questions have been answered correctly, select the End Exam button. Within a few seconds the results of the exam will appear on the screen before you and you will know right then if you have passed or failed. You will then quietly make your way out of the exam room so that you can pick up the section analysis and, provided you have passed, a certificate attesting to your success. The exam results should automatically be received by Lotus, but do not lose your "pass certificate," as it is the only physical proof that you passed the exam.

Should you not pass the exam, take solace in the fact that you can write it again. Use this experience as an opportunity to better prepare yourself for next time. After you leave the testing center, make some notes concerning what types of questions were asked. Try rebooking the exam again within a couple of weeks so that the material you have studied, not to mention some of the exam questions, are still fresh in your mind. As well, make use of the section analysis to determine which areas on the exam presented you with the greatest difficulty. However, be forewarned that just because you scored 100% on a particular competency area, this does not mean that you should ignore these topics while preparing for the your next stab at the exam. It may very well be that among the exam questions that you encountered in your initial sitting there was only one question on that particular topic and you happened to guess the answer correctly.

A FEW LAST THOUGHTS

For many individuals, the exam process proves to be a grueling ordeal. However, although it may be impossible to alleviate all the stress leading up to the exam, there are a few things you can do to help make you feel a little more relaxed in the time leading up to the exam.

First, do not leave your preparation to the last minute. Although you cannot fail an exam if you do not show up to write it, if you continually "blow off" the exams that you have scheduled (Sylvan requires 48 hours' notice to cancel an exam without the charges being incurred by you) it may take its toll on your bottom line. There is simply too much information for you to cover in the span of a couple of hours the night before the exam.

Second, if possible, study during times of the day when you are least tired. Certainly there have been times where, although very tired, you have been forced to read some text only to find yourself thinking "what was it I just read?". You need to be sharp to absorb the materials that are covered in this book.

Make yourself some study notes. Not only will you find these to be helpful tools for review purposes, but they will also help reinforce the material you have recovered. In fact, statistics have revealed that whereas we remember roughly 20% of what we hear and 40% of what we see, we can recall upward of 60% of what we write. Use these statistics to your advantage.

Finally, it is also a good idea to get a good night's sleep on the night before the exam. Although you may physically be capable of pulling an "all-nighter" to study for the exam, you will not mentally be as sharp as you can be if you are feeling sleep deprived.

Good Luck!

This is an exam preparation book. It's the belief of the author and publisher that it's difficult to get too much practice with sample exam questions. There are other study materials available—books and software—that enable you to practice extensively, and we recommend that you give strong consideration to using these in some form.

What follows in the next three chapters are practice tests designed to reflect the questions you'd likely be challenged with on the actual CLP exams. These questions tie in directly to the material covered in this book.

Sample Test Questions: Exam 520

QUESTIONS

1. *Fred would like to move a database through the Domino Administrator. What level of access must Fred have in the Server document on the destination server?*
   A. Reader access
   B. Create Database access
   C. Manager
   D. Manager with Delete Database access

2. *What tool allows you to delete a replica database in a cluster?*
   A. Cluster tool
   B. Pending delete command
   C. Domino Administrator
   D. Manual deletion

3. *How often should replication be monitored?*
   A. Monthly
   B. Weekly
   C. Daily
   D. Hourly

4. *Users of your database are reporting sluggish performance. Of the following, which would improve performance?*
   A. Move the database to its own disk.
   B. Move the database to a partition shared with other databases.
   C. Save Conflicts.
   D. Monitor all files.

5. *When a database has reached its size limit, what will happen?*
   A. The oldest data will be replaced with the newest data.
   B. Data older than seven days will be replaced with the newest data.
   C. The users will receive a warning dialog box, but their data will be saved.
   D. The users will receive a warning dialog box, and their data will not be saved.

6. *What is the maximum number of databases allowed in cache at one time?*
   A. 10,000
   B. 1,000
   C. 100
   D. 25

7. *Transaction log recovery does what after a system crash?*
   A. Checks every document in every database.
   B. Checks every document in the last accessed database.
   C. Applies or undoes transactions not written to disk at system failure.
   D. Triggers the Fixup command.

8. *What specifies the level of access users and servers have on a database?*
   A. ACL
   B. Privileges
   C. User types
   D. Roles

9. *What is the name of the field that records the name of the user or server that edits a document?*
   A. $Revisions
   B. $UpdatedBy
   C. $BusyName
   D. $Servername

10. *What does the agent log report?*
   A. The end results of an agent
   B. The last time a database was accessed by a Manager
   C. The last time an agent ran
   D. The last time an agent ran and if the agent completed or not

11. *Lotus Notes 5 allows users to have how many assigned names?*
   A. 1
   B. 2
   C. 4
   D. 8

12. *What is the default file name of the Domino Directory?*
    A. NAMES.NSF
    B. USER.NSF
    C. LOG.NSF
    D. DATABASENAME.NSF

13. *Mary has opted to delete a group from her Lotus Notes 5 Server. What will actually determine when the group is deleted on the server?*
    A. Replication timings
    B. ACLs
    C. Active Process on the server
    D. Free disk space on the server

14. *The People and Groups Look In field found within the Manage Groups tool provides what information?*
    A. A list of directories available
    B. A list of the groups you are managing
    C. All group hierarchies
    D. A list of servers

15. *When a Notes ID expires, what must happen before a user can use that ID again?*
    A. A new user account must be created for the user.
    B. An administrator must extend the expiration date on the Notes ID.
    C. The account must be re-certified by an administrator.
    D. The account must be re-certified with a new certificate.

16. *What is the default time before a Notes ID will expire?*
    A. One year
    B. Two years
    C. Three years
    D. Four years

17. *Fred would like to rename a user's account. Fred has been assigned the UserModifier role access to the directory but still cannot change the user's name? What additional access does Fred require?*

    A. Editor

    B. Administrator

    C. Author

    D. Reader

18. *Mary would like to migrate users from another mail system to her Lotus Notes 5 server. What course of action should Mary use to complete the migration?*

    A. Use the Migration tool

    B. Use the External Mail tool

    C. Through the Domino Administrator

    D. Migrate people in the Register Person dialog box

19. *Of the following, which mail system can Notes not migrate users from?*

    A. Microsoft Mail

    B. Novell GroupWise 4.1

    C. TOSS Mail Servers

    D. Netscape Messaging Servers

20. *What will happen if the save and edit count in both documents are the same during a normal replication conflicts process?*

    A. The most-recently saved document becomes the main document.

    B. The oldest document becomes the main document.

    C. The documents will be merged into one master.

    D. The document that has been open by users for the longest amount of time will become the master document.

21. *Which log keeps detailed information about replication of databases?*

    A. DATABASENAME.NSF

    B. LOG.NSF

    C. USER.NSF

    D. MTSTORE.NSF

22. *Mary would like to view the replication details. In Domino Administrator, how can she open the replication log?*
    A. Click the Analysis tab on the desired server.
    B. Click the Basics tab on the database properties.
    C. Click the Configuration tab in Domino Administrator.
    D. Click the Status tab on the desired server.

23. *Of the following, which cannot be collected through database analysis?*
    A. Replication history
    B. User reads and writes
    C. Design changes
    D. Template creations

24. *What command can you use to send and receive changes from a specified server?*
    A. Push
    B. Pull
    C. Replicate
    D. Synchronize

25. *The design task is run by default at what time on a daily basis?*
    A. Noon
    B. Midnight
    C. 1 a.m.
    D. 6 a.m.

26. *Martin is planning to expand his Lotus Notes mail system. He would like to create a report to see how busy his current mail system is. What type of report should Martin create?*
    A. Mail usage report
    B. Mail tracking
    C. Mail probing
    D. Mail usage summary

27. *The ISpy task monitors which mail servers by default?*
    A. Only the local mail server
    B. All mail servers
    C. All mail servers on the local network
    D. No mail server

28. **What command can be used to query which servers have mail in queue?**
    A. Tell Router Update
    B. Tell Router Config
    C. Tell Router Show
    D. Tell Router Reveal

29. **What does the Route command do?**
    A. Sends mail to or requests mail from a server immediately
    B. Sends mail to or requests mail from a server at the next regularly scheduled mail routing time
    C. Sends mail to or requests mail from a server in a different time zone
    D. Sends mail to or requests mail from a server at the next regularly scheduled mail routing time, or five minutes—whichever is sooner

30. **How can an administrator initiate a mail trace?**
    A. By using the route command
    B. By using the tracert command
    C. By using the Mail trace command
    D. By using the route tell command

31. **What is the default expiration date for a server at registration time?**
    A. 1 year minus one day
    B. 5 years minus one day
    C. 10 years minus one day
    D. 100 years minus one day

32. **The Domino log provides monitoring of the following resources, except for which one?**
    A. Mail routing
    B. Available memory
    C. Network transports
    D. Passthru connection

33. **What does the server task compact do?**
    A. Reduces the amount of data in cache
    B. Reduces the amount of whitespace in a database

C. Repairs corrupted databases

D. Loads calendar utility

34. *In the Domino Administrator client, where can an administrator view how long users have been attached to the server?*

A. Monitoring tab, Agent Manager

B. Monitoring tab, Domain Indexer

C. Status tab, top pane

D. Status tab, bottom pane

35. *Frances is running a Lotus Notes 5 Server in tandem with Microsoft IIS Server. What procedure allows this feature between Notes and IIS?*

A. Domino Services for IIS

B. Domino Services for HTTP

C. Domino Services for WWW

D. Domino Services

36. *When troubleshooting access to a Lotus Notes Server via the Web, what command should be issued to troubleshoot the connectivity to a specific IP address?*

A. Route

B. Tracert

C. Ping

D. Telnet

37. *What port should you use to telnet into when accessing a Lotus Notes Server during troubleshooting sessions?*

A. Port 80

B. Port 25

C. Port 1352

D. Port 4081

38. *The Domino Web Server log file (DONLOG.NSF) logs all activity on a Web server, except for which one of the following?*

A. The IP address of the user

B. The date and time the Web site was accessed

C. The IGMP packets to the client from any router

D. The success or failure of server access requests

39. **What is the maximum number of servers that can be in a Domino cluster?**

    A. 2
    B. 4
    C. 6
    D. 8

40. **What is required for users and servers to authenticate with each other?**

    A. Permissions
    B. ACLs
    C. A common certificate
    D. A Notes ID

41. **Where are the R5 certifier IDs that are created at an administrator's workstation stored by default?**

    A. Lotus\Notes
    B. Lotus\Notes\Data
    C. Lotus\Notes\Data\ids
    D. Lotus\Notes\Data\ids\certs

42. **What protocol is required to run SMTP Internet clients?**

    A. NetBIOS
    B. LDAP
    C. TCP/IP
    D. IPX/SPX

43. **Fred is having difficulty with his modem connecting to a Notes Server at the specified 56.6 connection. He has confirmed that the modem is working. What should he do on the modem next?**

    A. Lower the connection speed.
    B. Use a new modem driver.
    C. Ping the remote server.
    D. Enable hardware compression.

44. **Jenn would like to drop a user from her server. Where can she do this?**

    A. Server, Monitoring tab
    B. Server, Status tab, top pane
    C. Server, Status tab, bottom pane
    D. Server, Users tab

45. *What does a probe do?*
    A. Checks for available resources
    B. Checks for connected users
    C. Checks for User IDs
    D. Checks for available cache

46. *Which task is responsible for the gathering of system statistics?*
    A. Event monitor task
    B. Statistics collector task
    C. Statistics and Events database
    D. ISpy task

47. *Jane has configured Notes so that when a monitored event occurs, Notes can trigger an action. Of the following, which is not a valid action?*
    A. Send a pager message.
    B. Generate an SNMP trap.
    C. Automatically restart the server.
    D. Run a program in an effort to correct the problem.

48. *In what database are events and statistics stored?*
    A. EVENTS.NSF
    B. EVENTS4.NSF
    C. EVENTSR5.NSF
    D. EVENT4.NSF

49. *What tool can be used to help identify possible configuration errors within the Statistics and Events database?*
    A. Web Administrator
    B. Troubleshooting Wizard
    C. Agents
    D. Probes

50. *What Lotus tool allows for TCP/IP connections to be checked through a GUI rather than the command prompt?*
    A. IPconfig
    B. Winipcfg
    C. Notesconnect
    D. DHCP Manager

ANSWERS AND EXPLANATIONS

1. **B.**   For Fred to move the database through the Domino Administrator, he must have Create Database access on the destination server. For more information, refer to the section in Chapter 1 titled "Working with Domino Databases."

2. **C.**   In a clustered server environment, replica databases must be deleted within Domino Administrator. Incidentally, you must have Manager access in the database ACL. For more information, refer to the section in Chapter 1 titled "Working with Domino Databases."

3. **C.**   Replication should be monitored on a daily basis. An administrator can monitor the history of a database or events through the log, or the administrator can create a monitor. For more information, refer to the section in Chapter 1 titled "Working with Domino Databases."

4. **A.**   If database activity is high, and users report performance problems, the best resolution of those offered is to move the database to its own disk. For more information, refer to the section in Chapter 1 titled "Working with Domino Databases."

5. **D.**   When a database has reached it size limit, the users will receive a warning dialog box and no additional data can be saved to the database. For more information, refer to the section in Chapter 1 titled "Working with Domino Databases."

6. **A.**   The maximum number of databases allowed in cache at one time is 10,000. The minimum number allowed in cache is 25. The amount of databases kept in cache is directly influenced by the amount of available memory on your server. For more information, refer to the section in Chapter 1 titled "Working with Domino Databases."

7. **C.**   The transaction log replaces the Fixup command in most scenarios after a system failure. The transaction log applies or undoes transactions not written to disk at the time of system failure. For more information, refer to the section in Chapter 1 titled "Working with Domino Databases."

8. **A.** Every Notes database has an ACL (Access Control List) that specifies the level of access each user or server has to said database. For more information, refer to the section in Chapter 1 titled "Working with Domino Databases."

9. **B.** The $UpdatedBy field stores, by default, the name of the user or server associated with each document editing session. The $Revisions field includes the time stamp of the editing session. For more information, refer to the section in Chapter 1 titled "Working with Domino Databases."

10. **D.** The agent log is a view in the database that shows the last time an agent ran—and whether or not the agent ran successfully. For more information, refer to the section in Chapter 1 titled "Working with Domino Databases."

11. **B.** Domino R5 allows users to use alternate names for users in the Domino Directory. The first name would be the international name of the users, while the second name could be in the user's recognizable language. For more information, refer to the section in Chapter 2 titled "Localizing Address Books in Multi-Cultural Settings."

12. **A.** The default Domino Directory is called NAMES.NSF. For more information, refer to the section in Chapter 2 titled "Localizing Address Books in Multi-Cultural Settings."

13. **C.** When Mary deletes the group, the processes on the server will determine when the selected group is actually deleted. Mary will receive a confirmation dialog box when the group is deleted. For more information, refer to the section in Chapter 2 titled "Maintaining Groups."

14. **B.** The Manage Groups option on the Tools pane allows for quick-and-easy management of existing Domino groups. The People and Groups Look In field provides a list of directories available. For more information, refer to the section in Chapter 2 titled "Maintaining Groups."

15. **C.** When a Notes account expires, the account must be re-certified with a new certificate before it can continue to be used.

For more information, refer to the section in Chapter 2 titled "Maintaining Notes User IDs."

16. **B.**   By default, Notes IDs will expire in two years, but this setting can be changed if desired. For more information, refer to the section in Chapter 2 titled "Maintaining Notes User IDs."

17. **C.**   Fred requires Author access in addition to the UserModifier role access to change the user's name. For more information, refer to the section in Chapter 2 titled "Maintaining Notes User IDs."

18. **D.**   For Mary to migrate users from a compatible mail system, she would complete this task from Migrate People in the Register Person dialog box. For more information, refer to the section in Chapter 2 titled "Monitoring/Maintaining Users."

19. **C.**   Notes can migrate users from most popular mail systems, such as Exchange, Microsoft Mail, and GroupWise, but not from older mail systems, such as TOSS. For more information, refer to the section in Chapter 2 titled "Monitoring/Maintaining Users."

20. **A.**   When two or more users are editing the same document in tandem, the document with the greater number of saves and edits becomes the main document. Should each document have the same amount of saves and edits, the most recently saved document becomes the main document and the remaining documents are labeled replication conflicts. For more information, refer to the section in Chapter 2 titled "Troubleshooting Directory Problems."

21. **B.**   The LOG.NSF keeps information about the replication of databases. Specifically, this information can be accessed through the Replication Events view of the log file. For more information, refer to the section in Chapter 3 titled "Monitoring and Maintaining Replication."

22. **A.**   Within the Domino Administrator, Mary should select the server she is interested in analyzing and then click the Server Analysis tab. For more information, refer to the section in Chapter 3 titled "Monitoring and Maintaining Replication."

23. **D.**   Templates cannot be monitored through database analysis. Use database analysis to view replication history, user reads and writes, and design changes. For more information, refer to the section in Chapter 3 titled "Monitoring and Maintaining Replication."

24. **C.**   To send changes to and receive information from a specified server, use the Replicate command. The Pull command will receive changes only from a specified server. The Push command will send changes to the specified server. For more information, refer to the section in Chapter 3 titled "How to Force Replication."

25. **C.**   The design task runs automatically each morning at 1 a.m. For more information, refer to the section in Chapter 3 titled "Replicating Design Changes."

26. **A.**   Martin should create a mail usage report. The report will allow Martin see information, such as an overall usage of his mail system, top users, message volumes, and more. This report will help Martin predict future growth in his network. For more information, refer to the section in Chapter 3 titled "Monitoring and Maintaining Mail Routing."

27. **A.**   ISpy monitors only the local mail server by default. To monitor additional Domino mail servers, you must create probe documents. For more information, refer to the section in Chapter 3 titled "Monitoring and Maintaining Mail Routing."

28. **C.**   When using the Route command, if no mail is queued, Domino will simply ignore the Route command. To check which servers have mail queued, enter the command `Tell router Show` at the console. For more information, refer to the section in Chapter 3 titled "How to Force Mail Routing."

29. **A.**   The Route command sends mail to or requests mail from a server immediately. This overrides any pre-specified mail delivery timings. For more information, refer to the section in Chapter 3 titled "How to Force Mail Routing."

30. **C.**   From the Domino Administrator, click the Messaging, Mail tab. From the toolbar, click Messaging, Send Mail Trace. The

mail trace is delivered to the Administrator's mail database, with a report indicating the path traced. The Administrator then uses this information to troubleshoot where problems have occurred along the route. For more information, refer to the section in Chapter 3 titled "How to Force Mail Routing."

31. **D.**   The default certification for a server at registration time is 100 years minus one day. If desired, this figure can be changed. For more information, refer to the section in Chapter 4 titled "Maintaining Domino Server IDs."

32. **C.**   The Domino log does not provide information on network transports. Use the Domino log to view information on replication, disk space, memory, mail routing, and more. For more information, refer to the section in Chapter 4 titled "Monitoring Server Resources."

33. **C.**   The Compact task is used to remove whitespace in a database and optimize disk space. For more information, refer to the section in Chapter 4 titled "Monitoring Server Tasks."

34. **D.**   The Status tab's top pane displays running tasks on the server. The bottom pane displays users attached to the server, the databases they have open, and how long they've been idle. For more information, refer to the section in Chapter 4 titled "Monitoring/Maintaining Servers."

35. **A.**   New to Domino release 5 is the ability to run HTTP services using Microsoft IIS server. Domino performs this function using a procedure called Domino Services for IIS. For more information, refer to the section in Chapter 4 titled "Monitoring/Maintaining Web Services."

36. **C.**   If you are experiencing difficulty connecting to accessing a Lotus Notes Server via the Web, use the Ping command to test the connection. The syntax is Piing ip_address_of_the_host. For more information, refer to the section in Chapter 4 titled "Monitoring/Maintaining Web Services."

37. **C.**   If you are experiencing difficulty accessing a Lotus Notes Server via the Web and you were able to Ping successfully, attempt

to connect to port 1352 via a telnet program. If this fails, then a firewall is likely blocking access to the port. For more information, refer to the section in Chapter 4 titled "Monitoring/Maintaining Web Services."

38. **C.** IGMP packets are not recorded in the DONLOG.NSF. IGMP packets report errors to clients and to other routers about the path a packet may take from host to host. For more information, refer to the section in Chapter 4 titled "Monitoring/Maintaining Web Services."

39. **C.** Domino clusters range in size from a minimum of two servers to a maximum of six servers. For more information, refer to the section in Chapter 4 titled "Troubleshooting Cluster Problems."

40. **C.** Each Notes ID contains certificates that are electronically stamped by a Certifier ID. Users and servers may authenticate each other provided they share at least one common certificate. For more information, refer to the section in Chapter 5 titled "Maintaining Domino Certifier IDs."

41. **D.** By default, R5 Certifiers IDs are stored in Lotus\Notes\ Data\ids\certs. For more information, refer to the section in Chapter 5 titled "Maintaining Domino Certifier IDs."

42. **C.** TCP/IP must be enabled to run SMTP. Without TCP/IP as the connectivity environment, key services will not be available, such as POP3, IMAP, LDAP, and NNTP. For more information, refer to the section in Chapter 5 titled "Modification and Maintenance of Connectivity."

43. **A.** Fred should lower the connection speed on the modem. Some modems allow the user to set connection speed that is higher than the actual modem, to modem, speed. For more information, refer to the section in Chapter 5 titled "Modification and Maintenance of Connectivity."

44. **C.** The Server's Status tab will allow Jenn to monitor open ports, server tasks, servers, and users—including dropping a selected user. For more information, refer to the section in Chapter 5 titled "Modification and Maintenance of Connectivity."

45. **A.** Probes check for the availability of a resource for a specified timeframe. For more information, refer to the section in Chapter 5 titled "Monitor Connectivity."

46. **B.** The Statistics collector task is responsible for collecting system stats on multiple servers within a domain. For more information, refer to the section in Chapter 5 titled "Monitoring and Maintenance of the Domino System."

47. **C.** Automatically restarting the server is not an action that Notes can be directly configured to do when a monitored event occurs. Jane can configure Notes to send a page, generate SNMP traps, or run a program to resolve the problem. For more information, refer to the section in Chapter 5 titled "Monitoring and Maintenance of the Domino System."

48. **B.** Domino monitoring configuration is stored in the Statistics and Events database—EVENTS4.NSF. For more information, refer to the section in Chapter 5 titled "Configuring Active System Monitoring."

49. **B.** The Troubleshooting Wizard analyzes documents within the Statistics and Events database and attempts to identify common configuration errors. The Wizard will generate a report containing any problems it found and suggests solutions. For more information, refer to the section in Chapter 5 titled "Configuring Active System Monitoring."

50. **C.** Notesconnect is a GUI that allows the user to test connectivity to remote server. For more information, refer to the section in Chapter 5 titled "Troubleshooting Network and Protocol Problems."

CHAPTER 16

Sample Test Questions:
Exam 521

QUESTIONS

1. *Why should no North American ID or software leave the United States or Canada?*
   A. North American version uses 128-bit encryption
   B. International version uses 128-bit encryption
   C. Copyright laws
   D. Foreign language problems

2. *Which one of the following components would prove most suitable for usage as an organizational unit?*
   A. A server or first and last name of the user
   B. A company name
   C. A department or location name
   D. A country code

3. *What is a flat ID?*
   A. Country code and user name
   B. Organizational unit and user name
   C. Organizational and user name
   D. Name of the person or server

4. *What is required to create a new organizational unit?*
   A. Editor access
   B. Editor access and member of the Net Modifier role
   C. Net Modifier
   D. Editor access and certificate ID of the organization

5. *Of the following, which is not a group that can be created in Lotus Notes?*
   A. Multi-Purpose
   B. Mail Only
   C. Servers Only
   D. Domain Only

6. *What is the default for a newly created group?*
   A. Deny Access Only
   B. Mail Only
   C. Multi-Purpose
   D. Servers Only

7. *In a discussion of a Domino server infrastructure, which one of the following classes of server would we expect not to be mentioned?*

   A. Print server

   B. Mail server

   C. Hub server

   D. Application server

8. *What is recovery information used for in a Lotus Notes ID?*

   A. To re-create the user should the account be accidentally deleted.

   B. To restore the user's original certificate ID

   C. To re-create the public and private keys

   D. To restore a forgotten password

9. *What will the mail file be called for a user named Joe Fujiyama?*

   A. JoeF

   B. FJoe

   C. JoeFujiyam

   D. Jfujiyam

10. *What is an alternate name certifier?*

    A. A certificate for two accounts that use the same name

    B. An alternate certificate so users can work between multiple domains

    C. Allows a user to use a different name in a different country

    D. Allows servers to communicate with servers in different countries

11. *What is a partitioned server?*

    A. A Notes server that spans multiple partitions

    B. A Notes server that spans multiple hard drives

    C. Multiple server installations on one machine

    D. Multiple server installations on one partition

12. *Of the following, which option would you select to pull data from external resources so that the information can be used in a Lotus Notes database?*

    A. DECS

    B. Domino Server Planner

C. Domino Web Services

D. Notes program files

13. **During the setup of a new server, which one of the following tasks is not added automatically?**

A. Indexer

B. Replicator

C. Mail Router

D. LDAP

14. **What is required to set up an additional Notes server?**

A. An Administrator account in any Notes domain

B. An Administrator account in the local Notes domain

C. An ID registered with a certifier that can authenticate with another server in your domain

D. An ID registered with a certifier that can authenticate with another server in a remote domain

15. **What does the Maps Extractor task do?**

A. Loads a GUI Map of your local Notes domain

B. Loads a GUI Map of your remote Notes domain

C. Views router schemes only

D. Views router and replication schemes

16. **What is the NOTES.INI file responsible for?**

A. Contains settings for the administrator account

B. Contains settings for a Notes server

C. Contains settings for an entire Notes domain

D. Contains application-specific settings

17. **In the NOTES.INI file, what does the entry KitType=2 represent?**

A. The local machine is a Notes server.

B. The local machine is a Notes client.

C. The local machine has accepted all installation defaults.

D. The local machine has been installed through a custom installation process.

18. **What does the ServerTasks= line in the NOTES.INI file tell Domino?**

A. What users are logged in by default

B. What servers should be connected by default

    C. What tasks to start when the server is started

    D. What tasks to start when server is shut down

19. *Of the following, which choice is not one of the four installation options?*

    A. Lotus Notes

    B. Domino Designer

    C. All Clients

    D. Domino Web Designer

20. *Of the following, which is not a valid method of connecting to a Notes server?*

    A. SLIP

    B. LAN

    C. MODEM

    D. RAS

21. *What is a connection record?*

    A. A log of all users who have ever connected to the Notes server

    B. A log of all IP addresses that have ever connected to the Notes server

    C. A component that is used to establish a connection to a Notes server

    D. A component that is used to record all connections to a Notes server by a specific client

22. *What is Lotus Notes Domain?*

    A. Notes servers using a single directory

    B. Notes servers using a single Organization certifier

    C. Notes servers using a common NetBIOS name

    D. Notes servers connected to the same physical LAN

23. *Mary would like to create a new domain. Of the following, which is a valid concern with regard to the new domain?*

    A. All domains will automatically see all domains.

    B. All users will automatically be added to the new domain.

    C. Users and servers will never authenticate with each other.

    D. Users and servers will not authenticate with each other until you cross-certify.

24. *What will be the name assigned to a network if you choose not to assign the network a name?*

    A. Network

    B. Network1

    C. NNetwork

    D. Lnetwork

25. *Of the following, which port is not a valid option with Lotus Notes and Domino?*

    A. AppleTalk

    B. TCP/IP

    C. NetBEUI

    D. DLC

26. *What is a Passthru server?*

    A. A call-in server for remotely connected users

    B. A server that ties two domains together

    C. A server that passes through authentication requests

    D. A server that passes queries to a specified server

27. *What is a hub server?*

    A. A lone server connected to its own hub

    B. A server connected to all other servers through a hub

    C. A server used to deliver mail or replication for all other servers

    D. A server used to deliver mail, replication, and synchronization for all other servers

28. *Samuel would like to install a workstation for Karen, who will be developing databases for his company. Which install type should Samuel choose?*

    A. Lotus Notes

    B. Domino Developer

    C. Domino Designer

    D. Domino Administration

29. *What is an island workstation?*

    A. A workstation that uses a different protocol than other users on a LAN

    B. A hidden workstation

    C. A workstation that is not typically connected to a LAN

    D. A workstation that is installed on the same machine as a Notes server

30. **What is a directory catalog?**

   A. A record of the entire directory
   B. A separate database that includes the entire directory of users and server
   C. A record of the directory on each server
   D. A smaller version of the entire catalog

31. **Of the following fields on the Basics tab, which is not a default field?**

   A. FullName
   B. NickName
   C. FirstName
   D. ShortName

32. **What is the Merge factor?**

   A. Defines the point when Domino will merge entries from multiple catalogs into one catalog
   B. Defines the point when Domino will merge entries from multiple domains into one catalog
   C. Defines the point when Domino will merge duplicate entries in the catalog with the original entries
   D. Defines the point when Domino will merge duplicate entries in different catalogs with the original entries

33. **What does the Dircat task do?**

   A. Creates a directory of all catalogs for the specified servers
   B. Creates a directory of all catalogs for all servers in the domain
   C. Creates a directory of all catalogs for all servers in any specified domain
   D. Combines all defined data in the configuration document and deposits it into the directory catalog

34. **What is required to support users of Lotus Organizer and IBM OfficeVision?**

   A. A Foreign Domain Document
   B. A Foreign Domain Catalog
   C. A Foreign Domain Index
   D. Replication to a Passthru server

35. **How many certification log databases are required in a domain?**
    A. 1
    B. 2
    C. 4
    D. One per server

36. **Domino is designed to lock the MAIL.BOX database when processing is occurring in the database. How does Domino address this problem to resolve bottlenecks?**
    A. Allows additional messages to be queued in the cache
    B. Allows for multiple routers tasks and multiple MAIL.BOX databases
    C. Allows for message forwarding to Passthru servers
    D. Allows for messages to override the locked database

37. **What is the MTSTORE.NSF database?**
    A. Mail tracking store database
    B. Mail routing database
    C. Mail forwarding database
    D. Monitors multiple MAIL.BOX databases

38. **When participating in message tracking, which of the following is not a possible result?**
    A. Transfer failed
    B. In queue
    C. Mailbox full
    D. Unknown

39. **What is the message tracking collection interval used for when configuring message tracking?**
    A. Specifies how often Domino will log messages in the Mail tracking store database
    B. Specifies how often Domino will track existing messages in the Mail tracking store database
    C. Specifies how often Domino will log messages in all servers
    D. Specifies how often Domino will log messages in queue on the local server only

40. **What does Domino provide for direct Internet Mail Routing?**
    A. MTAs
    B. SMTP

C. LDAP

D. SNMP

41. **What is required for an IMAP client to access a Domino server?**

A. IMAP Certificate

B. Authentication between the client and server

C. HTTP

D. MTA

42. **What must be started before a mail probe can be created?**

A. IMAP

B. SMTP services

C. Domino services for Microsoft IIS

D. Ispy

43. **When configuring Agent restrictions on the server record, what does the field Run Personal Agents do?**

A. Allows only personal agents to run on this server

B. Allows only personal agents to run on a specified database

C. Allows only specified users to run personal agents on this server

D. Allows only specified users to run personal agents on the specified database

44. **When configuring the ACL for a database, what does the depositor entry allow?**

A. Allows users to create records

B. Allows users to create and view existing records

C. Allows users to create, view, and modify existing records

D. Allows users to create new records, but modify only records they've created

45. **Marcia is configuring a Passthru server and would like this server to automatically dial another server as needed. Which field should Marcia complete?**

A. Access This Server

B. Route Through

C. Cause Calling

D. Destinations Allowed

46. *What role must you be a member of to register new users in the directory?*
    A. GroupCreator
    B. NetCreator
    C. UserCreator
    D. ServerCreator

47. *What are roles used for?*
    A. Roles can be used to dynamically change rights for users in a specific server.
    B. Roles can be used to dynamically change rights for users in a specific database.
    C. Roles can be used to dynamically change rights for users in all databases stored on one server.
    D. Roles can be used to dynamically change rights for users in all servers within a domain.

48. *What does the Author Names field do?*
    A. Captures the time and date of when the author created the document
    B. Captures the name of the creator who created the document
    C. Captures the role of the creator who created the document
    D. Assign the name of the new author to a modified document

49. *What will happen without an Author Names field?*
    A. Author access will not allow the creator to change his own documents
    B. Author access will allow only the creator to change his own document
    C. Author access will allow only the owner to change any documents
    D. All users will be able to modify the document because no author is associated with the document

50. *When configuring security settings on a server, what does Compare Notes Public Keys Against Those Stored in the Directory accomplish?*
    A. Allows any ID to use the server
    B. Allows only users whose public key matches one stored in the Domino directory to access the server

C. Allows only users whose public key matches one stored in the Domino public directory to access the database

D. Allows users who provide a username and password that are stored in the Domino directory to access the server

ANSWERS AND EXPLANATIONS

1. **A.**   No North American ID or software should leave the United States or Canada because the North American version uses 128-bit encryption, whereas the International version uses only 48-bit encryption. For more information, refer to the section in Chapter 6 titled "Creating/Registering Certificates."

2. **C.**   An organizational unit is typically a department or location name. There can be up to four OUs. Each OU is limited to 32 characters. For more information, refer to the section in Chapter 6 titled "Creating/Registering Certificates."

3. **D.**   A flat ID contains only the name of the person or server. Flat IDs are not as robust as naming conventions in R5. For more information, refer to the section in Chapter 6 titled "Creating/Registering Certificates."

4. **B.**   You must have at least Editor access and be a member of the Net Modifier role to create an organizational unit. For more information, refer to the section in Chapter 6 titled "Creating/ Registering Certificates."

5. **D.**   You cannot create a Domain-Only group. The types of groups you can create are Multi-Purpose, which is the default; Access Control List Only, used to grant access to databases and servers; Mail Only; Servers Only; and Deny Access Only. For more information, refer to the section in Chapter 6 titled "Creating Groups."

6. **C.**   The default for a new group is Multi-Purpose. This type of group is allowed to send email and access databases and servers. For more information, refer to the section in Chapter 6 titled "Creating Groups."

7. **A.** A print server is not a viable choice for a Notes Server. You can create mail servers, hub servers, and application servers. For more information, refer to the section in Chapter 6 titled "Creating/Registering Servers."

8. **D.** This can be used to obtain a password that may have been forgotten by the user. For more information, refer to the section in Chapter 6 titled "Creating/Registering Users."

9. **D.** The user Joe Fujiyama will have a mail file named Jfujiyam for the mail file name box. This is because the first letter of the first name, plus seven characters of the last name, are used to create the file. For more information, refer to the section in Chapter 6 titled "Creating/Registering Users."

10. **C.** An alternate name certifier allows a user to use a different name in a different country. There can be only one additional name certifier added to an individual. For more information, refer to the section in Chapter 6 titled "Creating/Registering Users."

11. **C.** A partitioned server allows you to have multiple server installations on one machine. For more information, refer to the section in Chapter 7 titled "Installing Servers."

12. **A.** DECS is used to retrieve data from external sources so that the information can be used within a Notes database. For more information, refer to the section in Chapter 7 titled "Installing Servers."

13. **D.** LDAP, Lightweight Directory Access Protocol, is used to collect information from various Web sites and directories. LDAP, however, is not added by default and must be added as an optional task. For more information, refer to the section in Chapter 7 titled "Installing Servers."

14. **C.** To set up additional servers, you are required to have an ID registered with a certifier that can authenticate with another server in your domain. This makes Notes more secure so that unauthorized users don't try to add additional servers to your domain. For more information, refer to the section in Chapter 7 titled "Installing Servers."

15. **D.**   The Maps Extractor allows you to view router and replication schemes within the administrator client. For more information, refer to the section in Chapter 7 titled "Installing Servers."

16. **B.**   The NOTES.INI file contains settings for your Notes server. You can edit the INI file with a text editor, but changes will not be effective until the server is restarted so that the changes to the INI file will be loaded. For more information, refer to the section in Chapter 7 titled "Installing Servers."

17. **A.**   The KitType=2 in the NOTES.INI file means that the local machine is a server. For more information, refer to the section in Chapter 7 titled "Installing Servers."

18. **C.**   The ServerTasks= line tells Domino what tasks the server should start automatically when the server is started. For more information, refer to the section in Chapter 7 titled "Installing Servers."

19. **D.**   The Domino Web Designer is not a choice during the client software installation. For more information, refer to the section in Chapter 7 titled "Installing Clients."

20. **A.**   SLIP, Serial Line Internet Protocol, is not an option to connect to a Notes server. Your connection choices are to connect via a LAN or a modem, or through a RAS (remote access server). SLIP, for the most part, has been replaced by the dial-up protocol PPP. For more information, refer to the section in Chapter 7 titled "Installing Clients."

21. **C.**   A connection record is used to establish a connection to a server, provide an avenue to pass through a server, or set up news groups. It is not used to log information that may have happened during the connection. For more information, refer to the section in Chapter 7 titled "Installing Clients."

22. **A.**   A domain is defined as servers using a single directory. Don't confuse this idea with Internet top-level domains such as .com, .org, or .mil; or with Microsoft's NT Domains. A Notes domain may follow a similar structure but the domain is not restricted, either. For more information, refer to the section in Chapter 8 titled "Setting Up Infrastructure Domains."

23. **D.** Users and servers from each domain will not be able to communicate until Mary cross-certifies the servers in each domain. For more information, refer to the section in Chapter 8 titled "Setting Up Infrastructure Domains."

24. **B.** If you do not assign the Named Network a name, the registration process will automatically assign the name of Network1. For more information, refer to the section in Chapter 8 titled "Setting Up Infrastructure Domino Named Networks."

25. **D.** DLC, datalink control, is not a protocol that can be used with Notes and Domino. Most likely, Domino and Notes will use TCP/IP, as it has gained popularity with Internet-related activities. You may find your network to also be using IPX/SPX for connectivity with a NetWare environment. For more information, refer to the section in Chapter 8 titled "Setting Up Infrastructure Protocols/Ports."

26. **A.** A Passthru server is a central call-in server for remotely connected users. This allows users to dial in to the Passthru server and connect to many other servers through this one connection. For more information, refer to the section in Chapter 8 titled "Setting Up Servers for Different Functions."

27. **C.** A hub server is used to deliver mail or replicate information to all other servers in a company. It is analogous to a wheel: The hub server is in the center of the wheel and the other servers are spokes off of the hub. For more information, refer to the section in Chapter 8 titled "Setting Up Servers for Different Functions."

28. **B.** Samuel should install the Domino Developer for Karen as her workstation install type. The Domino Developer will allow Karen to create and change Domino databases. For more information, refer to the section in Chapter 8 titled "Setting Up Workstations for Different Clients."

29. **C.** An island workstation is disconnected from a network. The location is typical to some settings where connection is not possible, such as in an airplane, or a similarly remote location. For more information, refer to the section in Chapter 8 titled "Setting Up Workstations for Different Clients."

30. **D.**   A directory catalog should be used if you choose to replicate the directory to remote users. This will reduce the size of the catalog to save space and time for the remote users. For more information, refer to the section in Chapter 8 titled "Setting Up Workstations for Different Clients."

31. **B.**   NickName is not a valid option when creating user names. Should you want to use a nickname for users in your environment, you may want to use the shortname field. For more information, refer to the section in Chapter 9 titled "Setting Up/ Configuring Directories."

32. **C.**   The Merge Factor field is used to define the point when Domino will merge duplicate entries in the catalog with the original entries. The default entry is 5%. For more information, refer to the section in Chapter 9 titled "Setting Up/Configuring Directories."

33. **D.**   The Dircat task will combine all defined data in the configuration document and deposit it into the directory catalog. Run this task regularly to keep the directory catalog up to date. For more information, refer to the section in Chapter 9 titled "Setting Up/Configuring Directories."

34. **A.**   To support users of Lotus Organizer and IBM Office Vision, a Foreign Domain Document must be created. For more information, refer to the section in Chapter 9 titled "Setting Up/Configuring Directories."

35. **A.**   After the first Domino server in a domain is created, the first database that should be created is the certification log. Only one log per domain is required. As new servers and users are added to the domain, they are added to the original certification log. For more information, refer to the section in Chapter 9 titled "Setting Up/Configuring ID Backup and Recovery."

36. **B.**   Domino addresses the problem of a locked mail database by allowing multiple router tasks and multiple MAIL.BOX databases on the same server. For more information, refer to the section in Chapter 10 titled "Setting Up/Configuring Message Distribution Performance Enhancements."

37. **A.** The database MTSTORE.NSF is used to record message tracking data. For more information, refer to the section in Chapter 10 titled "Setting Up/Configuring Message Distribution Tracking."

38. **C.** When tracking a message, you'll see the end result of the tracking displayed as deliver, delivery failed, in queue, transferred, transferred failed, group expanded, or unknown. Mailbox full is not an option. For more information, refer to the section in Chapter 10 titled "Setting Up/Configuring Message Distribution Performance Enhancements."

39. **A.** The message tracking collection interval is used to tell the Domino server the frequency for logging messages in the Mail Tracking Store database. The default value is 15 minutes. For more information, refer to the section in Chapter 10 titled "Setting Up/Configuring Message Distribution Performance Enhancements."

40. **B.** SMTP mail routing is now accessible directly in the server configuration. SMTP allows users to send and receive mail directly from the Internet. For more information, refer to the section in Chapter 10 titled "Setting Up/Configuring Message Distribution Using Non-Notes/Internet-Based Mail."

41. **B.** An IMAP client must authenticate with the server in order to access it. The client can authenticate through user name and password, SSL, and SSL encryption. For more information, refer to the section in Chapter 10 titled "Setting Up/Configuring Message Distribution Using Non-Notes/Internet-Based Mail."

42. **D.** The Ispy task must be started before a mail probe can be created. You can start the Ispy from the prompt, or through the NOTES.INI file. For more information, refer to the section in Chapter 10 titled "Setting Up/Configuring Administration Tools."

43. **C.** This field limits who can run personal agents on the server. If there is no entry, then everyone can run personal agents on the server. For more information, refer to the section in Chapter 11 titled "Setting Up/Configuring Agent Access."

44. **A.** A depositor is person or group that can only create records. They cannot modify or even view records. For more information, refer to the section in Chapter 11 titled "Setting Up/Configuring Agent Access."

45. **C.** Cause Calling will force the server to call the destination as needed. If no entries are in the field, then the server will not automatically dial. For more information, refer to the section in Chapter 11 titled "Setting Up/Configuring Server Access."

46. **C.** You must be a member of the UserCreator role to register new users in the directory. For more information, refer to the section in Chapter 11 titled "Setting Up/Configuring Security for the Domino Directory."

47. **B.** Roles are used to dynamically assign or change rights for users in a specific database. A user could have different roles in several different databases. For more information, refer to the section in Chapter 11 titled "Setting Up/Configuring Security for the Domino Directory."

48. **B.** The Author Names field automatically captures the name of the author who created the document. For more information, refer to the section in Chapter 11 titled "Setting Up/Configuring Document Access."

49. **A.** Without any entries in the Author Names field, the permission author access will not allow the author to modify the document. For more information, refer to the section in Chapter 11 titled "Setting Up/Configuring Document Access."

50. **B.** When a client attempts to use the server, the public key in the ID must match the one stored in the Domino Directory. This option allows for a very secure server. For more information, refer to the section in Chapter 11 titled "Setting Up/Configuring Document Access."

CHAPTER 17

Sample Test Questions: Exam 522

QUESTIONS

1. *What must you use if you'd like to compact files on an R5 server but want to keep files as R4?*
   A. Compact –R4 command
   B. Compact –R5 command
   C. Compact –R command
   D. Compact command

2. *What is required to place new applications on a server?*
   A. Rights for that server
   B. A mapped drive
   C. A scheduled agent
   D. Domino Designer

3. *In what order are formulas processed?*
   A. Left to right, top to bottom
   B. Right to left, top to bottom
   C. Top to bottom, left to right
   D. Top to bottom, right to left

4. *What is a benefit of using JavaScript when servers are concerned?*
   A. Easier to use than any other scripting language
   B. More robust features than other scripting languages
   C. More processing happens at the server rather than at the client
   D. More processing happens at the client rather than at the server

5. *What is required to create JavaScript in an application?*
   A. Designer access only
   B. Author access only
   C. Designer access with the Create LotusScript/Java Agent check box selected
   D. Author access with the Create LotusScript/Java Agent check box selected

6. *What is the Idle Session Timeout value used for in conjunction with Java servlets?*
   A. Specifies total number of users at once
   B. Specifies total number of inactive users at once
   C. Specifies what time value constitutes an idle session. The default is 10 minutes.
   D. Specifies what time value constitutes an idle session. The default is 30 minutes.

7. *What is the default setting for maximum active sessions in regard to Java applications?*
   A. 10
   B. 100
   C. 1000
   D. 10,000

8. *What is restricted LotusScript?*
   A. LotusScript that is restricted from running on a server
   B. LotusScript that is restricted from running during peak hours
   C. LotusScript that references fields or changes data
   D. LotusScript that references the file system

9. *Of the following, which is not considered to be a design element?*
   A. ACL
   B. Forms
   C. Actions
   D. Navigators

10. *When creating a field, what is the maximum amount of data a text field can store?*
    A. 64K
    B. 65K
    C. 1024K
    D. 2048K

11. *When creating a field, what type of field should you use to hold a ZIP code or Social Security number?*
    A. Text
    B. Number
    C. Check box
    D. Dialog list

12. *Of the following, what cannot be included in a number field?*
    A. Numbers
    B. Periods
    C. Commas
    D. Negative sign

13. *What is a radio button?*
    A. A button the user checks to select more than one choice
    B. A button the user selects to make only one choice
    C. A design element that looks like a radio
    D. A button that requires the user to select at least two choices, but not more than four

14. *What is unique about rich text?*
    A. Allows for formatting of characters
    B. Allows for ASCII only
    C. Requires author access to format the characters
    D. Used to display formatting in a view

15. *Ben has created a "Computed when Composed" field in his form. The formula included in the value event for the field references an editable field that is located further down the form. When Ben tests the form, he finds that the Computed when Composed field remains blank, even after he enters data in the editable field and refreshes the document. Why?*
    A. Fields are calculated when saved.
    B. Forms are calculated when saved.
    C. Fields are calculated from left to right and top to bottom. Ben is accessing a field that has not been calculated yet.
    D. Fields are calculated from left to right and top to bottom. Ben is referencing a field that has not been calculated yet.

16. *What are forms and subforms?*
    A. Forms and subforms are the same as documents.
    B. Forms and subforms display documents in a row-by-row format.
    C. Forms and subforms are a collection of fields that users can use to view and input data.
    D. Forms and subforms are a collection of fields that have existing data only.

17. *Why would you choose to use the Display Images After Loading option when designing a form?*
    A. Allows users to view the text only
    B. Allows users to view the image only
    C. Allows users to cancel the loading of any images
    D. Allows all text to load before the images load

18. *If Mark is using OLE to share a file within Lotus Notes, what will happen when changes are made within Notes in regard to the linked document?*
    A. Only parts of the file that are stored within Notes will reflect the changes.
    B. Only the original document will reflect the changes.
    C. Both Notes and the linked document will reflect the changes.
    D. The link between Notes and the original document will be broken.

19. *When should sections be used?*
    A. To control access to parts of a form
    B. If the document *cannot* fit into one screen
    C. To start a new document
    D. To start a new form

20. *What is the default for new views and folders?*
    A. Private
    B. Private on first use
    C. Shared
    D. Shared on first use

21. *What does archiving do?*
    A. Deletes documents that are no longer needed
    B. Moves documents that are no longer needed to a separate file
    C. Moves documents that are no longer needed to a separate database
    D. Compacts the database by compacting files that have not been accessed recently

22. *What is required so that users will be able to edit documents they have created?*

    A. Author access
    B. Author names
    C. User name field
    D. Author access and author names field

23. *What is recommended if many users will authenticate to your server with a user name and password that are not part of your company?*

    A. Create a different directory to house the additional users.
    B. Allow anonymous entry.
    C. Use the internal directory and create each user account.
    D. Create a person record for each account that will access your server externally.

24. *What is the most common cause of replication failure?*

    A. Network lag
    B. Hardware problems
    C. Access Control List
    D. Time zones

25. *Why are servers needed in the ACL in regard to replication?*

    A. To identify other servers to replicate to
    B. To identify other servers to replicate from
    C. To assign permission for the servers to replicate
    D. To restrict users from forcing replication

26. *How many characters can be used in a newly created role?*

    A. 6
    B. 12
    C. 15
    D. 26

27. *What will the setting Replicate Based on Age of the Document accomplish?*

    A. Only documents older than the specified number of days will replicate.
    B. Only documents younger than the specified number of days will replicate.

C. Only documents that have been modified within the specified number of days will replicate.

D. Only documents that have not been modified within the specified number of days will replicate.

28. **When adjusting the properties for an index, what does the refresh index value control?**

A. How frequently the view will update

B. How frequently the document will update

C. How frequently the view will replicate

D. How often users may refresh a view

29. **Mary would like all text to load before images do so that users can see the text in a database before the graphics. What setting should Mary choose on the database properties?**

A. Allow Use of Stored Form in This Database

B. Don't Maintain Unread Marks

C. Display Images After Loading

D. Document Table Bitmap Optimization

30. **Why would you normally not enable the option Allow Use of Stored Form in This Database?**

A. Causes the database to grow in size

B. Causes the database to compact daily

C. Restricts forms to be routed to other databases

D. Anyone can make changes to the form

31. **What does the setting Don't Maintain Unread Marks do to a database?**

A. Associates tables with the forms used by the document appearing in the view

B. Will not reveal if the document has been read by the user

C. Degrades database performance

D. Will not notify users of new documents

32. **What does the tool Domino Server.Load accomplish?**

A. Captures real-time performance of your server

B. Captures replication load on your server

C. Simulates users attached to your server

D. Simulates replication on your server

33. *What does the tool NotesBench accomplish?*
    A. Vendor tool to test client and servers as they connect to other servers
    B. Vendor tool to test users only as they connect to other servers
    C. Vendor tool to test servers as they connect to other servers
    D. Free tool used to benchmark overall server performance

34. *Which one of the following factors would most likely cause a developer to alter his standard design strategy?*
    A. How many users will run the application simultaneously
    B. How many users will connect via the LAN
    C. How many users will connect via a modem
    D. How many users will use the application in peak periods

35. *David would like to send a routed document to another database. What command should David use to forward the document?*
    A. SendNow
    B. Replicate
    C. Actions, Forward menu
    D. Send

36. *Frederick has designed a workflow application that will be used by several users in his company, including remote users. Some of the documents will be routed to users' mail files. Of the following, what must the remote users have configured for them to properly view the documents?*
    A. The entire application database stored locally.
    B. The Store Form in Document setting or in their mail file.
    C. The Store Form in Document setting or referenced in their NOTES.INI file.
    D. No additional configurations are required. The users will be able to read the documents when the documents arrive in their mail files.

37. *What does the Lotus Notes Mail license type allow usage of?*
    A. A mail file only
    B. A mail file and the databases created with the basic set of Lotus templates
    C. A mail file and access to only one other database
    D. A mail file and up to ten databases

38. *What is required to automate replication between servers?*
    A. TCP/IP
    B. Cluster server
    C. Connection record
    D. Links to partner database(s)

39. *What task must be configured for a Web browser to access Domino objects on the server?*
    A. DIIOP
    B. HTML
    C. Domino services for Microsoft IIS
    D. JavaScript

40. *In order for a Web browser to access a Domino application, what needs to be configured on the server?*
    A. JavaScript
    B. SMTP
    C. HTML server protocol
    D. HTTP server protocol

41. *Of the following, which would be the best choice to improve performance on a server?*
    A. Run all agents at once.
    B. Run all agents at night.
    C. Run one agent per hour.
    D. Run agents each hour only.

42. *How can you specify when and how many agents will run?*
    A. NOTES.INI file
    B. Agent Controller
    C. Agent Manager
    D. Agent properties

43. *Why should agents be limited in use?*
    A. They are hard to configure properly.
    B. They cannot be used on databases derived from templates.
    C. They cannot be used on compacted databases.
    D. They use up server resources.

44. *Frank has hired a consulting firm to develop an application. The consultant warns Frank that he should sign the elements of the database. Why is this important?*

    A. The application will not run on Frank's server until he signs the elements.
    B. The application will not allow agents to be run by Frank unless he signs the elements.
    C. An outsider should not be allowed to run agents on a server.
    D. The consulting firm most likely cannot install the application until Frank signs the elements.

45. *You have made changes to an application's design. What is the best way to apply the changes?*

    A. Design changes are best applied with a template.
    B. Design changes are best applied directly to the application.
    C. Design changes are best applied with an agent to automate the process.
    D. Design changes to an application essentially means creating a new application and discarding the original application.

46. *You would like to distribute application design changes using replication. What is the easiest way to accomplish this task?*

    A. Create an agent to complete the replication.
    B. Force replication to occur immediately.
    C. Schedule replication to occur with an agent.
    D. Schedule replication to occur with connection records.

47. *What constitutes Notes Authentication?*

    A. A valid user name and password.
    B. An anonymous account.
    C. Passthru security.
    D. A user or server presents an ID to the server and the public and private key sets are verified.

48. *If you would like to force users to authenticate with your Notes server through a Web browser, what is required to force the user to offer a user name and password?*

    A. The default and Anonymous access should be set to Read.
    B. The default and Anonymous access should be set to No Access.

C. The default and Anonymous access should be set to Password Required.

D. The default and Anonymous access should be set to Depends on Password.

49. *Where can you import Java applets?*

   A. Database properties, applets
   B. Design pane, resource options, applets design
   C. Design pane, applets design
   D. Database properties, Java

50. *Of the following, which is not an example of what an action can do?*

   A. Call menus.
   B. Run agents.
   C. Disconnect idle users.
   D. Implement formulas.

ANSWERS AND EXPLANATIONS

1. **C.** If you compact files on an R5 server but want to keep files as R4, you can use the Compact –R command. For more information, refer to the section in Chapter 12 titled "Deploy Applications Based on Backward Compatibility."

2. **A.** To place new applications on a server, you will either need the rights for that server or you will need to send the database to the Domino Administrator. Rights are granted on the server record. For more information, refer to the section in Chapter 12 titled "Deploy Applications Based on Coding."

3. **C.** Notes will evaluate formulas from top to bottom, and left to right. For more information, refer to the section in Chapter 12 titled "Deploy Applications Based on Coding."

4. **D.** JavaScript requires more processing at the client rather than the server. This does reduce overhead and traffic. For more information, refer to the section in Chapter 12 titled "Deploy Applications Based on Coding."

5. **A.** If you'd like to create JavaScript in an application, you must have Designer access. For more information, refer to the section in Chapter 12 titled "Deploy Applications Based on Coding."

6. **D.** The idle session timeouts allow you to configure what constitutes an idle session. The default value is 30 minutes. For more information, refer to the section in Chapter 12 titled "Deploy Applications Based on Coding."

7. **C.** Maximum Active Sessions allows you to determine the total number of "users" for your site. The default is 1000. For more information, refer to the section in Chapter 12 titled "Deploy Applications Based on Coding."

8. **C.** LotusScript that references fields or changes data is considered restricted LotusScript. Unrestricted LotusScript refers to instances when operating system commands or calls to C programs are needed. For more information, refer to the section in Chapter 12 titled "Deploy Applications Based on Coding."

9. **A.** Design elements do not include applications. Design elements are individual components such as actions, agents, buttons, field, forms, and navigators. For more information, refer to the section in Chapter 12 titled "Deploy Applications Based on Design Elements."

10. **B.** The Text field type will accept a limited amount of data (64KB) and does not allow links, graphics, or attachments. Text fields can be shown in views unlike Rich Text fields. For more information, refer to the section in Chapter 12 titled "Deploy Applications Based on Design Elements."

11. **A.** When entering values that are not true numbers, such as figures or dollar amounts, use a text field to hold values such as phone numbers and Social Security numbers. For more information, refer to the section in Chapter 12 titled "Deploy Applications Based on Design Elements."

12. **C.** You cannot include commas in a number field. A number field can have only numbers, periods, and the negative sign. For

more information, refer to the section in Chapter 12 titled "Deploy Applications Based on Design Elements."

13. **B.** The Radio Button field type limits the user to a set of choices that can be changed. The user must select one choice from the alternatives given. For more information, refer to the section in Chapter 12 titled "Deploy Applications Based on Design Elements."

14. **A.** Rich text is the only field type that allows the user to do character formatting, use links, embed objects, make attachments, and much more. Rich text fields cannot be displayed in a view. For more information, refer to the section in Chapter 12 titled "Deploy Applications Based on Design Elements."

15. **D.** Fields are calculated from left to right and top to bottom. Therefore, you cannot reference a field that requires input if it is below or to the right because the referenced field will likely not contain data. For more information, refer to the section in Chapter 12 titled "Deploy Applications Based on Design Elements."

16. **C.** Forms and subforms are structures that hold fields so a user can view and input data. Subforms can make it easier to build and change an application because they can be shared by many forms. If you are requesting similar information on different forms, you can call subforms and decrease your development time. For more information, refer to the section in Chapter 12 titled "Deploy Applications Based on Design Elements."

17. **D.** You can enable the Display Images After Loading option to allow Notes to display all of the text of the document before loading the graphics. For more information, refer to the section in Chapter 12 titled "Deploy Applications Based on Design Elements."

18. **C.** Object Linking and Embedding allows you to share a file within Lotus Notes. When changes are made, the changes will also be made to the linked document. For more information, refer to the section in Chapter 12 titled "Deploy Applications Based on Design Elements."

19. **A.** Sections can control access or break up a form for the user. When documents are long and have areas that are easily divided, sections can be handy. For more information, refer to the section in Chapter 12 titled "Deploy Applications Based on Design Elements."

20. **C.** Views and folders will default to Shared and you must choose to make them Private (or Private on First Use). For more information, refer to the section in Chapter 12 titled "Deploy Applications Based on Design Elements."

21. **B.** Archiving can automate the task of moving documents that are no longer needed to a separate file. Archiving is typically set up with the Properties dialog box using a time criteria to determine when to remove documents. For more information, refer to the section in Chapter 12 titled "Deploy Applications Based on Document Characteristics."

22. **D.** To deploy applications with Author access, and Author Names field must be present. If you have not defined a field as Author Names, users will not be able to edit the documents they have created. The typical formula for an Author Names field is @Name([CN];@UserName). For more information, refer to the section in Chapter 12 titled "Deploy Applications Based on Document Characteristics."

23. **A.** If you intend to have hundreds of users authenticate with a user name and password that are not part of your company, you should strongly consider using a different directory to house the many person records that will be needed. For more information, refer to the section in Chapter 12 titled "Design Secure Applications."

24. **C.** The most common mistake is not including the servers in the ACL so that replication can occur. The server will need to be included either explicitly or within a group (usually the LocalDomainServers group). For more information, refer to the section in Chapter 12 titled "Design Secure Applications."

25. **C.** The server must have high enough rights to carry out changes you make. For more information, refer to the section in Chapter 12 titled "Design Secure Applications."

26. **C.**   A role may have to 15 characters in its name. For more information, refer to the section in Chapter 12 titled "Design Secure Applications."

27. **B.**   In the Replication Settings menu, you can specify a number of days for the age of a document. Only documents that are less than the days you specify will replicate. For more information, refer to the section in Chapter 13 titled "Capacity Plan Based on Application Size."

28. **A.**   You can select how frequently the view will update. For more information, refer to the section in Chapter 13 titled "Capacity Plan Based on Indexes."

29. **C.**   This feature will force the text to appear before graphics. This allows the user to focus on the content of the document. For more information, refer to the section in Chapter 13 titled "Capacity Plan Based on Performance."

30. **A.**   If you save each document with the form, it will make the database large and it will be difficult to make changes to the form. The primary reason to enable this feature is to allow the form to be routed to other databases (such as a mail file). For more information, refer to the section in Chapter 13 titled "Capacity Plan Based on Performance."

31. **B.**   Choosing this option will speed up access and performance of a database. You must compact the database before you will see a change in performance. The user will not know what documents he has read, so only use this if unread marks are not needed. For more information, refer to the section in Chapter 13 titled "Capacity Plan Based on Performance."

32. **C.**   Using a script, you can simulate users that will be attached to the server. You can evaluate the performance of the server and better determine the need for CPU, RAM, and disk. For more information, refer to the section in Chapter 13 titled "Capacity Plan Based on Server Size."

33. **A.**   NotesBench is available to vendors to test client and servers as they connect to other servers. For more information, refer to

the section in Chapter 13 titled "Capacity Plan Based on Server Size."

34. **C.** How users connect to the servers can have a significant impact on the design of an application. Especially if you will have any remote users, you must consider the point of view of the end user as you construct an application. You should determine how much will be replicated on servers and workstations. For more information, refer to the section in Chapter 13 titled "Deploy Applications Based on Connectivity."

35. **C.** You can accomplish this task with the SendTo field and a button or just by using the Actions, Forward menu. In either case, mail routing must be enabled on the server that is sending the mail, and there must be a logical path for the router to follow. For more information, refer to the section in Chapter 13 titled "Deploy Applications Based on Routing Fundamentals."

36. **B.** Users who receive the document must also have the form either included with the Store Form in Document setting or within their mail file. The Store Form in Document setting can be added to a form's property in the first Basics tab. For more information, refer to the section in Chapter 13 titled "Deploy Applications Based on Impact of Routing on Remote Users."

37. **B.** The Lotus Notes Mail license type can use a mail file and the databases created with the basic set of Lotus Notes templates. For more information, refer to the section in Chapter 13 titled "Deploy Based on License Types."

38. **C.** To automate replication between servers, you can simply create connection records. The connection records specify the action that will be triggered (replication, mail routing, or both) and what time and frequency are desired. For more information, refer to the section in Chapter 13 titled "Deploy Based on Server's Involvement in Replication."

39. **A.** If you intend to use Java, you will also need to run and configure the DIIOP task on the server. For more information, refer to the section in Chapter 13 titled "Deploy for Web Integration."

40. **D.**   To use applications with a browser, you must be running the HTTP server protocol. For more information, refer to the section in Chapter 13 titled "Deploy Server-Based Applications."

41. **B.**   Agents can take up resources; the more you have running, the more performance problems you may encounter. If you can run agents during off-peak hours and limit the number that run at the same time, you can gain some performance back. For more information, refer to the section in Chapter 13 titled "Deploy Server-Based Applications."

42. **C.**   Agent Manager allows you to determine times agents will run, limit the number of concurrent agents, and specify a maximum time out. You can also limit who can run agents on the server within the "Security" section in Chapter 13. For more information, refer to the section in Chapter 13 titled "Deploy Server-Based Applications."

43. **D.**   Agents should be limited in use because they can be damaging and they take up server resources. The use of agents can be restricted within the configuration of the "Security" section in Chapter 13. For more information, refer to the section in Chapter 13 titled "Deploy Server-Based Applications."

44. **C.**   Signing the design elements of a database will prevent problems running agents because an outsider should not be allowed to run agents on a server. For more information, refer to the section in Chapter 13 titled "Distribute Application Design Changes Based on Design."

45. **A.**   Design changes are best applied with a template. Depending on the complexity and number of users an application has, it may be best to also do testing with the changes you intend to apply. A template typically has the extension .NTF and is placed in the data directory of the server. For more information, refer to the section in Chapter 13 titled "Distribute Application Design Changes Based on Impact on ACL."

46. **D.**   The most common method of periodic replication is by scheduling the replication to occur with connection records. A connection record can be created within the Domino Directory.

A schedule can be established that will trigger the server to replicate with another at the times and frequency specified. For more information, refer to the section in Chapter 13 titled "Distribute Application Design Changes Based on Replication."

47. **D.** Notes authentication occurs when a user or server presents an ID to the server. It involves verifying the public and private key sets of both the server and client. For more information, refer to the section in Chapter 13 titled "Secure Domino Applications Based on Notes Authentication."

48. **B.** Users can authenticate with a server via a Web browser. To be certain that authentication is used, the Access Control List must be set low enough to require authentication. Ideally, the Default and Anonymous Access should be set to No Access. This will require the user to verify a name and password before proceeding. The password for the user is kept in the Person record for the individual. For more information, refer to the section in Chapter 13 titled "Secure Domino Applications Based on Notes Authentication."

49. **B.** Java applets can be created or imported in the applets design selection of the database. The applets design area is found by expanding the Resources option in the Design pane. For more information, refer to the section in Chapter 12 titled "Deploy Applications Based on Coding."

50. **C.** Actions can appear in the Actions menu or as buttons for forms or views. They can call menus, run agents, or implement formulas. For more information, refer to the section in Chapter 12 titled "Deploy Applications Based on Design Elements."

INDEX

W-Z

WE WANT TO KNOW WHAT YOU THINK

To better serve you, we would like your opinion on the content and quality of this book. Please complete this card and mail it to us or fax it to 317-581-4663.

Name _____

Address _____

City _____ State _____ Zip _____

Phone _____ Email Address _____

Occupation _____

Which certification exams have you already passed? _____
_____
_____
_____

Which certification exams do you plan to take? __
_____
_____
_____

What influenced your purchase of this book?
❏ Recommendation   ❏ Cover Design
❏ Table of Contents   ❏ Index
❏ Magazine Review   ❏ Advertisement
❏ Publisher's reputation ❏ Author Name

How would you rate the contents of this book?
❏ Excellent   ❏ Very Good
❏ Good   ❏ Fair
❏ Below Average   ❏ Poor

What other types of certification products will you buy/have you bought to help you prepare for the exam?
❏ Quick reference books ❏ Testing software
❏ Study guides   ❏ Other

What do you like most about this book? Check all that apply.
❏ Content   ❏ Writing Style
❏ Accuracy   ❏ Examples
❏ Listings   ❏ Design
❏ Index   ❏ Page Count
❏ Price   ❏ Illustrations

What do you like least about this book? Check all that apply.
❏ Content   ❏ Writing Style
❏ Accuracy   ❏ Examples
❏ Listings   ❏ Design
❏ Index   ❏ Page Count
❏ Price   ❏ Illustrations

What would be a useful follow-up book to this one for you?_____
Where did you purchase this book?_____
Can you name a similar book that you like better than this one, or one that is as good? Why?_____
_____
_____

How many New Riders books do you own? _____
What are your favorite certification or general computer book titles? _____
_____

What other titles would you like to see us develop? _____
_____

Any comments for us? _____
_____

Fold here and tape to mail

Place
Stamp
Here

New Riders
201 W. 103rd St.
Indianapolis, IN 46290